For Jenny

**Last Boat For**

with very best wishes

*J R Mill...*

Jenny,
Xmas 2005
Thought you would find this
interesting –
Much love, Happy Christmas
and let's hope 2006 is a
better year!

*Sara*

Sobhuza II, Ngwenyama and King of Swaziland.
*Photo courtesy of Swaziland Administration, 1966.*

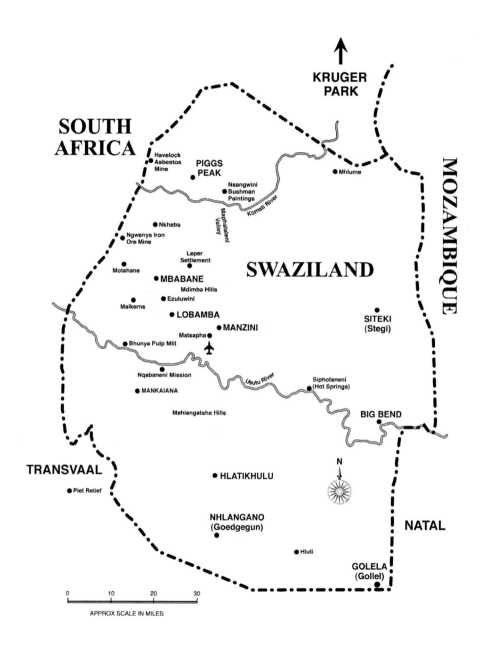

SOUTH AFRICA

KRUGER PARK

MOZAMBIQUE

Havelock Asbestos Mine

PIGGS PEAK

Mhlume

Nsangwini Bushman Paintings

Komati River

Maphalaleni Valley

Nkhaba

Ngwenya Iron Ore Mine

Leper Settlement

SWAZILAND

Motshane

MBABANE

Mdimba Hills

Malkerns

Ezuluwini

LOBAMBA

MANZINI

SITEKI (Stegi)

Matsapha

Bhunya Pulp Mill

Nqabaneni Mission

Usutu River

Siphofaneni (Hot Springs)

MANKAIANA

Mahlangatsha Hills

BIG BEND

N

TRANSVAAL

HLATIKHULU

Piet Retief

NHLANGANO (Goedgegun)

NATAL

Hluti

GOLELA (Gollel)

0    10    20    30

APPROX SCALE IN MILES

# Last Boat For Africa

A District Officer's experiences
during Swaziland's run-up to
independence in the 1960s

## J P Miller

Librario

Published by

**Librario Publishing Ltd.**

ISBN No: 1-904440-68-1


Copies can be ordered from retail
or via the internet at:
www.librario.com

or from:

Brough House
Milton Brodie
Kinloss
Moray
IV36 2UA
Tel / Fax: 01343 850617


Printed in Times.


Cover design and layout by Steven James
www.chimeracreations.co.uk


Printed and bound by
DigiSource (GB) Ltd.

*To the Swazi people, and to the
memory of Sobhuza II, Ngwenyama
and King of Swaziland (1899-1982)*

*All royalties from the sale of this book will go to the Swaziland Diocese HIV/AIDS
and ORPHANS Programme (for details of their work, see Appendix III).*

# Contents

# Foreword

By Sir Francis Loyd, KCMG, OBE
(Queen's Commissioner for Swaziland, 1964 - 1968)

John Miller's recollections of his first tour of duty as a young District Officer in Swaziland are of particular interest for two reasons. First he was one of the last Colonial Administrative Service cadets to be posted to any African Territory and secondly he arrived in Swaziland just as it was about to be given independence. This book has valuable things to say and good tales to tell about Swaziland and the Swazi people at this important moment in history.

**Frank Loyd, 19th September 2005**

# Acknowledgements

I am indebted to countless people without whose help this book would not have happened. It is invidious to try to name them; I am listing some below: many others should have been included in my thanks, but space forbids. I hope they will take the thought for the deed.

My parents, Archie and Muriel Miller assiduously kept all my letters from Swaziland; these have been an invaluable aid to my memory. Peter and Diana Simkin, former colleagues, besides innumerable kindnesses to me during my time in Swaziland, checked my manuscript for accuracy. Jean Hall typed it all and gave me the benefit of her years in publishing. Pat May and Barbara Belshaw also pitched into the fray at crucial times. Anthony Kirk-Greene let me tap his encyclopaedic knowledge of the literature of the Colonial Service.

When I left Swaziland in late 1966 the Government Information Service kindly gave me a number of prints with the right to reproduce them as a more than generous quid pro quo for the use they had made of some of my photos. I have shown when their material has been used. All the other photos are my own and Nicola Hinton gave good advice on photograph selection. Chris Ball and Paul Cracknell at GGS Creative Graphics coped skilfully with my ancient and often dusty negatives.

Dot Kent was a constant willing sounding board on word and phrase usage. Sir Frank Loyd, Swaziland's last Queen's Commissioner, despite ill health, gave me the benefit of his razor-sharp memory. Huw Jones and Canon Anthony Molesworth were able to put me right on several matters and our writer friends Barbara Nash and Jemma Smy encouraged and advised me, as did Barbara's agent, Sheila Ableman. I have been fortunate in my publisher, Mark Lawson at Librario who has been invariably helpful and tolerant. Anne Wilson, the text editor, was amazingly hawk-eyed yet used her red pen with sensitivity. John Brennan and his people at Digisource, the printers, were charming and enthusiastic and amazed me with their state of the art technology.

Besides those mentioned in the text, there are numerous people from all sections of the Swaziland community in the 1960s whose vibrant personalities made such an impression on me that my memories remained alive and fresh over the years.

My family have been unfailingly tolerant during the book's gestation period and never flinched from asking, "How's the book coming on?", knowing the enquiry would unleash a torrent of queries as to their opinion on this or that passage. Most of all my darling wife has sustained, helped and encouraged me from the start and has been a most valuable and understanding partner in the whole undertaking.


**John Miller, September 2005**

# Introduction

Readers may consider what possessed a young man leaving university in 1961 to join the shrinking British Colonial Service in the sunset of Empire. I put the same question the other day to a cousin of mine, Garry Philipson DFC, latterly Managing Director, Aycliffe and Peterlee Development Corporation. As with many others, his time in the Colonial Service did not prevent him from having an excellent subsequent career. Older than me, he went out to Sierra Leone in 1949 having, before his postponed university years, served with distinction during the war with the RAF. He had a longer time in Africa than I did; but even in 1949 there was never any chance of the Colonial Service giving him a full career. His reply to my question was immediate "I thought it would be fun"

It was the same answer as I might have given. I wondered however if there was something else, gratitude for having survived the war and being able to live in freedom, a sense of duty to help others and give something back for one's good fortune. "Yes" he agreed "There was that too; but it was not to be worn on one's sleeve." I admitted, despite having missed war service, being younger, that I felt the same. So I believe did my contemporaries in the Swaziland District Administration. For all of us there was more than just the desire to have fun: but fun there was in profusion and I hope my text brings out both elements.

I hope, too, that this book may make Swaziland a little better known. It is a gem of a country and its people, despite their present difficulties, are a joy and deserve to prosper.

## Chapter 1

# The Sea Voyage

July 1962

"Put him down, Jeremy!" I yelled as the four of us ran to rescue the man from our friend's grasp. The wretched fellow had spat derisively during the playing of God Save the Queen. Jeremy, brave as a lion and sometimes intemperate, was threatening to pitch him over the rail. As we were aboard ship and in mid-Atlantic, this was probably not a good idea. It was our fifth night afloat and much had happened to raise our hackles since we had embarked; but even righteous indignation must have bounds!

Five days earlier at Southampton when friends, well-wishers and family had finally left the ship and the last gangplanks had been hauled aboard, the *Athlone Castle*, with a deep-throated blast from its siren, started to edge away from the quay on a routine voyage to Cape Town. As the crowd on the dockside and the passengers lining the ship's rail variously waved, wept into their handkerchiefs or dealt with the lumps in their throats, the band struck up *Auld Lang Syne*. Although it passed unnoticed at the time, this was a defining moment, for the ship's full complement of passengers included the last four British Colonial Service Cadets ever to be posted to any African territory. In the shrinking Colonial Service this was indeed the last boat for Africa.

I was lucky enough to be one of those four.

The others were David Findlay, Jonathan Harlow and Jeremy Varcoe. David was a graduate of Edinburgh University, Jonathan was a First in Classics from Cambridge and Jeremy had been a contemporary of mine, both at Oxford and before that at school at Charterhouse. David and Jonathan were bound for Bechuanaland (now Botswana) and Jeremy and I were both going to Swaziland.

Before being posted to our territories, the four of us had been required to spend a year on the 'Devonshire Course' in preparation. Course students were based either in Oxford or Cambridge, depending on destination. For Jeremy and me this meant effectively a fourth year at Oxford and we were able to continue our university and college life. During this time Jeremy married Wendy, a charming girl from an army family, who had been Archbishop Fisher's secretary. She was the fifth member of our little group on the *Athlone Castle*. The Devonshire Course gave us an introduction to tropical agriculture, law, local government, economics and social anthropology, also the local language. For Jeremy and me this was Siswati, a variant of Zulu. The tutor who took us for anthropology was David Lienhardt. He was an authority on the Dinka, immensely tall people who lived in the Sud (the marshes of southern Sudan), who seemed to spend most of their time standing in the water on one leg, waiting to spear fish. Dr Lienhardt suggested we did some extra work outside the Devonshire Course syllabus so that we could sit the examination for the Certificate in Social Anthropology. We took his advice and in due course achieved our certificates, having read such diverse tomes as *Coming of Age in Samoa*, *Aluer Society* and, of course, *The Dinka*, by David Lienhardt.

Most of our fellow students on the course had come from territories that were already self-governing, or on the threshold of independence. Many of them were older than us, some quite senior in their particular service. We thus had the chance to learn about the ways of government administration in a cross-section of very different countries, including the Caribbean, Nigeria, Kenya, Uganda, Hong Kong, Mauritius and the islands of the Pacific. I particularly enjoyed the company of Sila Boit, who was already well up the ladder in the Kenyan Civil Service. He had been one of Roger Bannister's pacemakers in 1954 at Iffley Road

Stadium when Bannister became the first man to run a mile in under four minutes. A number of the Kenyans were Kikuyu and some had been involved, on one side or the other, in the Mau Mau unrest which had broken out in 1951 amongst the Kikuyu and, to a much lesser extent, the neighbouring Meru and Embu. They were grand chaps and seemed to get along well together, past enmities notwithstanding.

Like most Britons, I had absorbed inaccurate, received ideas about Mau Mau. Kenyans on the course were able to talk to me from personal experience about what had really taken place. It seemed there had always been factions within the Kikuyu tribe. Most people in Britain believed Mau Mau was a rebellion against the colonial power; that may have been how it started; but it became a struggle within the tribe itself with large sections of the Kikuyu bitterly opposed to the Mau Mau and their methods.. Over 10,000 people were killed during Mau Mau, less than 100 of them Europeans. However, in 1959 the killing by prison guards of Kikuyu detainees at Hola turned Mau Mau into a black/white issue, at least in the eyes of the world's press. Hola was dubbed British Africa's equivalent of the Amritsar massacre in India in 1919, when the intemperate Brigadier-General Dyer had ordered his sepoys to fire on a peaceful but unauthorised demonstration, killing 379 people and wounding over 1,500, thereby providing the fuel for much of the anti-colonial propaganda of the next forty years. Hola had re-cycled this propaganda and given it an African slant; but the facts, as opposed to the popular myth, showed that Hola was a totally different tragedy and on a much smaller scale. Sir Frank Loyd, who was to come to Swaziland from Kenya in 1964 as its last Queen's Commissioner, had been a District Commissioner and then a Provincial Commissioner during the Mau Mau years. I never felt it was my place to raise the subject with him while I was in the service nor later over the years when we met socially. But after I started to write this narrative I asked if I could come and speak to him about Hola and Mau Mau. I need not have been so shy.

Sir Frank was happy to talk at some length and although he was by then an old man and in poor general health, his mind and powers of recall were as sharp as ever. He had actually been on UK leave at the time of the Hola killings, but he knew all the details and made several points. Most importantly, the Hola tragedy was not, like Amritsar, the result of a senior figure deciding to 'teach the natives a lesson'. Instead the Hola killings arose from the neglect of established practice by junior African prison staff who panicked and used their batons when a situation with a work party of Mau Mau detainees ran out of control. Eleven detainees were killed. To put Hola into context Sir Frank spoke of the Mau Mau activists' countless vicious attacks on their fellow Kikuyu and the intimidation they inflicted on members of the tribe, particularly the practice of forcing them to take repulsive oaths. He stressed that whereas Hola became a byword in anti-colonial rhetoric, little publicity was given to the atrocities the Mau Mau had routinely inflicted on their own people. For instance, in 1953 the whole population of the Kikuyu village of Lari, near Nairobi, a total of 120 men, women and children, had been slaughtered by the Mau Mau in cold blood; but Hola is the name that is remembered, not Lari.

However, for us idealistic young British colonial service cadets going out to our first postings in 1962, the happenings at Amritsar and Hola were both horrors, the embodiment of colonial rule at its worst and far removed from the benign paternalism and rule by consent which, we believed, were the hallmark of the best of British imperial practice. But we encountered people on the boat who would have been only too keen to fire the first shot and who would have applauded Amritsar and Hola as 'the smack of firm government'. Additionally, to our surprise, by no means all such reactionaries were Afrikaners (South Africans of Boer, i.e. Dutch descent); many were 'English' South Africans, some quite recently arrived.

When we went into the dining room on our first evening aboard ship, Jeremy, Wendy, David, Jonathan and I found ourselves placed at a table for six. The sixth person was a well-dressed man in his seventies who had been born in Carlisle, qualified as an architect and then went out to South Africa where he had remained ever since. He was still running his practice in Cape Town and was returning after visiting relatives in the UK. The dining room was set up with the Captain's table in prime position; at this were placed passengers of note and the remainder of us were allocated to tables of six or so. One table, however, was set for only two people. These turned out to be a Methodist clergyman and a barrister, both returning to Nyasaland (now Malawi) after study leave in England. Within a day or two we had made their acquaintance and found them to be well mannered, quiet spoken, articulate and interesting. But they were black, hence the table on their own. We felt the least we could do to counter this *de facto* apartheid aboard a British ship was to invite them to join us at our table one evening and we hoped that thereafter other tables would follow suit. We checked with the steward that this was feasible and then asked our architect friend if this was all right by him. We were totally unprepared for the outburst our request provoked from this seemingly pleasant, cultured and agreeable old man. He exploded – ignorant young people like us with our communist ideas were ruining Africa – only South Africa could save the continent by holding out against the tide of savagery – give the native an inch and he would take a mile – the good natives knew their place and that was how they liked it – the only people who wanted change were a few agitators, so that they could line their own pockets and exploit their fellow Africans – hand the place over to the *munts* (a derogatory South African word for Africans) and within a few years there would be famine all over Africa – Africans were lazy; bribery and nepotism were a way of life for them – etc. etc.. This was a refrain we were to hear over and over again during our time in Africa, not only from 'poor whites', whose livelihoods could be threatened by African advancement, but from educated and cultured people too. Shamefully, at times, we even heard this wretched mantra from white employees of the British Protectorate Administrations of Bechuanaland, Basutoland and Swaziland. (These countries were technically not colonies but protectorates, having through their paramount chiefs at the end of the 19th century petitioned to be allowed to "nestle like fleas in Queen Victoria's blanket" to avoid being overwhelmed by the advancing Boers.) It could not have been more of a shock to us to hear this sort of tirade from people born and brought up in the UK.

Although shaken to the core by the Cape Town architect's reaction to our suggestion that the two Nyasas dine at our table we stood our ground. The invitation was made and accepted and the architect arranged to be moved to another table.

I have rather laboured the matter of racial attitudes to underline our astonishment at the rampant racism we were to find, not only on the ship and in South Africa, but also in Swaziland, one of the 'Lands of Opportunity', as a Commonwealth Office pamphlet described the High Commission territories. The people running the Devonshire Course should have given us some warning of what to expect. As a ten- year-old I had learnt in school music lessons the chorus 'Hold him down, the Swazi Warrior, Hold him down, the Swazi Chief, Chief, Chief,' – a relic of the 19th century Zulu Wars in which the Swazi were marginally involved, long before the establishment of the Protectorate. It never occurred to me that in 1962 we would meet people of British birth who still regarded it our proper role to hold the Swazi down rather than prepare them for independence. Of course, we encountered many enlightened Europeans in Southern Africa and also others who were happy to be friendly and pleasant, yet agree to disagree on the racial question. Entrenched pro-apartheid attitudes and 'Brit-bashing' kept cropping up in the most unlikely places. An example was the fellow who spat on the deck during the playing of the National Anthem, mentioned at the start of this narrative.

Generally, however, the voyage passed agreeably enough. I shared a cabin with a tall, gangly District Officer from Nyasaland, a bachelor some twelve years my senior. He was a pleasant fellow and a considerate room-mate. One would not have called him good-looking and he had a shy, almost retiring nature. We nicknamed him 'Percy'. Early on he struck up a friendship with a fellow passenger, a girl of similar age, physique and temperament. They became partners in the deck sports and, amazingly, the deck tennis court transformed them both into the most extrovert and noisy players on the ship. Soon they were at the same table at dinner and rarely seen apart. Wendy, only very recently married herself, felt they were well suited to each other and quietly tried to encourage each of them. "After all," she said to the rest of us, "it could be the last chance for them both." In those days, unlike today, any girl over thirty and unmarried was more or less considered to be 'on the shelf'.

Another girl, slightly younger than us and highly unlikely to be left on the shelf, was Jenny Salmon, who was accompanying her mother, Lady Salmon, on a visit to her brother, a missionary in KwaZulu (the Zulu homeland). Jenny joined in our deck sports and was a good companion for Wendy in our male-dominated group. It turned out that the Salmons would be coming to Swaziland to stay with their friends, Brian and Riva Marwick at the Residency after the visit to KwaZulu. Brian Marwick had been Resident Commissioner since 1957 and besides having a reputation as an able administrator was known outside the Colonial Service for his anthropological text, *The Swazi*, published in 1940.

Jenny Salmon, Wendy and Jeremy Varcoe at the Fancy Dress Ball.

To break up the gentle pace of shipboard life there were various deck sports competitions, dances and entertainment. Jeremy won a prize at the fancy dress ball with his imaginative, ultra-simple costume as a gatecrasher. He turned up clad in pyjamas and dressing gown, with his head poking through a hole in a packing case lid. I, against the odds, reached the final of the table tennis competition. My opponent in the semi-final had swept dramatically through the earlier stages of competition, obliterating his opponents with unplayable services and sensational smashes. After being thrashed in the first set, I realised my only hope was to alter my game to suit the moment. By this stage we were into the South Atlantic and the ship was rolling and pitching in gale force winds; I decided to use the rough weather to my advantage. I stonewalled, waiting for the ship's motion to deliver me point after point. The strategy worked. Increasingly a sudden lurch by the ship to port or starboard carried my opponent's decisive shots an inch wide or long and he became rattled. The great player was a surly loser, accusing me of being merely a 'ping pong' player. The following day in the final I was comprehensively beaten by a very good player. Even Aesop's tortoise, as far as we know, could not repeat the trick the next day.

Our only stop on the voyage was at Funchal, Madeira. We were glad to be off the ship for a few hours, but soon tired of being pursued by little boys offering us dirty postcards or their sisters. "Velly nice, velly clean, mister!" As the voyage wore into the second week I found the enforced leisure and the artificiality of it all was beginning to pall. I reflected that prison must be fairly similar to life as a ship's passenger. You shared a small space with a cell-mate; meals were taken communally at fixed times; there were organised leisure activities and boundless opportunities for reading and thinking; but, until the predetermined date of your release there was no prospect of going off site even for a few minutes. In our case it was only a ten day sentence and we had been granted the short release on parole at Funchal so ours was a pretty easy incarceration, but I determined in future to settle for the short, sharp shock of a jet flight rather than lose time through a sea voyage.

Of course, there had been much to enjoy on the voyage, the companionship of our close-knit group, the casual friendships made aboard ship, several magnificent sunsets and sunrises, flying fish, dolphins and albatrosses and, most enticingly one night, the smell of Africa, of the sand, dust and heat in the dark as we skirted the unseen Senegal coast near Cape Verde.

The last evening's dinner and dancing gave us an opportunity to say our goodbyes before the scramble of leaving the ship the next morning. We wished the Salmons a happy time in Zululand and Lady Salmon suggested she rang me on their arrival in Mbabane to fix a time for them to come and visit me in my bungalow. For 'Percy', the end of the voyage was more momentous. He was not the sort of fellow one could ask, "What are you going to do about that nice girl with whom you have been getting on so well?" Nor did he ever raise the subject of his intentions. Certainly they danced very close all evening, but the next morning he was more than usually silent and he and his bounding deck tennis partner left the ship by separate gangplanks.

For Jeremy and Wendy, Jonathan, David and myself, our African adventure was about to start. On the ship we had learned a thing or two about life in Southern Africa. The next stage of our journey was to teach us more.

## Chapter 2

# Cape Town to Swaziland

On the morning of our docking at Cape Town we awoke to a full gale, driving rain and poor visibility. We were thus denied the renowned picture postcard view of Cape Town spread out beside the ocean with the mass of Table Mountain separating the city from the deep blue sky to landward and the even deeper azure of the South Atlantic to seaward. Cape Town was generally held to vie with Athens for the title of the world's finest seaboard city. Argentinian friends give the palm to Rio de Janeiro; my vote, as a Scot, goes to Edinburgh.

Certainly our landing was not in the same style as the most notable recorded disembarkation at the Athens of the North. I refer, of course, to George IV's visit to Edinburgh in 1822. Entering into the spirit of the Scottish romantic revival engineered by Sir Walter Scott and his cronies, the stout King pranced down the gangway from the Royal Yacht at Leith docks resplendent in a mini kilt and voluminous pink trews. The apparition apparently prompted one of the society hostesses of the time, Lady Nithsdale, to declare when presented to him at Holyrood Palace later in the day, "Your Majesty, it is a great joy, though we see you so seldom, that when you do come to us, we see so much of you."

There were no witty ladies waiting to greet us at Cape Town; instead we had to do battle with the Afrikaner customs officials. Jeremy and I had brought our cars out with us as this saved money and their unloading and customs clearance had to be negotiated before we could move northwards. Eventually, after what seemed like endless bureaucratic obfuscation and delaying, the cars were cleared and Jeremy, Wendy and I were free to head for Swaziland. Manzini, in the middleveld, was the Varcoes' destination; Mbabane, the capital, in the highveld, was mine. Both towns, we imagined, would be very different from Cape Town which, on a cold, wet, windy winter's day, felt more like Greenock on the Clyde at its most dour, than the jewel of Africa.

We had organised ourselves a leisurely schedule so as to have a chance to look around on our journey north and we agreed to meet at pre-arranged hotels during the trip to compare notes. My first detour was up the Outeniqua Pass through the mountains to Oudtshoorn, in the Little Karroo, a centre for ostrich farming in an area dominated by European landowners. By now the sun was bright and the air crystal clear and the scenery resembled the Southern Uplands of Scotland. But, as I had felt in Cape Town this was not the Africa I had come to see, so I quickly pressed eastwards along the 'Garden Route'. It was near Wilderness, midway between the towns of George and Knysna, that I saw my first African mammals. These were hyraxes, or rock rabbits, called *dassies* in South Africa. They are similar to the biblical coneys, which are mentioned in the Book of Proverbs: "The coneys are but a feeble folk, yet they have their habitation among the rocks". These particular coneys had their homes among rocks beside the main tarred road, so I pulled over and watched them for several minutes. They did not seem to be bothered by me, possibly because living on a famous tourist route they felt they had a duty to entertain passers-by. However, unlike some baboons I was to encounter several months later in the Kruger Park they had not learnt to beg.

Wilderness, which I reached shortly after my dassie-watching, was one of the most charming places I saw on the Garden Route. The name 'Wilderness' goes back to the early 19th century when a man named Van den Berg fell in love with a girl of fanciful nature. According to the story she agreed to marry him only on condition that he would take her out into 'the wilderness' where they could live untainted by the evils of civilisation. She had probably read too much Rousseau and romantic poetry for her own good; history does not relate whether the rural idyll lived up to expectation, but at least the small town remains as a memorial to her dream.

Baboons that had learnt to beg.

My destination for the night was Knysna. This town had been developed by George Rex, allegedly the son of George III of Great Britain and the Quaker Hanna Lightfoot. Whether Rex's claims of royal blood were genuine or mistaken he certainly left his mark by developing the area from his estate of Melkhoutkraal (Afrikaans – meaning 'Milk Wood House'). He drew on the local forests to create a timber industry and a seaport and started shipbuilding by constructing the brig *Knysna*, using local stinkwood. Furniture made from the stinkwood planks used for the brig's slipway could be seen in the local council offices. The hotel where the Varcoes and I were to rendezvous stood by the lagoon close to the Knysna Heads, which towered over the narrow entrance to the sea. It was a glorious spot on a clear evening as the rocks and aloes by the water's edge stood out in relief against the backdrop of the Outeniqua range. I arrived before Jeremy and Wendy and went into the hotel bar, where the talk was about a family on holiday from Cape Town who had been overtaken by tragedy. They had driven off the main road onto a dirt track through the forests and their car had overturned.

This misfortune provoked one of the locals to lecture me on the dangers that such roads presented to the inexperienced. "Don't take liberties with dirt roads, man," he instructed, "and don't swerve for an animal like that poor man from Cape Town." Apparently the father, who was driving, swerved to avoid a Cape hare, the car skidded and went down a *donga* (a ravine created by flood water). The crash broke the man's leg and killed his wife; the two children suffered multiple fractures; but the hare escaped.

I was soon to learn, or think I had learnt, how to drive on dirt. Apart from deep soft sand often encountered in the dry season, the main problem was the corrugation of the road surface caused by the passage of vehicles. The only way to avoid being shaken to pieces was to accelerate until the car was going fast enough to float over the surface. The sensation was similar to planing in a high performance sailing dinghy and there was the same inherent lack of control. The roads were periodically levelled by the Public Works department, using 'graders', which skimmed off the top surface with huge blades. Some cars had a better reputation on dirt than others. For instance, most local insurance companies charged an additional premium for Volkswagen Beetles, then in their heyday, because their rear engines made them difficult to control off the tar. The excess usually lasted only for the first year of ownership on the theory that after a year the owner would either have killed himself or would have learnt to handle the car on dirt.

Early next morning I lay in bed watching a pair of pied kingfishers working off the hotel jetty. What a paradise this whole area must have been when Van den Berg first arrived and built his stone house

'Wilderness', the perfect fulfilment of his bride's romantic dream. Jeremy, Wendy and I, however, had a full day's driving ahead of us, so after a quick breakfast we hit the road, making a mental note to come back one day. My itinerary was to take me past Port Elizabeth, into the Ciskei, one of the smaller Bantustans (African reserves). It was the homeland of the Peddie people, neighbours of the much larger Xhosa and Zulu tribes. I was booked to spend the night in Hamburg, a little fishing port at the mouth of the Keiskama River and was expecting an interesting day. I was not disappointed.

The road went through Grahamstown, which is both a university town and the home of St. Andrews, a renowned boarding school whose pupils frequently gained places at Oxford and Cambridge. Being so close to the Ciskei the town attracted large numbers of Africans from the overcrowded reserve who were unable to make a living there or even find space for a kraal and drifted into Grahamstown in search of work. I had hitherto on my trip avoided the main population centres, so this was my first sight of the urban African problem. I turned a corner to be confronted by a group of African children gesturing me to slow down, holding out their hands, crying *"Tikki, tikki!"* (sixpence in pre-decimal terms). I had never before seen children in rags, begging, barefoot and alarmingly thin. I stopped the car, got out and shared out among them all my change and small notes. They reacted as if Christmas had come early. I went back to the car and drove off, basking in the happy feeling of having helped and made a difference. Round the next corner was a similar group of children. Clearly I could not continue as the munificent benefactor all the way up to Swaziland so I started to behave like a normal European. I didn't slow down, kept the car windows shut and the doors locked, smiled, waved and continued on my way. I reflected that, had they been there, some of my fellow passengers from the *Athlone Castle* would have been smirking, "the *rooinek* (red neck) was beginning to learn!"

Driving into the Ciskei one could quickly grasp why the Grahamstown shanty-dwellers had left their homeland. Gently rolling hills were dotted with the neat kraals of the Peddie; bands of horsemen sped across the veld on their little ponies, stirrups long, leaning back in the saddle doing the 'triple gait' so popular with the Ngoni peoples; others plodded on foot beside oxen dragging sledges loaded with firewood; small children herded cattle and goats, old men sat in groups under the trees, drinking beer, smoking pipes and talking men's talk in the luminosity of a winter's afternoon. All this is what the tourists come to see and hear. But the downside hit me in the face, the sheer density of the population, the soil erosion caused by overgrazing and the dongas made by rainwater biting into topsoil stripped of grass or tree cover because too many animals and people were trying to live off an area palpably too small for them. Quaintness put no food on the table.

A Donga.

Apologists for apartheid argued that different races lived more happily if allowed to develop at their own pace and in their own separate areas. The theory may or may not have been sound, but it was applied unfairly. Although Africans made up 70% of the population they were allocated only 18% of the land. The lion's share, 82%, went to the whites. The Coloureds (mixed race) did not feature in the carve-up at all. The Ciskei confirmed the dire analysis of African land shortage, which I had read about in the UK. People would tell you that appearances were deceptive, that it was the Africans who caused their homelands to deteriorate. In some cases this was true; but it is hard to stick to good farming practices if there is simply not enough land to go round.

On my way through the Ciskei I passed a sign to Fallodon and I thought of Edward, Viscount Grey of Fallodon, British Foreign Secretary at the outbreak of the First World War, and his famous remark: "The lamps are going out all over Europe; we shall not see them lit again in our lifetime". I reflected wryly that if the other African reserves were anything like the Ciskei the lamps would soon be going out on White South Africa.

There were no other guests that night at the little hotel in Hamburg so I spent some time talking to the owner, an agreeable woman who had lived in the area most of her life. She knew the Peddie well, spoke their language and understood their ways. The Africans from the reserve who worked for her at the hotel were loyal and the local *nduna* (sub-chief) was always helpful. So how did she feel about them? "I hate them," she said. "Why?" I asked, when her experiences of them were so good. "Because they are so many," she replied. I guess the South African Nationalist Party had her vote every time; and yet she was a pleasant woman and, according to her lights, fair minded; but she was caught in the politics of fear.

Next day I continued northwards through the Transkei, home of the Xhosa people. It seemed more structured than the Ciskei; the homesteads were larger and the individual huts looked more substantial and generally better kept than those I had seen the day before. There were more cars and more of the people seemed to have horses, suggesting greater prosperity; but here too there was obvious overcrowding. As I pushed on via the north-western parts of the Transkei towards the Drakensbergs the picture was the same – these Bantustans made a marvellous spectacle for the tourist, but they would never support their population. Anywhere else Africans could only live courtesy of a Government pass.

By contrast, nestling under the massive Drakensberg escarpment was a semi-circle of holiday hotels, high enough to be an escape from the heat of the lower districts or the humidity of the Natal coast. They offered walking, climbing and horse riding as well as golf, tennis and trout fishing or simply the opportunity to relax in considerable comfort amidst stunning scenery. A particular attraction of these resorts was the opportunity to swim in the bilharzia-free mountain streams. The resorts had enticing names, Mont-aux-Sources, Cathedral Peak, Cathkin Park, Champagne Castle, White Mountain Inn, Solitude Mountain Resort and Drakensberg Garden. It was to Drakensberg Garden that I headed for my night's stop. This was a paradise for anyone who enjoyed the outdoor life – anyone, that is, who was white. Like all 'whites only' facilities these places were barred to Africans and Coloureds, who could only come there as cooks, waiters, maids, gardeners and other manual workers, or be lodged in scruffy huts well away from the main buildings, as the servants or chauffeurs of white holidaymakers. It was the same with the buses, trains, hotels, libraries, schools and universities - even the beaches and the park benches. Everywhere in South Africa outside the 'native reserves' Africans and Coloureds were humiliatingly segregated into their own second-class facilities. At times this descended into farce. I was later to come across a notice behind Johannesburg Central Railway Station proclaiming "Lavatory for European females, non-Europeans' entrance" – i.e. it was the cleaners' entrance! It seemed unlikely that intelligent and ambitious Africans would knuckle under such humiliation for long; instead they would increasingly turn to those who were aiming to bring about change by force.

The next day's driving took me, via a detour into Zululand, to Vryheid, within striking distance of the Swaziland border. In the hotel bar, when my destination was discovered, I was treated to an earbashing even more virulent than hitherto, about the iniquities of the British during the Boer War and their failure to grasp the basic difference between the white man and the African. The locals gave me a picture of what to expect in Swaziland. "The erosion, man, they just let the natives (pronounced 'jest' and 'nightives') do what they like.

There are dongas everywhere, and the poverty, man – the idea that those nightives will be able to run the place in a few years' time – that's crezy, man. What you people from England got to understand is jest this; the nightives are inferior and will never be able to look after themselves" – and more of that ilk.

I could not wait to shake off the dust of South Africa and cross into Swaziland the next day to see things for myself.

## Chapter 3

# Mbabane

The following morning I was up early and soon across the border into Swaziland. The countryside looked reasonably tidy and not overcrowded and the people appeared happy. The roads, all dirt except for a short stretch in and out of Mbabane, were no worse than in South Africa and soil erosion, although apparent in places, was nothing like as bad as in the Ciskei, the Transkei and parts of Zululand. I was in an optimistic mood as I parked my car in front of the Secretariat in Mbabane and reported for duty to Eric Broadbent, the Establishment Officer.

My posting was as District Officer, Mbabane District. Eric introduced me to Peter Simkin, who was coming to the end of his first tour of duty, currently working as the Resident Commissioner's Private Secretary. He would show me around and, incidentally, there was a reception that night at the Residency to which I was invited. Peter took me to the District Office to meet Mr. Elliot, my District Commissioner, who suggested I use the day to settle into my bungalow and then report for duty the next morning. He would see me at the function at the Residency – "Wear your best suit." For me, that meant the suit.

Peter next led me up the hill from the town centre into a residential, almost suburban area where, down a dirt street, a characterless bungalow with a red tin roof lurked behind an overgrown hedge surrounded by unkempt lawns. But the place was redeemed by masses of huge scarlet poinsettias, magnificently in full flower. The bungalow, similar to hundreds I had seen on my drive up from Cape Town, was shaded in the front by a substantial verandah or *stoep*. At the back was a separate block forming the servants' quarters. The house cried out for a woman's touch; but that was not to be forthcoming. The form appeared to be that bachelors should employ 'schoolboys' as their servants. That way any hint of possible scandal was avoided and the schoolboy was provided with rations and somewhere to live, as well as money for his books and general expenses. Most such schoolboys came from country districts, where they were required to herd cattle until a sibling was old enough to take over. As a result, many had to start their schooling in their teens and were at school into their early twenties. This was the case with Cornelias, whom Peter's servant had found for me. Swazi men were not natural house-servants, deeming housework 'infra dig' and 'women's work'. If a reasonable level of domestic sophistication were required it was necessary to find a Nyasa or, failing that, a middle-aged Swazi lady who had been well trained by an accomplished hostess. Cornelias would be fine for me. Hopefully he would benefit, and I was not planning sophisticated entertainment (although in that respect I was to be proved embarrassingly wrong within a fortnight).

Cornelias could start at once – he needed somewhere to live – and we agreed a rough schedule of his duties, which he said would be compatible with his schoolwork. Peter told me where to buy the various items I needed, particularly the khaki bush-jackets and shorts which were the accepted alternative to a suit for everyday working dress. The Indian tailor in Mbabane measured me up for these and also suggested a lightweight suit; but that, I said, would have to wait. I had spent much of my outfit allowance clearing my overdraft before leaving UK and all but the barest necessities were delayed until my first Swaziland pay day.

The tailor's prices were a fraction of what I had paid at Airey and Wheeler in Piccadilly for the few items of tropical kit I had brought out with me and I was pleasantly surprised how little my bush jackets and shorts cost, complete with matching stockings and desert boots (the 'brothel creepers' of Eighth Army parlance). My purchases were restricted to one of everything, apart from working clothes, plus the essentials to get the kitchen going and the various items Cornelias needed to set up his little domain in the servants' quarters.

There was just time to do all this and have a quick bath before setting off for the reception at the Residency. Peter was keeping an eye open for me and introduced me to the Marwicks. Brian Marwick, the Resident Commissioner, was a fine looking man with a strong face and a kind expression; he talked pleasantly to me and then introduced me to his wife. She was extremely smartly dressed and obviously a lively conversationalist. She asked if I had any experience of amateur dramatics. "None," I replied, "excepting a walk-on part in Macbeth at my prep school." This was clearly not the answer she had been seeking and her interest in me quickly waned. I later learned that acting ability, or a good singing voice, gave instant access to her inner circle and that her theatrical productions were the highlight of the Mbabane social scene. I had probably not made a good first impression on the redoubtable Mrs Marwick, but otherwise I think I survived the evening without rubbing people up the wrong way. I had to be careful. A member of the European Advisory Council (EAC) was kind enough to take me aside and advise me to keep my ideas to myself until I had been in Swaziland long enough to grow out of the stupid liberal notions I would have picked up at Oxford or Cambridge or wherever I had come from. Another EAC member, Robert (Bob) Stephens, chairman and managing director of Peak Timbers, the large forestry company in the north of the country, asked me sensible questions and wished me good luck, ending by saying he hoped I would one day be posted to Pigg's Peak, but not before I had served a good apprenticeship elsewhere! Representatives of the King's Council, The Swazi National Council, were also there. These included Mnt (abbreviated form of *Mntwanenkhosi* - Prince) Mazini Dlamini, one of the King's many sons. On hearing that I was posted to Mbabane District Mazini told me that his oldest brother, Mnt Makhungu, was on the DC's staff there as Chief Clerk. I also met the King's private secretary, A K Hlophe. I immediately liked Abednigo Khuseni Hlophe and my regard for him was to increase as time went by. He was a Christian and active in church affairs, yet was able to bridge the divide between traditional Swazi and European ways.

A. K. Hlope

A few minutes later I was introduced to another EAC member, Carl Todd. He was a South African lawyer and was chairman of the EAC. My immediate impression was that if he had been a bull I would be very cautious going into his pen. Mr Elliot was also there with his wife and he pointed out to me some of the more notable people in the room including Mnt Makhosini Dlamini, once headmaster of the Swazi National School and then a Rural Development Officer and a chief in the Hlatikulu area. By 1962 he was playing an increasingly important role in the Swazi National Council. "He is a coming man," said Mr Elliot, a prediction fully borne out when Makhosini became the first Prime Minister of the

Independent Kingdom of Swaziland six years later. Peter Simkin had kindly asked me to dinner after the reception. The other guests, all around his age, were "Bunny" Theale, a government vet originally from Dorset, and Julian and Rosemary Faux. Julian had grown up in Natal and then gone on a Rhodes scholarship to Cambridge. There he met and married Rosemary, the daughter of Dr Wynn Wilson, a former Welsh Rugby International. Julian was working in the Secretariat and he and Rosemary had a young family.

It was natural that the conversation, perhaps partly for my benefit, should turn to the rapidly developing Swaziland scenario and how some of the people who had been at the Residency that evening fitted into the political jigsaw. Until the mainly Afrikaner South African Nationalist Party defeated Jan Smuts' United Party in 1948 it was tacitly assumed that the purpose of the 'Protectorate' in Swaziland was to gently nurture the country until it was appropriate to hand it over for incorporation into South Africa. Even into the late1950s this was still the expectation of most European Swazilanders. This assumption explained their hostility when the administration changed policy and moved in the direction of universal suffrage leading to independence for Swaziland as a nation state. It was a shock to me to learn that racial segregation had not been proscribed in Swaziland until March 1962 (i.e. less than six months before my arrival) when the Anti-Discrimination Proclamation came into effect to prohibit segregated facilities in bars, banks, cinemas, hotels and theatres. There had been, and to some extent still was, a pathological fear of upsetting South Africa and providing an excuse for its army to march in and annexe Swaziland on the pretext of protecting South African citizens and property. This fear probably explained the delay in abolishing segregation. There were lesser fears in the other two protectorates, Basutoland and Bechuanaland, as they were not nearly so attractive to South Africa as the fertile and mineral-rich land of the Swazis. (Bechuanaland only started to develop its diamonds in the late 1950s. Basutoland, now Lesotho, is still a very poor country.)

As elsewhere, it was racial discrimination probably more than anything else that pushed talented Swazi men into the 'new'politics.

I had read that Kwame Nkrumah, who had spearheaded the independence movement in Ghana and was its first President in 1957, had as a young man been fiercely pro-British until he went to Britain and America and found himself discriminated against because of his colour. In Swaziland John J. Nquku, a Zulu who had been appointed Supervisor of Native Education (*sic*) in 1937, resigned ten years later because of racist ill-treatment. Sobhuza, the *Ngwenyama* (King) immediately gave him a position as National Adviser to the Swazi National Inner Council and in 1960, following extensive travels abroad, Nquku had formed the first modern Swazi political party, the Swaziland Progressive Party (SPP).

Sobhuza II with Charles McSeveny, then a member
of the European Advisory Council.
*(Photo courtesy of Swaziland Administration, 1964)*

Perhaps because he was a Zulu Nquku never had much of a following. The strong man of the party was Dr Ambrose Zwane who was soon to split with Nquku and form his own party, the Ngwane National Liberatory Congress (NNLC). He had been the first Swazi to qualify as a doctor and he too resigned from the government service, in his case the Medical Service, because of racial discrimination and specifically discrimination in matters of salary. He was another protégé of Sobhuza, who had helped to pay his university fees. However, the man to watch, Julian and Peter agreed, was a high-born young prince of real charisma, the leader of the party's youth wing, Dumisa Dlamini. "Wait till you meet him, you'll be impressed." He could be dangerous, they suggested; it was not known to what extent he had been communist influenced or communist funded. Like Nquku and Dr Zwane, he had been helped by Sobhuza, who had paid for him to attend the University of Basutoland, Bechuanaland and Swaziland at Roma in Basutoland. While there he had failed to graduate but had worked with the anti-colonial Basutoland Congress Party, which had links with the African National Congress in South Africa.

"What prospects are there for the multiracial Swaziland Democratic Party?" I asked. I mentioned I had met their leaders, Simon Nxumalo and Vincent Rozwadowski at the Residency party. "Oh yes," said Peter, "you'll meet them everywhere. The party is a grand idea; but it only really appeals to ultra-westernised Swazis and a sort of Bloomsbury set in the European community, people like Bunny, who is well dug in at the Residency." (I later heard the SDP described by some wag as "the political wing of the Mbabane Dramatic Society!"). Bunny, who for all his friendship with the Marwicks was nobody's poodle, agreed with Peter, Julian and Rosemary that senior members of the administration and particularly Athel Long, the Government Secretary and Mike Fairlie, the Labour Secretary, had too high hopes of the SDP. A final party, just formed, was the Mbandzeni National Convention, led by Dr George Msibi and Clifford Nkosi, a Swazi lawyer. This party seemed to be placed midway between the SDP and the NNLC. Not much was yet known of them, but their leaders were people who had worked in the outside world. George Msibi had trained in India and Clifford Nkosi had been with a law firm in the Republic.

"What about those Europeans who are not caught up with the SDP?" I asked, mentioning I had met Todd and Stephens. "Ah, Todd," said someone, "they say of him, parodying Ogden Nash,

'Two Ds in Todd,

How very odd,

When one's enough for God'"

Todd, they said, was a forceful character and had close links with Verwoerd, the President of South Africa. Stephens, by contrast, was his own man and was thought to be pragmatic.

"Where did Marwick stand in relation to all these political developments?" I asked. I was told that he had gradually lost patience with his old friend, Sobhuza and the Swazi National Council, partly because of the King's reluctance to row in behind the Colonial Office's recipe for movement towards independence on the 'one person one vote' principle, or 'one person, one vote, once' as the cynics called it. The rift derived partly because of the promptings of Marwick's senior lieutenants, Long and Fairlie. The latter, an acerbic Aberdonian bachelor, whose talents included haute cuisine and flower arranging, made no attempt to disguise his contempt for the Swazi National Council. It seemed that Marwick felt that the King was a spent force and that the Swazi National Council had become an anachronism, out of touch with the younger and particularly the urban Swazis. One only had to go down to Lobamba, the Swazi National Council's headquarters, they said, and look at the scruffy old guards there, to sense an air of decay and hopelessness. How the future would unfurl was very uncertain. We were, Julian said, on the cusp of new times. It was already becoming apparent to me that the political scene was much more complicated than I had been led to believe back in the UK. I had plenty to ponder as I drove home to my bungalow and prepared myself for my first working day.

Mr Elliot, to whom I reported for duty at the District Office the next morning, had spent most of his service in Basutoland and on retirement had settled in Swaziland and bought a little farm half way down the hill from Mbabane overlooking the Ezulwini valley. Mr Marwick, who had served for a time with him in Basutoland, soon coaxed Mr Elliot out of retirement to do a final stint as DC Mbabane. He was a big man and in his youth had been a considerable polo player. I was told that on marriage he had sold his polo ponies, believing that he could not afford to keep a wife and family as well as a string of ponies, and he never played polo again. This, I was to discover, was typical of his straightforward decisiveness. He spoke briefly about what my job would entail and then took me round the offices to meet the other staff. He prefaced the round of introductions with a warning not to expect instant warmth or even civility from the Swazi staff. Mr Elliot (and in those formal times it was always to be 'Mr Elliot') told me of his first posting to Basutoland, where he was 'sent to Coventry' for six months before the Basuto staff gave him any sort of friendly recognition. It would probably have been longer but for his prowess on the polo field, for the Basutos are great horsemen. I was, therefore, not surprised to be received by the office staff with something less than rapture.

Three people particularly caught my attention. The first was the Chief Clerk, Mnt Makhungu Dlamini, whose half-brother I had met the previous evening. Although he was the King's first son there was never any possibility of Makhungu becoming Ngwenyama. Succession was not a matter of primogeniture and was only determined after the death of the reigning king. According to tradition a committee of senior counsellors would meet and decide which son was to be chosen to become the new king. Often it was a young boy; Sobhuza had been only a few months old when he had been selected in 1899. There would then be a regency until the boy was old enough to be installed as Ngwenyama. The whole process of selection is set out in detail in Hilda Kuper's *Sobhuza II, Ngwenyama and King of Swaziland*.

Makhungu, although not in the frame for succession, was nevertheless a respected figure in Swazi society. It might be thought strange that a prince of his standing should be serving in a government office; but Sobhuza had always encouraged members of his family to go out and do real jobs, rather than spend their time in idleness and pleasure seeking. Makhungu, a large man with an open face was to become a

41

great help to me, and a good friend. But that morning, as far as his impeccable manners allowed, he gave me a cool greeting. My predecessor had been the country's second Swazi District Officer and there was general disappointment that he was not being followed by another Swazi. If Makhungu was cool, Amos Mamba, the revenue clerk, was icy. A small chap with a bright face but eyes full of hostility, he doubtless resented the arrival of a young man from Britain to fill a post that could have been given to a local, possibly even himself. The third person to stand out in the round of introductions was Ntshalintshali. He was the *Ndabazabantu* (literally 'affairs of the people'), the Swazi National Council's representative at the District Office. Unlike the other staff he spoke practically no English and wore traditional Swazi dress. His only concession to European attire was the almost obligatory fashion accessory for middle-aged Swazi men, an old British Army great-coat. Swazi soldiers returning from the North African and Italian campaigns at the end of the Second World War had brought their army uniforms back with them. Thanks to army surplus wholesalers great-coats later became available in most Swaziland stores. The Swazi said that the thick cloth absorbed the heat in summer and kept out the cold in winter. Early August was the height of winter, approaching the end of the dry season and cold enough, even in the bushveld, for a fire in the evenings – certainly it was great-coat weather in the highveld.

While I was being taken on my round of introductions there was suddenly a great commotion emanating from the reception office, much shouting and laughter and exclamations of *"Hau! Hau!"* the multi-purpose Swazi expression of surprise. The cause of all the excitement was a snowball that had been brought in from the Bomvu Ridge, a high hill on the Transvaal border fifteen miles to the west of Mbabane. The name meant 'Red Ridge'. The red colour of the soil came from deposits of iron ore and a contract had recently been signed with a Japanese consortium to mine the ore and build a railway to carry it down through Mozambique to Lourenco Marques for shipment to Japan. None of the Swaziland hills was much more than 6,000 feet above sea level and snow was a rarity. The snowball was shown round all the offices and duly admired; for my part I was much taken by the office staff's ability to be so enchanted by a natural phenomenon. One thing was quite certain, they were much more impressed by the snowball than they were by me!

By coincidence I was going out to the foot of the Bomvu Ridge that morning as Mr Elliot had arranged for the District Agricultural Officer, Peter Millin, to take me with him on a visit to agricultural projects in the Swazi area of Motshane. It was a place where Swazi farmers were making excellent progress in advanced husbandry practices. We met the local Agricultural Field Officer (Umlimi), Peter's resident man on the spot, together with the local cattle guard, who advised on animal husbandry and supervised the fortnightly dipping of cattle against tick-borne diseases. Ntshalintshali came too. He seemed to play little part in the proceedings; but his presence was a token of the Swazi National Council's approval. This expedition had an effect on me quite as dramatic as that of the snowball on the office staff earlier in the morning. These rural Swazi, seen in their own environment, with their natural grace and charm, made me want to grab a knobkerrie (stick with a knob handle, originally used for fighting and still a source of many cracked heads) and dance around shouting "*Hau! Hau!*" What struck me was that these people had a bearing and independence of spirit totally different from what I had seen in my travels through South Africa.

On the drive back and later in the privacy of his office, Peter explained that Motshane was not typical of the general state of agricultural development in the rural areas. Allocation of land was entrusted to the local chief and much depended on his attitude. Some carried out their duties with scrupulous fairness; but it was not unknown for a chief to allocate the best land to his own kinsmen, or allow a progressive farmer to develop a vegetable growing business through irrigation and the use of fertilisers and then, when the market garden came to fruition, to decide that "this is a lucky piece of land", take it for himself and push the unfortunate farmer off to some uncultivated rocky outcrop. Other chiefs did not go that far, but demanded unreasonable favours as the price of continuing tenure. Various loan schemes to enable Swazi farmers to buy machinery tended to come to grief through such practices, with tractors and pick-ups being prematurely worn out through joy-riding and use as unpaid rural taxi services. Also, just as in the UK, where many 'gentlemen farmers' were keener on the rural lifestyle than on getting their hands dirty, equally in Swaziland many would-be 'progressive farmers' were more attracted by the kudos of owning new machinery than they were by the daily grind of small-scale agriculture.

There was a further barrier to widespread agricultural progress, Peter explained. What he told me echoed some of the teaching at the Devonshire Course. Traditionally, amongst the Ngoni tribal grouping which included the Swazi, the grown man was a warrior. His role was to fight, which included cattle rustling and general pillage and if this was proscribed, as it was under Colonial rule, then to *xoxa* (discuss affairs over a pot of beer) – shades of the gentleman farmer again. His cattle were herded by his children and his womenfolk tilled the land. The system worked well; the land was fertile and well watered and the rainfall, even in the bushveld, was sufficient to allow the average family to feed itself and even amass a little capital in the form of cattle and goats. These could be used for *lobola* (bride price) as necessary. But such a relaxed attitude was no proof against drought or overgrazing when the cattle weakened or died and the reduced crops were insufficient to feed the family, let alone provide seed-corn for the next year. Without cash reserves people could be in desperate trouble. Happily in those days the contingency plans for famine relief were very rarely needed. It had to be conceded, Peter continued (although he was a South African), that British colonial rule had brought peace, law and order and impartial justice to the High Commission territories and these benefits should not easily be disregarded.

The next day Mr Elliot asked me my impressions of my day out with Peter. I told him briefly what I had seen and, I hoped, learned. He spoke about tax collection. Poll tax had been introduced to help kick start the cash economy. The tax was a minimal amount, then four rand (£2.00) per adult male, single or with one wife. There was a higher band for men with two wives and a third band for those with three wives or more. The tax probably did not cover the real cost of collection, but made it necessary for all heads of Swazi households to have some hard cash. Hopefully more and more people would start to alter their attitude to a cash economy and stop relying on a purely subsistence approach to farming. In earlier years, if people wanted money they sent their sons to work in the mines in South Africa. Over time the proportion of the Swazi population going to the mines had decreased as more and more families benefited from home-earned wealth in the gradually expanding Swaziland economy. Even so, in 1962 around nine thousand Swazi men were still working in the South African mines, but the statistics showed that this source of income was becoming less important to the Swaziland economy. In 1926 the number of adult males working in the South African mines amounted to 9.97% of the total population (men, women and children). In 1962 the equivalent figure was 2.6%.

My next trip out into the District with Peter Millin was to an area very different from progressive Motshane. We went to Maphalaleni, east of Mbabane. This was a scenically impressive valley running north to the Komati River, which formed the boundary between the Mbabane and Pigg's Peak Districts. Even in a Land Rover and in the dry season when there was no mud or flooding it was a moderately challenging drive. The area had been effectively without a chief for some time as the present chief, Mashila, was ill, probably incurably, so it was difficult for the Field Officer to raise any enthusiasm for growing crops or vegetables, despite excellent opportunities for irrigation as no one knew whether, if Mashila died, the new chief would reallocate land. Likewise, cattle-dipping discipline was breaking down without an active chief to back the cattle guard's authority. There was little that could be done except apply gentle pressure through Ntshalintshali; but, like elsewhere, one could use one's contacts. Makhungu, in particular, was well placed to put in a judicious word at Lobamba to authorise interim arrangements during Mashila's illness.

For me this was a time for watching and listening; but at the end of the week I was given my first proper task. The Secretariat had recently decided that each District Commissioner should produce a 'District Plan'. The envelope had lain untouched in Mr Elliot's in-tray since its delivery. "There you are," he said to me, "get on with it. With your

Oxford education you should be able to write decent English. You can't write about things you don't understand, so go out and about in the District and see what you find. Apart from anything else you will be bringing a completely fresh mind to the task, which could be interesting." This was a shrewd move by Mr Elliot. I now had a focus for practically every working moment of each day, a reason to travel extensively throughout the District, acquainting myself with the problems of each community. I also had a cast-iron excuse for enlisting the help of the senior Swazi staff, as well as the specialist European officers - Agriculture, Veterinary, Education, Public Works, Police and Medical. I negotiated a period of three months to come up with the draft plan.

On our first Saturday in Swaziland Jeremy and Wendy Varcoe and I were invited to join a walking party organised by Peter Simkin, to visit the bushman paintings at Nsangwini, almost due north of Maphalaleni but on the Pigg's Peak side of the Komati River valley. We drove as far as we could and then had a long walk through rough scrub country. It was to be the first of many Simkin expeditions in which I participated, characterised by Peter striding confidently ahead, usually with his faithful servant, William, at his heels, but not quite convincing the remainder of the party that he knew where he was going. The infantryman's jibe about British cavalry regiments' typical approach to battle sprung to mind. "Having lost sight of their objectives, they redoubled their efforts." (William's surname, Mahlalanga, was misleading. It meant 'those who are left behind'. In fact, he kept up with Peter better than most people, but not on crocodile hunts. He was unconvinced by Peter's theory that crocodiles did not attack at night!)

Soon the midday heat, trapped in the steep valley, started to affect some of the party. Jeremy, who had not brought a hat, draped a towel on his head. His detractors said he had the temperament of a swirling dervish; now, bizarrely turbaned by his towel, he looked the part. Wendy began to realise that her attire for the day was more suited to a stroll in the Parks at Oxford than to a trek through the rocks and thorn trees of the middleveld. Another of the party, a middle-aged nursing sister from Mbabane hospital, found the terrain increasingly taxing and the group became widely strung out.

Bushman Paintings at Nsangwini.

Several of the women were particularly challenged when we had to cross the fast-flowing Nkomazane River (little Komati). Eventually, after several feints at the wrong rock overhangs we found the paintings. They were totally unguarded and unprotected yet remarkably were not desecrated in any way. Most of the paintings were thought to date from the 18th century. Thus many generations of people, including herd-boys bored out of their minds watching their beasts, had resisted the temptation to make their own additions to the artwork. Two years later when revisiting the paintings, I found a group of Swazi children amusing themselves at the site. They were using the sun's rays to project hand and finger shadow-patterns onto the rock face, and were making these hand figures dance amongst the painted creatures on the stone. These children were totally respectful of the paintings themselves, being careful not even to touch them. However, when I took my family back to Swaziland for a visit in 1982, we were told that the paintings were railed off and only open for visitors at specific times. 'Civilisation' had caught up. In 1962 and for some years to come, however, there was complete freedom for anyone to go and view the amazingly clear paintings. The showpiece was a pair of winged human figures, featured at that time on one of the everyday Swaziland stamps. These figures were thought to be unique; nothing remotely like them has ever been found anywhere else. Theories abounded as to what they represented, ranging from warriors or medicine men in ceremonial dress to creatures from outer space. The rest of the paintings, though interesting, were unremarkable and similar to many others all over southern Africa. They depicted animals, birds and hunting scenes, but they lacked the quality and precision of the winged figures, which the experts thought were considerably older.

Mission accomplished, we were a tired but happy group who set out to trudge back to our cars, buoyed up by the realisation that we had seen something rather special. On the way we suddenly noticed a figure running towards us from a Swazi homestead. It was Amos Mamba, the stand-offish revenue clerk from the Mbabane District Office. "Mr Miller, Mr Miller," he cried, "what are you doing here?" I introduced him to our party and explained where we had been. "That is very good," he said, "you must all come and meet my wife and the children." This was not his weekday lodging, but his real home, the *khaya* to which he returned every weekend to be with his family. We were shown round and asked him about irrigation possibilities in the valley. I then talked to him about his cattle. What did he think, for instance, about the government bull-breeding project at Mpisi? "You know about the Mpisi bulls then?" "Oh yes," I replied, stretching the truth a little, "I heard all about them from Professor Masefield at Oxford University." "Hau," he said, "that is extraordinary." Having grown up in a prime dairy farming area of southern Scotland, which was also the home of the Galloway and Belted Galloway beef breeds, it was easy for me to talk cattle with him and to discuss the finer points of individual animals. We were given tea and little home-baked cakes and the whole interlude was a delightful surprise addition to the day's programme.

Amos Mamba was the first person into my office on the Monday morning, wanting to talk about our Saturday encounter and my impressions of the paintings. From that day onwards the Swazi office staff were friendly towards me, including even Ntshanintshali, who started to give me the occasional incomprehensible grunt in reply to my best attempt at a Swazi "Good morning" greeting. Why had this inconsequential leisure time encounter broken the ice? I suspect because we had been spending the day learning something about Swazi heritage rather than disporting ourselves with other Europeans on the tennis courts at the Mbabane Club.

On the subject of clubs, most towns had a sports and social club. These had been for Europeans only, but after the passing of the Anti-Discrimination Proclamation the clubs had to open their doors, at least in theory, to Africans and Coloureds. The doors were not opened very willingly, nor very wide, and in some places not at all. The Mbabane Club had admitted Edward Zwane, the territory's first Swazi District Officer and he could not have been a better pioneer. His charm and tact meant that he had soon been welcomed by all but the most diehard members. At Hlatikulu, where he was next transferred, the principle of African club membership had already been established. Dr Sidney Shongwe, an able and delightful doctor originally from Zululand, had been appointed as a Government Medical Officer at the Hlatikulu Hospital. The Club President was Colonel Loringh van Beeck, a retired Dutch Cavalry officer and former ADC to Queen Juliana. He was quick to propose Sidney's membership, which was seconded by the Hospital Superintendent Jack Klopper, a liberal South African of Afrikaner descent. Sidney and his charming wife June were happily assumed into the club, likewise Edward Zwane when he arrived. Another excellent development was the opening of Swaziland's new multi racial Boarding School, Waterford, founded by Michael Stern, a teacher from South Africa. It was an instant success with 100% passes in the British O-level exam in its first year. Pupils came from all over Southern Africa.

At Manzini, however, where Jeremy Varcoe had been posted, the situation was very different. The town might have shed its Afrikaans name of Bremersdorp in favour of the Swazi 'Manzini' (by the riverside); but Afrikaner attitudes persisted amongst many of the European population. Jeremy, no sluggard in matters of conscience, invited a Swazi to the club as his guest during his first week of membership. Other members reacted angrily and Jeremy was shocked. He was further incensed when Frank Fleck, his DC, refused to take his side in the matter. Frank Fleck, tall and in his fifties, was an able administrator; but he had been born and brought up in South Africa and was no advocate of Africanization, nor of relaxing the social boundaries between the races. By advising Jeremy to take things quietly and slowly he was waving a red rag at an already stirred up young bull. Things did not improve for the Varcoes the following weekend when I stayed with them. Jeremy suggested we play tennis, so we went down to the club relatively early in the morning and, finding none of the courts in use and the place deserted, we had a few games. Suddenly, an enraged South African matron descended upon us, asking what we were about. Apparently there was a booking list and, anyway, they were preparing for a tournament. The *rooinek* had done it again!

The Swazis, incidentally, call the skin colour of all Europeans (Afrikaners included) red, not white, and say that we "smell of the sun", analogous to the Chinese view that Europeans "smell of meat". It is all relative. I am told, for instance, that Nairobi prostitutes say that European men smell like chicken feathers in the rain! Smell, of course, is largely a question of diet. Swazi millet beer, *utshwala*, white and acid, usually served in huge black communal pots passed from person to person, played a large part in Swazi social life. On a hot day the sweat of a Swazi who had copiously imbibed took on the beer's bitter smell - giving such a person a lift in one's car could be an unpleasant business especially as you often had to close the windows to keep out the dust. I soon found, however, that if I drank *utshwala*, and it could be a social obligation to do so, my sweat smelt just as rank as that of any bush Swazi. Drinking the beer from the communal pot also had hygiene implications in a country where tuberculosis was rife. Additionally, it would not create a good impression pitching up at one's next appointment reeking of drink!

I could not complain if drinking *utshwala* was really the worst trial I had to undergo. Sir Arthur Grimble's memoirs *A Pattern of Islands*, was the book which seriously set me thinking about the Colonial Service. Grimble's ordeal in his early days in the Gilbert and Ellis Islands was to be the decoy man in an octopus hunt. He had to dive into the harbour, let a vast octopus envelope him in its tentacles until, just before his breath gave out his partner rescued him by diving down onto the preoccupied octopus and killing it by biting it between the eyes. Even though ordeal by Swazi beer was not in the same league as Sir Arthur's octopus embrace I nevertheless devised a way of avoiding drinking in the line of duty. The technique, which I am sure was not original, was to poke my face well into the vast upturned beer pot and swallow ostentatiously, with intermittent burping, all the time keeping my lips tightly closed. Nobody told me that I was ever found out. The Swazi are polite people, but not that polite, and if they had rumbled me I am sure they would have shared the joke, if not with me, certainly with a service colleague. It was amazing what you found out about others from the casual talk of Swazis, especially when they imagined you could not understand what they were saying.

As well as thinking of us as red rather than white, Swazis had great difficulty in distinguishing between individual Europeans. "All whites look the same." Many Europeans, newly arrived in Africa, said the same about Africans. The trick, of course, is not to focus on what people have in common – colour or hair texture etc – but on what differentiates them – features, height, stature, bearing or body conformation. Growing up in a rural part of Scotland one absorbed this technique with livestock. Even chickens are quite easy to identify individually if you take it seriously! With these considerations in mind and to make myself distinguishable by rural Swazis who would only see me from time to time, I worked out a recognisable identity for myself. This consisted of the standard DO's khaki bush jacket with Government brass buttons, khaki shorts (or long khaki trousers in winter), khaki stockings with garters and suede desert boots. In addition, to aid recognition, I would carry a Scots shepherd's crook with a ram's horn handle. This I asked my father to procure for me. When it arrived it was an instant success.

Most Swazi, even in the towns, were interested in livestock and the ram's horn handle would generally set a conversation going.

Another request was that my parents should start to use airmail for their letters. When my father had been in Singapore and Jahore in the 1920s and 1930s, there had been no airmail so it probably never occurred to him or my mother that by 1962 there was an alternative to surface mail. They had always been punctilious in their correspondence. It says as much about the Royal Mail's reliability in the 1950s as it does about my parents' care for us that my sister and I, when at boarding school, could tell the day of the week by whether there was a letter for us in the morning post. Our father wrote to each of us on Sundays and our mother wrote on Tuesdays and Thursdays. The letters were put out for the postman to take the next morning when he delivered their mail; and the letters always arrived the following day. So, if there was a letter from my father it was Tuesday; a letter from my mother meant it was Thursday or Saturday – no letter meant it was Sunday, Monday, Wednesday or Friday. This routine was typical of the sense of duty which ran so strongly through most of my parents' generation. They made rules for the way they lived and stuck by them. Anyone who did not was a 'bounder' or the female equivalent. It was a surprise therefore that there were no letters from my parents awaiting my arrival at Mbabane, nor indeed for another fortnight. However, two airmails from my sister, living in London, had indicated that all was well at home. Telephoning the UK from Swaziland was an uncertain business and it could take up to two days to get connected, so airmail was the easiest way of keeping in touch. Once such contact was established my parents and I conducted a regular correspondence. They kept all my letters, which have been a very useful aide-memoire in writing this narrative more than forty years later.

From the very start it was clear to me that Mr Elliot was well experienced in training new DOs, so I was lucky to start my service under him. I soon discovered that the first DO to be posted to him when he was a DC in Basutoland had been another Galloway man, recently appointed Chief Secretary in Bechuanaland, Arthur Douglas, whose uncle, Sir James Douglas of Barstibly near Kirkcudbright, was a friend of my father. Sir James had been the founding chairman of the Scottish Milk Marketing Board which had done so much to re-establish Scottish dairy farming on a sound basis after the decline that followed the First World War. He had been extraordinarily kind to me when I was growing up and had often included me in his excellent shooting parties and other enjoyable social functions when I was at home. I was soon to meet Arthur Douglas when he visited Mbabane and found him to be cast much in the same mould as his delightful uncle.

Just as I was beginning to find my feet and settle into a comfortable routine I had a phone call which brought me up with a jolt. It was from Lady Salmon, whom we had met on the *Athlone Castle*. She and her daughter Jenny had finished their visit to Zululand and had now arrived to stay with the Marwicks at the Residency. As had been suggested when we went our separate ways at Cape Town, she was asking if she and Jenny could pay me a visit. "Of course," I replied, "come and have supper one evening if you don't mind bachelor fare." "That's fine," she said, "we didn't exactly encounter haute cuisine with Anthony in Zululand; but I'd better check with the Marwicks which evening will be convenient for us to be out." She was quickly back on the line. "Friday will be fine and the Marwicks would like to come too, if that's all right." That I had never expected!

I had four days to prepare. Cornelias and I set about the garden in a frenzy. Although what we achieved was not in the same league as the Count of Monte Cristo's pre-party landscaping in Alexandre Dumas's eponymous novel, the garden was transformed. I bought a uniform for Cornelias and rehearsed him in the intricacies of table service, while at the same time borrowing from my new friends the crockery, cutlery, glassware, table linen, rugs, picture and lamps to make the evening a viable possibility and render the bungalow remotely worthy of the occasion. The borrowed items included a huge entrée dish on which to serve the evening's pièce de résistance, a splendid joint of beef. This was in line with a culinary strategy to allow maximum preparation before the guests arrived. Swaziland beef was good, if you could find something tender (flavour was never a problem as it was all slow matured) and the joint I had bought was large enough to be allowed to 'rest' after cooking and not grow cold. Brightly coloured vegetables were selected to contrast with the glorious deep red of the beef and I drew a plan for Cornelias as to how they should be arranged. He was rehearsed on making his entry with the beef and, by now fully into the spirit of the endeavour, summed it up as being "a bit like Herod's feast with John the Baptist's head on the platter". (He went to a Mission School!) I felt like saying it would be his head on a platter if he messed up; but I knew from a friend in the Oxford University Dramatic Society that you did not make chancy remarks to your male lead just before the curtain went up.

Peter Simkin and Bunny Theale, the vet, had been enlisted to come and steady the ship for me. Peter knew the Marwicks well, having done a considerable stint as the RC's Private Secretary and Bunny was very much *persona grata* at the Residency and a friend of the Marwicks' daughters. Mr Elliot and his wife were also invited. It was politic to include them as I had asked for the afternoon off work in order to make things ready. I also thought they would hit it off with Lady Salmon and, of course, they were old friends of the Marwicks from the latter's time in Basutoland. Additionally, the Elliots had been very kind to me, inviting me to meals and introducing me to people in my first few days in Swaziland. Finally, there were Jeremy and Wendy, whom I knew the Salmons wanted to see. Thanks to my afternoon off work we were as ready as we were ever likely to be when the guests started arriving.

The Marwicks and the Salmons came in the RC's official car with the Resident Commissioner driving, rather than Jo Abner, a member of a well respected 'coloured' ( mixed race) family who was the official chauffeur, since this was a private function. Somewhat to my surprise, the RC parked the car on my newly manicured lawn. (People did not do that in Galloway, not even the Lord Lieutenant!) The car in question was an Austin Princess, much used at that time in the UK by undertakers, but in this case kitted out to be something of a mobile office for the RC and those accompanying him when he went around the territory. It looked the part; but I was later to discover was a pig to drive, uncomfortable and very slow.

Joe Abner, the RC's driver.
*(Photo courtesy of Swaziland Administration, 1964)*

The minor affront to my lawn notwithstanding, all started rather well. Mr Marwick asked Jeremy if he had met the American Roving Ambassador to Africa who had visited Manzini two weeks earlier on a whistle-stop fact-finding tour of Africa. No, replied Jeremy, he had just missed him, but the good American had caused considerable comment. Half an hour after his plane touched down the Roving Ambassador had held a press conference. When this finished much earlier than expected because of almost total lack of interest by the local press, Mr Fleck, the DC, had filled in time before the Ambassador's next appointment by taking him round the Manzini Government Offices and introducing him to the various staff. It so happened that when they reached the Revenue

Office they found the revenue clerk, a very bright, intelligent Swazi, busy dealing with someone who had walked in from the nearby Swazi Area to pay his tax. This old man was barefoot, clad in traditional dress and was wearing a red loeri-bird feather in his hair, the mark of a Dlamini, the royal clan. Mr Fleck mentioned the significance of the red feather and then introduced the Ambassador to the revenue clerk, whereupon the American, inexplicably mistaking who was who, completely ignored the clerk but seized the old man by the hand exclaiming, "I sure am glad to meet you, Mr Dlamini. The DC has been telling me what a good job you are doing here." The old rural Swazi, totally mystified, bowed and scraped, shielding his eyes in the traditional gesture of submission, humbly greeting him *"Nkos"* (Chief). Nobody disillusioned the Roving Ambassador who possibly started to question his earlier assertion at the press conference that "these educated Africans are perfectly capable of governing themselves".

Mr Marwick offered another story, which concerned the Ambassador's visit to the Swazi national headquarters at Lobamba later in the same day when he met the Ngwenyama and senior chiefs and counsellors. There was a liberal supply of gin and one old chief took such advantage of the hospitality that he fell off his seat and started crawling around the ground, draining the dregs from any glass that came within his reach. The American, seeing him on his knees, once again reached the wrong conclusion and said to Athel Long in a confidential tone, "Isn't it remarkable what respect some of these fellows have for their chief!" I followed this tale with my own illustration of the apparent tendency for Americans of that generation to make their observations tally with their preconceptions. In my second year at Oxford I was one of the University Yacht Club's bosuns, responsible for the upkeep of our fleet of racing dinghies. One afternoon I was walking across the quadrangle towards the bicycle shed to go down to the river to work on the boats. I was wearing the old clothes I kept for this purpose, all liberally spattered with the dark blue paint we used on the boats' hulls. There was a group of American tourists admiring the façade of the college library and as I passed them I heard the *sotto voce* comment, "You see dear, it is what I was saying, it is not only rich men's sons who come to Oxford these days!"

After drinks on the stoep we sat down in the dining room. There was a cold starter, which I had prepared and laid out earlier. When that was finished Cornelias cleared away the dishes impeccably. I had feared that he might have fortified himself with a little Dutch courage, but there was no sign of this. So far, so good! The Salmons were their normal charming selves and the Marwicks chatted happily with everyone; but then there was a hiatus – no sign of the main course. I rang the bell to no avail. So I excused myself to investigate. There, on the kitchen table, was the meat dish with the colourful vegetables arranged around the edge according to my diagram, but of the joint itself and Cornelias there was no trace.

I had a sudden flashback to the Devonshire Course when someone had said that the Swazi, because of their pastoralist origins, were obsessed with cattle and were great meat eaters. Cornelias had probably never seen such a fine joint of meat and presumably the temptation had been irresistible. However, this was no time to ponder anthropological explanations. I had ten guests to feed, including the two men best placed to make or break my Swaziland career. As in the feeding of the five thousand it was a question of using what was available. Unfortunately I had no loaves and fishes, only a small tin of corned beef. This unexpected entertaining so early after my arrival had stretched my finances. The larder was bare as I was expecting to live for the next few days off the dinner party leftovers. So it had to be the corned beef.

I plonked the pathetic lump of Argentinian pressed meat onto the middle of the great platter and carried the dish in, making feeble apologies and trying to explain what I thought had happened. My guests were generally amused, although Mrs Marwick made some remark about people needing to be less naïve about whom they employed. I forebore to say that perhaps a food pilferer was better than the prohibited immigrant who had almost conned me into employing him before Peter had produced Cornelias; nor did Jeremy and Wendy volunteer that the first girl they had taken on as their part-time servant turned out to be a member of the oldest profession! I kept filling up the glasses to promote bonhomie and help kill off my guests' appetites, wondering all the while whether Cornelias and his dining chums would beat us to the pudding and the cheese. They didn't, so that at least was a relief. When the Marwicks, Lady Salmon and the Elliots drove off home, the younger folk stayed on for another whisky. Within a minute of the cars leaving Cornelias reappeared, clutching in one hand the mangled remnants of the joint, covered in soil and saliva and, in the other, a makeshift lead attached to Bruce, Peter Simkin's yellow Labrador. Unbeknown to me, Peter had brought Bruce with him and had left him in the car with the door open, so that the dog could roam around a little. He was a peaceable creature, Peter explained, and never strayed far from the car. That night, however, Bruce had wandered far enough to find the open kitchen door. Coming in with the tray of dishes from the first course Cornelias was just in time to see Bruce making off with the joint and had given chase. He eventually caught up with Bruce but was so horrified at what had happened that he went and hid in his quarters till he saw the RC leave. We gave the poor chap a drink to steady his nerves and thanked him for his efforts and then we all collapsed with mirth. Jenny was able to carry the full explanation back to Government House, but Mrs Marwick dined out on the story for weeks, how this new DO, straight out from the UK, had invited the RC and his lady and their house guests to dinner and fed them corned beef. To have explained that it was she who had done the inviting and that the corned beef was not the dish of choice would have spoilt the story. The Salmons, for whom the dinner was designed, claimed to have enjoyed themselves and the Elliots were much amused by the evening's typically African outcome.

For my part, this was to be just the first of many illustrations of the ability of Swaziland and its people to reduce one's best-laid plans to farce or chaos.

Chapter 4

# First Steps as a District Officer

The next three months passed happily and without undue incident. I confirmed my excellent first impressions of Mr Elliot. He formed his own opinions and was not afraid to apply radical solutions. For instance, a few days after my arrival I was in his office, looking out of the window with him, when he suddenly interrupted what he was saying, pointed to a uniformed figure walking by and said, "You see that fellow, we should have hanged him for ritual murder; but we made him District Orderly instead."

Routine work involved a certain amount of supervision of tax collection, but I tried to concentrate on familiarising myself with the District, usually with Makhungu or one of the Swazi Agricultural Field Officers as guide/interpreter. The next area I visited was Nkhaba, in the high ground to the north of Motshane. Here the atmosphere was totally different from Maphalaleni, mainly thanks to the efforts, over the years, of the local chief, Mnisi Dlamini. His son Bekhimpi was a major figure in the Swazi National Council and was to step in as leader of the SNC delegation to the Constitutional Conference four months later, when Mnt Makhosini was unexpectedly taken ill. Bekhimpi went on to play a prominent part in the events of the next decade and was a Cabinet Minister after independence. He had served in the Second World War, becoming a sergeant at the age of twenty. Whether Bekhimpi was the product of his father's perspicacity or had brought back from his soldiering new ideas, which the old man espoused, I do not know. Most likely they cross-fertilized each other's views. Whatever the cause, Nkhaba was a model of how a chief's area should be run and after the old man died another son kept up the good work at Nkhaba.

Chief Mnisi had embraced the ideas of the agricultural and veterinary departments, with the result that the local field officer and cattle guard were key figures in the area. A fenced cattle camp had been constructed which both eliminated the need for constant herding of farm animals and protected the horticultural and arable areas from damage by the cattle and goats. This released children to go to school at an early age rather than much later, which was the norm in rural areas where children had to do the herding until a sibling was old enough to relieve them. Reputedly, once the grazing camp had been completed, Chief Mnisi fined parents if their children played truant. Irrigated plots produced excellent vegetables, which were sold in the Mbabane market and also at stalls beside the Mbabane/Pigg's Peak road.

*Mvangati* wood bowls from Nkhaba.

Bright-eyed children danced and waved at the passing motorists, drawing attention to the stalls and to their own wares, carved animals, birds and bowls made from *mvangati* wood – a type of mahogany. It took a hard-hearted motorist not to stop and buy. Unsurprisingly, the local primary school was a model of good attendance, discipline and achievement. By the same token, when we arrived for our meeting we found the people ready and waiting, unlike Maphalaleni the previous week where we had to hang around almost two hours for them to trickle in. Nkhaba exemplified the adage that what matters is people, not systems. If one only saw Nkhaba one would think that the traditional way of working through the Swazi National Council was the only way to run a rural area; if one only saw Maphalaleni any other system would seem preferable. But all was not lost at Maphalaleni – before long the old chief died and his brother was appointed and showed himself to be receptive to progressive ideas and the valley started to become forward looking and prosperous. We really had not done much, but we had given a gentle push to bring about a quick appointment when it was needed and then continued to give encouragement and imperceptible guidance. This was surely what our job entailed, helping the people to help themselves.

I had started to tackle the Swazi language in preparation for the government's Proficiency Examination, Grade III, which I hoped to be able to sit within the year. At the Devonshire Course Jeremy and I had gone up one day a week to the School of African Studies, at London University, to be taught the basics of Zulu, of which Swazi (or Siswati) was a variant. Zulu and its kindred languages are tonal, which makes them difficult to learn and easy to mispronounce, with the resulting malapropisms causing bafflement, amusement or grave offence, according to one's error. The Swazi language had not been written down until the coming of the Europeans and the orthography varied according to the extent of the writer's determination to distinguish Swazi from 'standard' Zulu. As a general rule, Swazi is 'Zulu with a lisp'. How much you use the lisp seems to be very much a matter of personal preference. For instance, on the Chamber of Commerce map of Swaziland, published in the late 1970s, one finds both the Zulu 'Usutu' and the Swazi 'Lusutfo' used randomly at different points on the same map for the same river. There is no need to labour the matter further; suffice it to say that both pre and post-independence, official proceedings were conducted in English, increasingly the lingua franca of Africa, and then laboriously translated into Siswati, or *vice versa*. This procedure was not without advantages for it provided an interval for reflection before replying to the previous speaker. It was inevitable that there were mistranslations at times. In my early apprenticeship I once corrected Makhungu in public. Afterwards, in the privacy of my car he told me I had humiliated him 'and he an Mntwanenkosi'. I apologised, acknowledging my fault and was more tactful in future, "excuse me, Mntwanenkos, I don't think I have made myself clear," etc.

It was perhaps that incident and no doubt others unnoticed by me, which led to the choice of the Swazi name I was given. Sometimes these names simply derived from the European's name or appearance. Thus Julian Faux (pronounced 'Forks') was 'Ndatcha' (Fox) – i.e. a play on words. In fact, there was nothing fox-like in Julian's character; but his colouring suited the name, as did his subsequent employment after independence, for he was recruited by MI6 and spent much of his time trying to out-fox the KGB, rising to high rank in the process. A former government secretary, Dan Fitzpatrick, was 'Malamba' (The Lean One) and his successor, G. J. Armstrong was called 'Mathendele' (The Partridge) because of his physiognomy. However, most names were descriptive of the person's character and where they cut close to the quick there was usually a second more innocuous interpretation for the benefit of the name bearer. Bruton, appointed RC in 1937, was 'Mcindzeteli' (The Oppressor) or put more kindly 'The Strong Man'. Featherstone, who followed him in 1942, earned himself the sobriquet of 'Magandeyane' (The Pounder) because the Swazi considered him unreasonably obstinate. Doubtless there was a euphemistic translation like 'The Determined'. By contrast, Beetham, Featherstone's successor, was 'Hlangabeza' (He met them half way) and David Morgan, who followed him, was 'Mazithulele' (The Quiet Peaceful Man). (David Morgan retired in 1957, bought a farm near Manzini and was still there when I arrived, living, true to his name, quietly and peacefully in retirement.) Brian Marwick, RC from 1957, had the full name of 'Musawendvodza' (Son of a Trusted Man), often shortened to 'Musa', which means 'kindness', although that was not the proper meaning of his name. His uncle, A. G. Marwick, who had come to Swaziland in 1902 and was appointed RC in 1935, was simply known as 'Ndlavela', the name of his age regiment, had he been a Swazi. I, too, was given the name of my age regiment, 'Malindzane'. This name, like others, was capable of dual interpretation for the 'Malindzane' were the 'Angry Young Men' of the 1960s. I never had a plausible explanation of the name's other connotations, but I suspect that 'Young Man in a Hurry' or 'Bull in a China Shop' were not far wide of the mark. Europeans, on the whole, were not very good at coming clean on the real meaning of their Swazi names. Purcell, Secretary for Swazi Affairs, would tell you his name 'Sigwili' meant 'The Cheerful One'. Everyone else knew it meant 'The Swank' and he must have known this too, for he spoke fluent Siswati. Of my generation of District Officers perhaps the most complimentary name belonged to Chris Anderson, the DO at Goedgegun. He was 'Mvulazinyango' (The Man who Opens Gates) because he would always jump out of the Land Rover to open a gate when being driven through fenced pastureland, rather than, as tended to be the wont of older officers, leave it for his Swazi driver to open. I am sure, too, that he opened other gates with his natural charm and linguistic fluency. Born into a well-established Scots farming family in East Griqualand in Western Natal, at the foot of the Drakensbergs, he had grown up speaking Xhosa as fluently as English.

Like most farmers' sons in South Africa, Chris had spent much of his time in his early years with an African nanny or playing with the young sons of the African farm labourers. Girls were strictly excluded from their games, which were all about men's activities – fighting, hunting and story telling. Girls had their own groups and their own activities. The boys' hunting games tended to be an enactment, in miniature, of the real thing. For Chris and his companions the favourite game was mouse hunting. The small boys armed themselves with tiny staves and home-made little bows and arrows and went out into the veld to hunt. Their quarry was field mice. When they found the mouse runs in the grass, one group, the 'beaters', would comb the land beyond, driving the mice towards the other group, the 'guns', who would wait, ready to strike, at the far end of the runs. The 'beaters' sang the mouse-hunting songs, for instance:

*"Hey Imbibo, hey Imbibo*
*Hey Imbibo, hey Imbibo, mdala!"*

"Hey mousie, hey mousie
Hey mouse, hey little old mouse."

Or perhaps others, more evocative of adult hunting or poaching:

*"Iyoyo, iyoyo,*
*Igusha zama Bhunu zidla zodwa*
*Iyoyo, iyoyo!"*

"Hey-ho, hey-ho
The Afrikaner's sheep is grazing on its own,
Hey-ho, hey-ho!"

Disturbed by the 'beaters' the mice would scamper down their runs and the waiting 'guns' would shoot them with their little bows and arrows or *boboza* them with their tiny spears. The mice would then be skinned while still warm and roasted on twig spits over little wood and grass fires and eaten with delight. Occasionally, the fires would fan out of control, setting the veld alight and the boys would rush off and make their presence very obvious somewhere else before the veld fires were discovered. Another cause of fires was a different sport – smoking out wild bees to steal their honey.

When the boys reached the age of six or so all this inter-racial childhood bonding came to an abrupt end. The white boys went off to school and the African boys would start herding cattle, sheep and goats. The easy, equal friendships stopped too. The white boys soon learned to behave like sons of the *baas* (boss) and the little African boys took their place as members of an 'inferior race'. Of course, by no means all European employers were hostile or unkind to their employees; quite the reverse. But the kindnesses and friendship that many Europeans and Africans showed to each other were overshadowed *de jure* in South Africa and more or less *de facto* elsewhere in the southern part of the continent by the hateful notion that there could be no social relations between persons of different races – hence the hostility which Jeremy Varcoe had encountered in his first weeks in Swaziland. He was trying to swim against a social tide, which had been running for two hundred years.

One of the positive things in Mbabane was the multi-racial 'Amadube' (Zebra) Tennis Club, founded by Julian Faux. I quickly became a member and enjoyed some good tennis there, including a match against the High Commission staff from Pretoria. I also joined the Mbabane Club, which, although it had admitted Edward Zwane, was fairly reticent about opening its doors to non-Europeans more than a symbolic chink. It irked me that many of its more reactionary members were government servants, but I felt that as a new arrival it would be counter-productive to pick a quarrel with people who had been around much longer than myself. Apart from other considerations, I might well want some of these people to do things for the District. Most rural Swazis needed roads and clinics much more than they needed to play tennis at the Mbabane Club!

Besides tennis there were all manner of social activities to keep me busy in my spare time. An early highlight was a weekend trip under canvas in the bushveld, once more organised by Peter Simkin. It was a thrill to be able to camp amongst the thorn trees and see and hear impala, zebra and wildebeest roaming around us, apparently unperturbed. We were now into summer, the night was hot and I slept in the open, outside the tent. I would have been very comfortable but for periodic visitations from Peter's Labrador, Bruce (the villain of my dinner party), who took it upon himself to wake me several times during the night by licking my face. When I complained in the morning to Peter he told me I was lucky it was just Bruce and not a hyena, which would have eaten my boots and, if I had been sleeping with my boots on, my feet as well. Apparently hyenas find leather irresistible.

Left to right: William, Bruce and Peter.

This trip gave me a taste for the bushveld and a few weekends later I took a tent down to the same area, this time on my own. By wandering about in the evening and early morning I was able to find large numbers of impala and wildebeest, a fair number of zebra and also, to my delight, a few kudu with their graceful gait and imperious bearing. While I was trying to stalk wildebeest, something disturbed a herd of impala and they and the wildebeest stampeded towards me. I fell flat in the grass and thought I was unnoticed. Suddenly the impala started running round in a vast circle, several animals deep, with the wildebeest forming a smaller circle in the centre. This went on until I could see nothing for dust and then they suddenly all broke off and rushed away. It was like an animal enactment of a scene from a western, with the pioneers and their families crowded inside their circle of wagons and the Red Indians galloping round the outside, whooping and waving their tomahawks in the air. I had heard of wildebeest forming a protective laager against predators; but I had never seen any record of two species being involved in such an exercise. It is possible there could have been a predator in the vicinity – lions were spotted very occasionally and leopards were around but seldom seen; or possibly it was I who had spooked the two herds.

The real delight of the bushveld, however, was its birds. I set about identifying them with the aid of *Robert's Birds of South Africa* and also I tried to learn their Swazi names. Asking Swazis about birds and trees was almost as good a conversational gambit as cattle talk. Swazi bird names are often remarkably evocative like 'Ingulingulu' (Bataleur Eagle, where the long vowels evoke this majestic bird's soaring flight as it works the thermals to glide across the sky) or onomatopœic like 'Itsitsihoya' (the Blacksmith Plover with its clinking call, resembling the blacksmith's hammer on the anvil). I had my own views about the Secretary Bird, which struts self-importantly around the veld, rather like one or two people in the Secretariat who regarded themselves as a race apart, superior to those of us who got out and about amongst the Swazi in the heat and dust of the day. One such secretary bird, well protected through his wife's friendship with Mrs Marwick, had his framed wartime DSC citation hanging in his office so that no one could miss it. When he left his office in the evening he would leave the light on and his car in its parking space outside to create the impression he was still hard at work, while he repaired to the Tavern Hotel bar opposite for an hour or so before going back to switch off the light, collect the car and drive home. By contrast people like Julian, Peter, Chris Anderson and older officers like Mr Elliot, or even, in his own funny way, Mr Fannin, the DC at Mankaiana (who looked like a small-town bank manager) all concentrated on useful and productive work, not always to their career's advancement. Even in romantic little Swaziland we were not entirely protected from the universal rule that the way to the top is to keep your in-tray empty and your nose clean, steering well clear of saying or doing anything controversial.

An exception to this rule was Athel Long, the Government Secretary, who was very much his own man and never afraid to be unconventional. In his case being true to himself did him no harm. I ended up feeling that his interpretation of the Swazi political scene was mistaken, but one could not help liking and respecting him. In a shrinking service he went on to be Governor of the Cayman Islands and I imagine that his sharp humour, offbeat ways and Swedish wife brought a welcome breath of fresh air to the Islands' social scene. Certainly he seemed to have been appreciated by the community there, for after his time as Governor he embarked on a major business career and became chairman or chief executive of many large companies and ended up as one of the Grand Old Men of the Islands. Educated at Westminster and Brasenose College, Oxford, commissioned into the Royal Artillery in 1940 and seconded to the Indian Army, he was posted to Malaya in 1942 and spent three years as a Japanese prisoner of war. He had come to Swaziland in 1961 as Government Secretary after a post-war career with the Indian Political Service, the Burma Civil Service and thirteen years in Nigeria. With such experience behind him it is not surprising that he found the traditional Swazis, King Sobhuza and his Council, a trifle unsophisticated compared to the slick Indians and Burmese or the plenitude of Nigerian graduates he had left behind in Lagos.

Athel Long found a ready-made multiracial group of people with whom he could socialise amongst Mike Fairlie's circle and by the time I arrived in Swaziland many people felt that he and Mike were running more or less in tandem and had become a significant influence on Brian Marwick. This was certainly the view of Hilda Kuper, the liberal South African anthropologist. As a young woman she had lived for two years in Queen Mother Lomawa's village at Lobamba. Much later, while working on the manuscript of *Sobhuza II, Ngwenyama and King of Swaziland* she was for seven months a guest of the King's influential daughter Princess Gcinaphi and her husband. It is perhaps a fair assumption, because of her long-standing friendship with Sobhuza and his entourage, that much of what she wrote represented the opinions of the Ngwenyama and his closest associates. With regard to Long and Fairlie, she wrote as follows (Ch XIV):

"The following years, 1961 – 1963, were heavy with danger of violence. Brian Marwick relied increasingly on the advice of senior officials in the service who had worked for 'progress on the British model' in other countries. Anxious to transform what they described to me as 'a feudal society' and also as 'a top-heavy monarchy' into a 'modern democracy' under a constitutional king, they underestimated the strength of the Swazi system."

She then added, as a footnote:

"Two senior expatriates who were particularly influential in shaping this policy (ie Marwick's) were Michael J. Fairlie and Atholl (*sic*) Long."

With the benefit of hindsight it is possible to make two comments on what Hilda Kuper wrote. First, she refers to the adoption of the standard British approach to the run up to Swaziland's independence as being "his" (i.e. Marwick's) policy. It is more than likely that Marwick was simply acting under orders from Westminster. This would explain his apparent weariness in his last years in Swaziland and his increasing frustration with Sobhuza's efforts to block a policy, which Marwick may have felt could not be changed. Secondly, the Colonial Office and people like Long and Fairlie had little experience of one-tribe countries. Practically everywhere British policy makers were faced with a diversity of peoples or a multiplicity of tribes as in Kenya or Nigeria (with their strong local loyalties and hostilities) or well-entrenched local rulers of portions of the country (like the Maharajahs in India and the Kingdoms in Uganda). In such circumstances a viable unitary state could only be created through a new tier of national government. This was unnecessary in mono-tribe Swaziland as it had always been a nation and the King and his Council were themselves the unifying forces. Thus Sobhuza felt that Swaziland Government officials, by opening the way for the new political parties, were denying, rather than granting self-determination to the people.

Homestead in the Highveld.

As it turned out the eighteen months after my arrival were to hold the key to Swaziland's future development; but I had to give up my ringside seat in the capital and follow the main events from a distance, down in the south. Early one morning at the end of November I was wakened by heavy hammering on my bungalow door. It was Mr Elliot. (I was not judged senior enough to be allocated a telephone, so Mr Elliot had been forced to get dressed and drive up to Mbabane to contact me!) Mr Fannin, the DC at Mankaiana, had been taken ill during the night and was in hospital. It was the smallest District, with just a DC and no DOs, so with Mr Fannin gone someone had to be sent to deputise for him. I was to go down and hold the fort. I would have to look sharp as it was a court day and I was to take his roll, starting at 9am. A message would be sent to say I was coming, but might be a few minutes late. I should stay at the Mankaiana Hotel and if I had any problems I could refer to 'Sigwili', John Purcell, the Secretary for Swazi Affairs. The main event on the horizon was a meeting at Mahlangatsha, in the hills near Mankaiana, concerning the enforcement of a court order to evict squatters from a nearby European-owned sheep farm. Sigwili would come down and hold my hand over that. Something more permanent would soon be sorted out and Mr Elliot expected to see me back within a few days.

I was a fairly obvious choice for this assignment. Being a bachelor I had no family responsibilities so I could move at the drop of a hat. Fortunately I had completed my draft of the District plan and I believe Mr Elliot simply submitted it to the Government Secretary as it stood. The idea for these plans probably came from some 'secretary bird' in the Secretariat; but events were to move so fast in the next months that I suspect the new plans all became quickly outdated and I never heard of them again. I paid Cornelias a week in advance and gave him a float for unexpected needs and told him to expect me back within a few days.

I was off on an adventure and, as it transpired, a longer one than I anticipated.

Chapter 5

# Mankaiana

Two hours later I was in Mankaiana and found the local staff were friendly and efficient and glad to have someone to keep the administrative machine running. There was plenty to be done. It was not my first spell on my own. Mr Elliot had gone on leave for a fortnight some six weeks after I arrived in Swaziland, leaving me in charge of the District and all had gone pretty well. Mr Fannin, whom I had already met on one of his visits to Mbabane, was not 'Sanders of the River' and Mrs Fannin, it seemed, kept a fairly low social profile; but it was clear to me from the feel of the office that Mr Fannin was an able administrator and he also had the reputation, although self-taught, of being a good Swazi linguist.

The day before the Mahlangatsha meeting Mr Purcell (Sigwili) telephoned me: "Bring comfortable folding chairs and a good lunch and be prepared for a long day," he said, "this thing is neither pleasant nor easy; but if we are conciliatory and polite and are prepared to listen to everyone who has something to say, in the end the shadows will lengthen and the air will grow cold and people will become tired, hungry and thirsty and that is when they will probably cave in and agree to do things our way."

The Mankaiana Hotel, where I was quartered, was little more than a bar and bottle store, with rare overnight guests as nobody stopped much at Mankaiana. Thus the packed lunch I brought the next day left much to be desired; but Mr Purcell had generously brought extra food, which sustained us through the long day. And it was indeed a long day, just as he had predicted. After brief opening words by the local chief and the Ndabazabantu (the counterpart of Ntshalintshali at Mbabane), Mr Purcell suggested I should say a few words and then he would take over. So I started with the traditional courteous Swazi greeting *Nina wekunene* – literally 'you of the right hand' meaning 'you important people'. Then, through an interpreter, interspersed by a few of my own phrases in Siswati, I explained that I was the *Nkosincane enkantole Mbabane*, literally 'the little chief in the office at Mbabane' (i.e. the DO Mbabane), and that Mr Fannin had been taken ill and was in hospital. I had been sent down until he returned. I did not know the Mankaiana District; I would listen; (*"ngiyisithunjwanje sakwahulumende"* – 'I am just the government's messenger'). Because this was such a serious matter, Sigwili, whom many of them knew, had come. He was the important government official who dealt direct with the headquarters of the Swazi Nation at Lobamba and he would explain the government's position.

With typical good manners the chief replied that I was welcome, "Did I have a Swazi name?" I said, "Mnt Makhungu has given me the name of 'Malindzane'." "That is good, you have a name we can understand", he replied, "however this is a bad business; an injustice has been done and these are my people who have been wronged." Then Mr Purcell (Sigwili) spoke, if I recall correctly, almost entirely without an interpreter, along these lines, "As you know probably better than me, in the days of King Mbandzeni the Boers came and asked to be able to settle in the land of the Swazis. The King welcomed them as protection against the nation's enemies. The Boers asked him to make marks on pieces of paper to show that they had the right to stay on his land. That was not the Swazi way of doing things, but the King consented. By the time of King Bhunu the Boers were saying that because of these papers they had right to the whole of the land of the Swazis. The King and his Council sought the protection of the British and claimed it was impossible for the Boers to say they owned the land because no one, not even the King, could say they owned the land. The land belonged to the nation, not to the King. The Ngwenyama himself has said that King Mbandzeni had inserted controls in all documents regarding land in order to ensure the protection of his people. In the time of our grandfathers there was a big convention to examine the land claims of the Boers. Some were found to be false but many were held to be genuine and those lands were registered as the legal property of the farmers in question and of their successors in title". As they knew, he continued, much land had been bought back by the Swazi nation through the 'Lifa Fund' (administered by the Swazi National Council and derived from a tax on Swazi owned cattle), but the land in question at Mahlangatsha had been confirmed by the Court as being legitimately owned by the farmer and he had the right to it.

The people who were required to move off the farmer's land had not been given permission to live there. They were in breach of Swazi custom. Nobody might settle in a chief's area without the permission of the chief. It was the same with land which belonged, not to the Nation but to a farmer, like this European who owned the freehold. Sigwili wondered, if the local chief were generous, if he could find places for those who were being required to leave the farm, which would be sufficient for them and save them from their difficulties. He hoped this could happen.

There were murmurs that Sigwili had spoken well; nevertheless, speaker after speaker stood up to say that the situation was not right. The farmer had thousands of acres yet he hardly ever came to the farm. For a few months in the year he would send sheep there from his other lands in the Transvaal, but otherwise it was deserted. He had all that land in Swaziland, yet was not even a Swaziland citizen. What right had he to the farm? His grandfather had tricked the Swazi out of the land for a few bottles of whisky or some hunting rifles. The government should be protecting the Swazis and not foreigners – and more besides. Occasionally Mr Purcell would answer a point, always courteously. At one stage the heat was turned on me. What did this young man, this 'Malindzane' think? Had he come all the way from England just to oppress people? I asked Mr Purcell if I should answer. "Go ahead," he said, "but be brief and polite." So I said, rather feebly, that I felt the people from Mahlangatsha had made some pretty fair points and continued, "All those years ago the Swazis had asked Britain to protect them by establishing the rule of law so that people could be secure from those who sought to attack or rob them. Rule of law could only continue if people accepted the judgements of the courts. If two people went to court to settle a dispute and one lost and the other won, there was no safety for anyone if the loser could then defy the court. In this case the court had found in favour of the South African farmer." The Ndabazabantu, possibly prompted by Mr Purcell, backed me up by saying that the Ngwenyama recognised that the courts had authority over all the people of Swaziland.

On and on it went, seemingly endlessly, with most speakers making more or less the same points. But then there was the first chilling of the air and a lengthening of the shadows and gradually people started to drift away. Eventually the chief spoke privately with several of the old men sitting around him and then rose to his feet. "We have discussed this matter very thoroughly," he said, "Sigwili and the Nkosincane have listened to everyone who wanted to speak; but, as they said, they are just the messengers of the government. All we can do is help these poor people who now have nowhere to live. I and my Ndunas feel we can find room for them here in Mahlangatsha."

It had all worked out as Sigwili had hoped. After courteous farewells we climbed into the Land Rover and drove off. The vehicle left behind a cloud of dust, orange in the sunset and through it we could see groups of men setting off for their homes, some on horseback, some on foot, to drink *utshwala* and *xoxo* (talk) about the day's events, sitting round wood fires outside their huts, attended by their womenfolk, with their children playing in the background, sometimes creeping closer in the shadows to eavesdrop on grown-up talk. There would be grunting from the cattle, kraaled for the night, the occasional barking of a dog or cries from a woman calling her children in from their games. Darkness comes quickly in Swaziland; there is little twilight. Soon the moon was rising and the stars appearing. Perhaps through the darkness they glimpsed a shooting star or watched the *imBongola* (the donkey – the name they gave to the Russian Sputnik) as it traversed the sky, a reminder that there was a whole wide universe beyond the enchanting little world of Mahlangatsha.

I went back to the dubious delights of supper at the Mankaiana Hotel, while Mr Purcell had the long, lonely drive on dirt roads back to Mbabane. It had been an instructive day.

A day or two later I was confronted by a different situation, but one which could well have linked with events at Mahlangatsha; I was visited by a representative of the NNLC. This young man, who in truth was probably several years older than myself, was a complete contrast to the rural Swazi with their easy bearing and traditional dress. Small, with dark glasses, he was recently returned from Dar-es-Salaam, which was something of an ANC training ground. He wore a cheap city suit and square-ended tie and looked the very image of a *tsotsi* (gangster or spiv). He answered anything I said with a patronising sneer and a torrent of freedom fighter's clichés, all delivered in the tone much beloved by comedians back home to mock the stream of emergent African politicians who passed through London. He wanted permission to hold political meetings in the District.

Thoughts rushed through my mind as I held him in conversation. My initial feeling was that we did not want him stirring up the Mahlangatsha problem just when we thought it was settled; but more rational thoughts followed. How could one back up a refusal of permission and how could one be sure whether he held a meeting or not? I knew from school and National Service that there was nothing so destructive to authority as giving orders that could not be enforced. Anyway, why should he not hold meetings, which were all part of the run-up to a democratic transfer of power? Also, as we talked, I began to sense something else. Did he really want to hold meetings, or was his target, perhaps, not the scattered rural people of Mankaiana, but myself? Was he trying to talk me into abuse of my authority so that he could make political capital out of my error? They had probably taught him a trick or two in Dar-es-Salaam. He was more likely to be after a quick sensation rather than the hard graft of turning people's hearts and minds. So, oozing sickly charm from every pore, I told him that of course he could go and hold meetings; it was a free country and everyone had the right to freedom of speech and assembly. Would I give him a permit he could show to local chiefs? "No," I replied, "the government does not give permits where no permits are required." He thanked me rather perfunctorily, left and, as far as we knew, there were no meetings. The new political parties were gathering support in Mbabane and Manzini and amongst the workers in the major industrial concerns, like Turner and Newell's Havelock Asbestos Mine at Emlembe, or the Commonwealth Development Corporation's Pulp Mill at Bhunya on the Usutu River north of Mankaiana and at the Sugar Mills at Big Bend and Mhlume in the bushveld; but the majority of the people looked to the Ngwenyama and not to the politicians.

Bottle feeding an orphaned Kudu in the Mankaiana 'zoo'.

One of the ventures Mr Fannin had started at Mankaiana was a little zoo, which was tended by the local prisoners. It was not a high profile undertaking, but most valuably it gave local schoolchildren the chance to come and see, at close quarters, some of the animals that had roamed the country a few generations earlier. The collection included several species of buck; and there were tortoises and monkeys, not creatures that featured high on most tourists' 'tick lists', but enough to give those who could afford the time en route from the Transvaal to Mbabane or Manzini a pleasant half hour's respite from the dirt roads. Like many good things in the Third World this little enterprise cost practically nothing. The animals were brought in, sick, injured or orphaned and they were lovingly cared for by selected prisoners who found in their zoo duties an outlet for their innate kindness.

The Mankaiana District Office.

Swaziland prisons, especially in the smaller settlements like Mankaiana, tended to be rather jolly places. Many of the prisoners were serving their time for crimes of domestic violence or assault in which alcohol often played a major part. Few of their crimes were premeditated although, in the larger centres, theft and burglary were beginning to become a problem. Some of the basic services, like rubbish collection, were carried out by the prisons department and they also did minor constructional or horticultural work. Detachments of prisoners would march happily from one task to another, often singing as they went and if their warder became diverted en route, they knew their way and would carry on until he caught up. While the prisoners were working away on a project, you would see the warder standing with his rifle, keeping watch.

Sometimes the warder would sit down on a rock or bench and on a hot day it was not unknown for the warder to doze off, when an obliging prisoner would take his place and hold his rifle until the warder awoke. The lawns and flower beds around the district offices were tended by the prisoners and 'trusties' would be provided to help with the chores if administrative or agricultural officers had to camp on their visits to outlying spots. Many people would specifically ask for a murderer for such missions and certainly, jumping forward three years, I can remember my godson, Michael Simkin, being devotedly looked after by the same trusted prisoner (a murderer) each time he and his mother accompanied Peter on tax camps. Murderers were usually 'good chaps', unlikely to harm anyone and could be relied upon not to pilfer from the camp. Most bore out the adage that the murderer usually only needs to kill one person and, having done that, presents no further danger. Local wags said that there had to be a certain level of security in Swaziland prisons to stop non-prisoners breaking in. The prisons were, by Swazi standards, comfortable, the food was good and many prisoners enjoyed the life.

At Mankaiana the prisoners looked after the two district horses. They advised me that one would be suitable for me; the other, they said, would be too much of a handful. I took their advice. Jeremy and I had treated ourselves to riding lessons while on the Devonshire Course, but neither of us was a horseman. Riding was a splendid way of seeing the countryside and sociable pursuits were not in abundance at Mankaiana. I was soon using the recommended horse and mentioned him in a letter home as being "an amicable, willing animal" and continued, "the prisoner who looks after him is an excellent groom. What would we do, especially in a place like this, if crime subsided and there were no prisoners? I cannot imagine".

We used the prisoners to carry out a tree-planting scheme, which I devised for some spare Crown land on the outskirts of the village. It was likely that in about five years' time the local Swazis would have no timber left for fuel and building work, largely because most of the wooded areas were unfenced, so any regrowth was at the mercy of the livestock as they roamed free, particularly goats. It seemed a good idea to plant a few acres of eucalyptus that could be coppiced and grew like fury, provided the plantation was fenced. We went to a nursery in the Transvaal and bought four thousand baby gums and also a hundred pines to provide a little variety at the edge of the wood. The prisoners duly planted and fenced them. I hoped that some of the chiefs would replicate the scheme in their areas and perhaps prisoners, on their release, would carry the tree-planting gospel back to their home areas.

Tree-planting.

Whereas the country as a whole was well provided with commercial forests at Pigg's Peak and at Usutu, Swazi areas were becoming denuded of trees. The rural Swazi had not grasped the need to keep replanting despite the relatively quick return for the effort involved. A pine tree may take fifty years to mature in Scotland, in Swaziland it takes only twelve to fifteen. But even that seemed a long time to people who had always been used to having timber to burn *ad lib*. As regards the commercial forests, most Swazis' attitude was ambivalent. Many welcomed the local employment the forests created, reducing the need for young men to go to work on the Rand in South Africa. But others, particularly the older men, said that the trees had dried up the streams that used to water the lands lower down the valleys. This view contradicted the received wisdom of development agriculturists, who contended that afforestation increased rainfall as well as preventing soil erosion near the hilltops, which dried up the river sources. Of course, coincidence is often confused with causation and possibly it was not afforestation but global warming (although the term was not then in general use), which was drying up the springs. Another possible cause might be the growing population, which put pressure on the land, increasing the risk of springs being damaged.

Two weeks before Christmas I was told to move into the DC's house, as it had become clear that Mr Fannin would not be coming back for some months and it would be a while before my replacement arrived.

The DC's residence was an old whitewashed ramshackle colonial style house which was said to be haunted. However, there were numerous swallows that roosted under the eaves of the stoep and in the absence of any domestic animals they gave a good feel to the place. I fed them bread and they soon became very tame. I also concluded that the 'ghosts' were rats. I was initially prepared to accept that they had acquired squatters' rights and felt the house was big enough to share with them. Christmas could have been a lonely time for a bachelor in Mankaiana; but a kind South African couple who lived in the village and farmed nearby entertained me and the local police inspector, also a bachelor, to Christmas Eve dinner with all the trimmings. The timely arrival of letters and presents from home created a festive feeling.

One night the rats stretched the limits of co-existence by running over my bed and waking me up, so I soon had them consuming vast quantities of Warfarin. This was a mistake. I believed that Warfarin made rats go down to water to die; not mine. They died in inaccessible places under the floorboards and in the walls. The stench was appalling. We found most but not all of them and the smell continued for some days after the clean up. The Chief Clerk, an efficient and genial Swazi, was much amused by my troubles. Doubtless I was typical of young expatriate officers in the way they approached a problem. First, they are too laissez-faire – in this case ignoring the rats, perhaps hoping a friendly python might move in – and then they overreact - Warfarin! Turning to the Ndabzabuntu he said, *"ifuna nge umangobe"* – 'all he needs is a *man-gobi'*. What the dickens was 'a man-gobi'? Not wishing to lose face by betraying my ignorance, I meekly repeated, with my best, forced smile – *"Yebo ngifuna a-man-gobi"* – "Yes, I do need a man-gobi". As soon as possible I went to the dictionary: *umangobe* – 'a female cat' – not any old cat, but specifically a female cat. The usual Swazi word for cat was *ikati* – like many Zulu/Swazi words, a corruption of the English or the Afrikaans. I reflected on the matter of overreacting and made a mental note to be more sensible in the future. Was not one of the interpretations of my Swazi name Malindzane 'a bull in a china shop'? Such a creature in such a situation, if he does nothing is at worst a nuisance, whereas if he starts throwing his weight around he will reduce the china shop to a pile of broken crockery. So, when in doubt, do nothing or don't act precipitately.

As for getting a female cat, a couple in the Agricultural Department, the Murdochs, offered to *"siza"* their cat to me while they went on overseas leave. The 'siza' system was an arrangement whereby a person could lend his cattle to another with the title to the cattle remaining with the lender, but the person to whom they were siza'd kept the produce, i.e. the milk and the progeny. In modern times the system worked well for a man in danger of having his goods and livestock attached by court order. Most rural Swazis' wealth was in their cattle. A creditor might obtain an order for attachment of cattle and then be disappointed to find, on execution of the order, that the cattle had disappeared. They would have been siza'd. Equally, the siza system enabled people to move cattle around in time of drought under a system that gave a fair return to those who made their grazing available to others.

In truth the Murdochs were not siza-ing their cat to me in the proper meaning of the word as it had been spayed, so there would be no progeny to remain with me after the end of the siza period. Also, as I was later to realise, they were not wanting it back. The cat was duly brought for inspection. I thought at the time that I and my household were also under inspection; but perhaps this was not the case, for when I said I would be happy to look after the cat while they were overseas they jumped at the offer and suggested they leave it with me there and then. Despite having recognised my earlier stupidity I had immediately repeated the same mistake. We are never so blind as when we determinedly set about a course of action and this was an illustration. I needed a cat to keep my house rodent-free, which would also be an agreeable companion at my hearthside; yet, without a moment's hesitation, I landed myself with an animal which I soon found would run a mile at the sight of a mouse, let alone a rat, and which had as cold a nature as any domestic pet I had encountered. However, Abednego, a 'schoolboy' even older than Cornelias, whom I had taken on at Mankaiana and who was to be with me for the next twenty months, was fond of the cat. This was just as well as it was a semi-Persian and clearly considered that grooming itself was *infra dig*; that was humans' work. Abednego kindly took on this duty and kept the cat in excellent order. It was no real surprise when the Murdochs returned from leave that they did not want the cat back. The poor thing had a sad demise several months later, choking on a piece of meat in front of us. Before we could do anything to help it was dead.

Just after I had cleared the house of rats I had a fleeting visit from the recently appointed Minister (i.e. the No 2) at the High Commission in Pretoria, accompanied by his wife. I had to give them coffee and then show them something of the District before dispatching them to Goedgegun for lunch with Chris and Val Anderson. On arrival at my house the Minister and his wife both opted for tea, rather than coffee. I imagined it would be within the compass of the Fannin's maid to produce this, but she served it with hot boiled milk. To make things worse, the biscuits, bought for the occasion from the local store, turned out to be decidedly musty. It was the Minister's first posting to Africa. He seemed to relate everything he saw to 14th-century England, so the musty biscuits were probably in line with his expectations. Anyway, I felt it did them no harm to discover at first hand some of the minor hazards of a rural DO's life.

Once out of the house the rest of their brief visit was more successful. Part of a nearby royal kraal was being repaired that day and I took my visitors to see this. Since the work was for the Ngwenyama it was the equivalent of a royal call to arms and there was much dressing up and ceremonial, which the Minister and his wife were able to watch and photograph. I gave the detachment commander a small sum to buy beer for the warriors, which triggered traditional effusions of gratitude, much genuflecting and shielding their gaze from our faces as a gesture of deference, which the diplomat doubtless considered all very 14th century. Anyway, they both seemed pleased with their short visit and invited me to stay with them in Cape Town if I was ever down there. I later compared notes with Chris. He confirmed my impression that the Minister actually seemed very little interested in Swaziland except in so far as it coincided with his vision of 14th-century England. We concluded that it would have saved us all trouble if he had just stayed in his office in Pretoria and read Chaucer.

Mocking other branches of the service was one of our amusements when DOs came together. The story of the lions was typical. Beyond Mbabane, up in the Mdimba hills where the Swazi Kings were buried, lived two lions. It was a rocky, inaccessible place, a safe haven for members of an endangered species. Whereas the older of the two lions was fat and well-liking, the younger lion found food hard to come by. So he asked the old chap how he managed to find enough to eat. "It's easy," said the old lion. "When I can't find anything better to eat I just go down to the Government Secretariat in Mbabane and take a government servant; nobody notices, nobody cares." The young lion thanked him and promptly put the advice into practice. He sloped into the Secretariat, spied a suitable looking young Swazi who was walking down the corridor carrying a tray, grabbed him and made off. Contrary to his expectation, all hell broke loose. Senior members of the administration rushed into the corridors, shouting and throwing files and alarms went off as the lion made it out of the main door. Half way down Alistair Miller Street the lion ran into the police mobile reserve, who had turned out in record time. They chased him up through Msunduza Township and out into the hill country beyond. He dumped his quarry early on and only managed to throw off his pursuers when he reached the craggy Mdimba outcrops. After he got his breath back he went and confronted the old lion. "That was a filthy trick you played on me," he expostulated. "I've just been down to the Secretariat to take a Government servant like you said. You told me no one would notice or mind, but it was even worse than trying to steal the Ngwenyama's cattle. I was chased for miles and very nearly shot." The old lion looked at him despairingly, "You bloody fool," he said, "you took the young chap who makes the tea."

Shortly after Christmas my house in Mbabane was allocated to someone else as apparently after Mankaiana I would be going to Stegi, the District bordering Mozambique. Then there was a change of plan and I was to be posted to Hlatikulu, in the south. Cornelias did not want to leave Mbabane, or to change schools, so as soon as he found another job I paid him off. I was sorry I would not to be going back to Mbabane to carry on some of the initiatives I had started; and I had enjoyed working for Mr Elliot and had begun to establish good working relations with the staff in the office. For a newcomer, too, there were advantages in being the DO, Mbabane District. You knew what was going on without the tedium of being part of the Secretariat machine.

I spent the New Year holiday in Manzini with the Varcoes, who had Jonathan Harlow from Bechuanaland staying with them. It made a very sociable break. Jonathan then came back with me and I took him around the District for a day. It was fascinating talking to him, not least because there were lessons for Swaziland in what was happening in Bechuanaland. Its present situation had sprung from events in the 1940s when Seretse Khama had succeeded to the Chieftainship of the Bamangwato, the territory's pre-eminent tribe, at the age of four. Until he grew up his uncle, Tshekedi Khama, was installed as tribal regent. Meanwhile, Seretse was extensively educated and after reading law at Balliol College, Oxford, moved to London in 1948 to complete his legal studies. There he met an English girl, Ruth Williams, and decided to marry her. This caused uproar and Tshekedi, reflecting the tribe's first reaction, unsuccessfully tried to stop the wedding. However in a series of tribal meetings held at Serowe (the tribal headquarters) during 1948 and 1949, feeling gradually shifted in favour of Seretse and the tribe eventually designated him as chief. Tskekedi, who had hoped to secure the chieftainship for himself, now found himself thwarted and requested the UK Government to decide the issue through a commission of enquiry. This decreed that Seretse was not a fit and proper person to discharge the functions of chief because he and his wife had been declared prohibited immigrants by both South Africa and Southern Rhodesia on account of their mixed race marriage. The British Government gave Seretse an allowance and banished him from Bechuanaland.

From the perspective of 21st century Britain, or even that of Swaziland in the 1960s, this was an extraordinary decision, but in the light of the circumstances of the time it had a certain logic. In those days the headquarters of the Bechuanaland administration was not in Bechuanaland itself but at Mafeking, a few miles across the South African border. Because of their mixed marriage Seretse and Ruth would never have been able to visit the territory's administrative capital lest they be arrested and imprisoned for breach of South African race laws, for although the Bechuanaland Government enclave in Mafeking, the so-called 'Imperial Reserve', was under British administration and thus safe from the South African racial laws, Seretse and Ruth would have been in constant danger while travelling between Bechuanaland and Mafeking. Secondly, since it was still official policy that the three High Commission territories would eventually be incorporated in South

Africa, if Seretse was appointed as chief this might have provoked South Africa to annexe Bechuanaland. There was a general perception that Britain could not divest itself of its colonies quick enough and would not be much bothered if a neighbouring state saved it the trouble by annexing some minor territory. Such, doubtless, was General Galtieri's thinking over the Falklands, thirty-odd years later.

The whole saga is clearly narrated in the Bechuanaland chapters of Mike Fairlie's autobiography *No Time like the Past*. People reading his narrative might wonder why someone who was so impressed by the tribal peoples of Bechuanaland and who so obviously admired Seretse should be so dismissive of Sobhuza and his advisers when he came to Swaziland. Admittedly neither Sobhuza nor any of his immediate circle had an Oxford degree like Seretse or Moshoeshoe, the Basuto King; thus Mike, like Athel Long, may have considered Swaziland's traditional aristocracy inferior to others whom he encountered in his earlier service. Unfortunately he never knew Sobhuza and his advisers sufficiently well to be disabused of his assumptions.

Seretse used his six years of exile in London to widen his contacts. His banishment helped focus sections of British public opinion on what was happening in South Africa and people began to grasp the enormity of the South African Nationalist Party's policy of apartheid. British politicians eventually accepted that the three protectorates should never be incorporated into South Africa, but would have to be developed to the point where they could stand on their own feet as viable sovereign states. By the time Harold Macmillan gave his 'Wind of Change' speech to the South African Parliament in 1960 he was probably echoing, rather than leading, British public opinion. In the meantime, Seretse, along with Tshekedi, had renounced all claims to the chieftainship of the Bamangwato and was allowed to return home. He then formed his own cross-tribal political party, the Bechuanaland Democratic Party, which subsequently dominated the scene in Bechuanaland's placid progress to independent nationhood as the Republic of Botswana. Seretse became the country's first President. Ruth was soon a much loved figure in the land and together she and Seretse symbolised the racial harmony which has so distinguished Botswana ever since.

Seretse's story was relevant to Swaziland because of the similarity between Seretse's and Sobhuza's situations. Seretse's traditional role had been denied him by the British, but he had used the imposed electoral process to his advantage and the British Government were hoist with their own petard. There was no reason why Sobhuza could not do the same. Botswana, a little-known country in those days, has now, of course, gained world-wide recognition, partly because of the development of its diamond mines, but principally, in the quirky way that things happen in the 21st century, thanks to Alexander McCall Smith's sensationally successful *No 1 Ladies' Detective Agency* books about a 'traditionally built' Swana lady who opens a detective agency in Gaberone (No 1 paperback bestseller in UK and US in 2003!).

Jonathan Harlow spent the morning accompanying me on my weekly gaol and hospital inspection, followed by a visit to a local chief and a number of local traders who were finding themselves in trouble over the famine relief maize scheme. Because the rains had more or less failed the previous growing season most rural Swazis had not been able to live off their home-grown maize and had to buy in supplies. This created a huge demand, which the smaller rural shopkeepers could not meet because they lacked the cash reserves to buy in the necessary quantities; so the government had introduced a scheme to underwrite the shopkeepers' purchases from the wholesalers. The shopkeepers then had to reimburse the government out of their retail sales, but many of them had spent the money from their sales before repaying their loan. It then fell to the District Administration somehow or other to get the Treasury's money back. We returned to Mankaiana for a late lunch to find a five-page coded telegram from the Government Secretary on my desk. I immediately assumed that there was some sort of emergency. Chris Anderson had been predicting trouble for weeks. With his fluent Swazi (albeit spoken with a Xhosa accent) I reckoned he had his ear closer to the ground than most people in the Administration who tended to rely on interpreters and thus often only heard what people thought was good for them. Most of the older generation of officers took the line that everything would always be all right as 'the old Swazi was an idle fellow who would never be gripped by political hysteria'. This might be so; but many of the younger urban Swazis had a very different approach and resented the discrimination they felt they encountered. Some had difficulty finding work near home and therefore had to move to the major Swaziland towns or even go for months at a time to South Africa. Once they were removed from their roots, it was easy for them to come under the influence of firebrands from the NNLC or ANC. I had seen such young men at Msunduza, the African township at Mbabane, walking around with hate in their eyes. It was such as these who were the potential threat to the old order, British or Swazi.

There was another sign that trouble could be brewing. Traditionally, Swazi men were modest in their toilet habits. If they needed to relieve themselves when out and about they would do so privately, away from other people, crouching down to be inconspicuous. But increasingly, and particularly in the towns, one saw young men urinating in full view of the public, standing up and pointing their urine at passers-by, as if to say "Here is one in the eye for tradition and respect". Older people shook their heads and muttered that the young people were being 'got at' by the politicians, and that the Ngwenyama should be more assertive. The telegram had been sitting on my desk since 9am and I imagined riots already sweeping the country. However, on decoding, the telegram turned out to be nothing more than notification of the New Year's Honours for the High Commission territories; so after a quick lunch we continued our whistle-stop tour.

Jonathan could not stay long enough to attend the public day of the most important traditional ceremony in the Swazi year, the Ncwala – the great annual ritual of Kingship. The Ncwala is extensively described by Hilda Kuper in *Sobhuza II Ngwenyama and King of Swaziland*. Its main purpose is to protect the King's potency and his ability to maintain the fertility of the land. Secondly, it is an annual re-affirmation of the Ngwenyama's position and finally, spanning as it does the last weeks of the old year and the start of the new year, the Ncwala incorporates a first fruits ceremony in its climax.

The Ncwala's Zululand equivalent had been prohibited since 1846, on the grounds that the gathering of the regiments for their *umkhosi* – celebration of Kingship – could be used as a ruse to mask mustering for war. The British administration never had such anxieties about the Swazi Ncwala, even though it produced a huge concentration of Swazi warriors at the national headquarters. On the final day, when the King danced with the regiments, Europeans were invited and in pre-independence days the Resident Commissioner was traditionally asked by Sobhuza to inspect the lines of regiments before the celebratory dancing commenced. Up in Mankaiana, long before the climax of the ceremony, there had been streams of Swazis passing through the village en route for the Ncwala, some in buses filled to overflowing, others in cars of every size and vintage. Many people strode along on foot, singing as they went, burdened with their luggage; and there were even those who passed through on bicycles, wearing their great-coats and felt hats, with all their finery for the festival, their shields, spears, knobkerries and skin *carosses* precariously attached to their saddle bags.

As this is not an anthropological text it is not appropriate to describe all the varied facets of the ceremony. Key elements include the journeying of priests to bring back purification water from rivers all over the country and also from the sea near Lourenco Marques. This is used to strengthen the King, together with selected plants and other medicines. Days later, in the Sibaya, the Royal Cattle Kraal, young men, using only their bare fists, pummel a black bull to death so that its intestines can provide further ingredients for potions and medicine and for offerings to the ancestors. On another day the Ngwenyama dances in the mud of the cattle kraal, naked but for an ivory penis sheath, enacting the isolation of kingship. Finally, at the climax, resplendent in symbolic finery, the King consumes the medicated first fruits of the harvest and throws an empty gourd, representing the past year, onto the shield of a warrior from his own regiment. The old year is gone and the new year begun and from that moment the nation can start to eat the first produce of the early harvest, knowing that the King has secured, for another year, the continued fertility of the land and the vitality of its people.

I duly went down to Lobamba for the public day of the Ncwala and watched the Ngwenyama dance in the Royal Cattle Kraal with his age-regiment, the Balondolozi. There had been some fears as to what the long-drawn-out Ncwala would do to his suspect health, but he seemed in fine fettle, thoroughly enjoying himself. His was indeed an extraordinary role: one day he was the pagan rainmaker stomping around in the mud of the Sibaya, clad in feathers and skins; on another he had to be the complete westernised leader, wearing morning dress and discussing mineral rights or like matters with businessmen and senior civil servants. What amazed people was the way he was equally at home in either role; and that day at the Ncwala, resplendent in full traditional finery, he looked fit and happy. People had been too quick to write him off, as the next twelve months were to show. The Ncwala was considered so important to Sobhuza's identification with the people that this year, 1963, many leading Christian Swazis, whose churches forbade attendance at the Ncwala, nevertheless had thought it vital to turn out and had donned ritual costume and danced with their age regiments in the Sibaya as a public show of their support for Sobhuza. Their numbers included some of the most influential members of the Swazi National Council. It was perhaps not generally appreciated how many of the King's trusted counsellors were Christians and Sobhuza was certainly much influenced by Christianity. William Duma, the astonishing Zulu evangelist, was a periodic visitor to Lobamba and his biography suggests that in May 1973 Sobhuza personally acknowledged his acceptance of the Christian Gospel.

Another Christian, who became a friend of the King and his family was a remarkable missionary, Joan Scutt, who ran the Mankayane Mission at Encabaneni, ten miles down the hill from Mankaiana. Encabaneni was a splendid place, which exuded joy and peace. Joan Scutt's achievements are best described by reproducing her obituary in *The Times* October 25th, 1993.

"Joan Scutt, the missionary who has died in Swaziland aged 84, made a remarkable contribution to the lives of the Swazi people. 'Blue Sky' as she was known for her clear blue eyes, spoke Siswati and Zulu. She learned the Swazi culture and customs and formed a close friendship with the late King Sobhuza II. The present King Mswati III hailed Miss Scutt as a 'Friend of the People' in 1987, on the Jubilee of her arrival in Swaziland.

Joan Frances Scutt was born at Poole, Dorset, in 1909 and trained as a teacher. She left England to become a missionary in 1937.

In 1953 she moved to Mankayane Mission in Encabaneni, where she stayed as the only missionary for 30 years.

From a small hut, she developed a Christian mission complex including a primary school, a secondary school and a health clinic. She raised the rural community from poverty to prosperity by pioneering one of the first handicraft centres in Swaziland, enabling women of the community to be self-sufficient by making and selling grasswork, weaving, mats, carpet and batik. It became a showpiece for Swaziland craft work. She led the building of a craft workshop and, with the profits, built a new church.

While at Encabaneni she was the architect, contractor, block-maker and builder of five schools in the surrounding communities. Consequently she was summoned by King Sobhuza to advise on education.

In 1982 Miss Scutt retired from Mankayane to Bethany, where the King gave her land on which to build her own home. She did so with her own hands and the new house attracted a buzz of people – not least orphans such as Katie, who had been with her since a small girl.

While pursuing her missionary work Miss Scutt also took a number of external degrees, including a BA from Natal University at the age of 48 and a diploma in Theology at 83.

Joan Scutt wrote more than 15 books and her *Story of Swaziland* was widely acclaimed. Shortly before her death she completed her last work, *The Church in South Africa*.

She served as secretary of the Swaziland Conference of Churches and was a fluent broadcaster in Siswati. In 1988 she survived a bad motor car accident. 'Blue Sky' celebrated her 50 years of service to Swaziland by supervising the building of a fine primary healthcare clinic for the Bethany Community and a year later, a nurses' home for the staff. Miss Scutt was appointed MBE in 1982. She was unmarried.

Her funeral was attended by a thousand people (95% African), with 10 speakers at a five-hour service.

One of the addresses described her guiding principles as being 'The greatest thing in the world is to find out the will of God and to do it'."

In the hills above Joan Scutt's mission.

There was another mission at Mankaiana, run by Pastor Liland of the Norwegian Alliance Mission. It struck me as a very cold place compared to Joan Scutt's domain. The pastor and his wife were pallid folk whose lifestyle embodied to me that dreadful phrase 'awful purity' in F. W. Faber's hymn *My God, how wonderful Thou art*. It seems that Mike Fairlie, DC at Mankaiana ten years earlier, formed a similar view. He wrote of the Lilands: "Apart from preaching sermons on Sundays in various parts of the district and supervising the one or two Swazi schools which their mission could afford to finance, it was hard to believe that they had a fruitful life". I did not eventually see eye to eye with Mike Fairlie on some topics, but in this matter he was spot on. The Lilands had two teenage children, a son, well scrubbed and monosyllabic, looking like a lad from the Hitler-Jugend in a 1950s film and a daughter, fifteen, coming on ten. One felt that both, and especially the girl, were ill prepared for the time when adult life would catch up with them. They were doubtless the type of children whom Philip Larkin was to have in mind when he wrote his well-remembered poem 'This Be the Verse': "They f**k you up, your mum and dad . . ." It was probably wrong for me to have felt uncharitably towards the Lilands. They doubtless believed they had a calling to be in Mankaiana and thought that the children's isolation was a price that had to be paid.

In addition to the Ncwala, there is another national ceremony, which includes a day when Europeans and foreigners may attend. This is the Umhlanga, or Reed Dance, which is intended to involve all unmarried young women of marriageable age. The Umhlanga takes place towards the end of the Swaziland winter and lasts about a week. In many ways it has similarities, as a bonding exercise, with a British Girl Guides' summer camp. Its overt purpose is for the young women to renew the reed screening at Lobamba around the Queen Mother's great Kraal. To this end the girls set out from all over the land and, once arrived at the designated reed bed, they cut bundles of reeds and proceed with them to the Royal Kraal at Lobamba. However, for most modern Swazi girls there is a snag. Part of the ritual involves the girls dancing bare-breasted in front of the King – and the King has the right to pick a new bride for himself from the dancers. By 1962 Sobhuza was sixty-three, an old man by Swazi standards, not in the best of health and he already had over a hundred wives. In recent years he had tended to forego his prerogative at the Umhlanga, but this was never certain, hence the growing tendency of many girls to find reasons not to be there.

Of course, it was an honour, both for herself and her family, for a girl to be chosen as a royal bride; but for a modern Swazi girl the honour held the promise of a lifestyle far removed from her dreams. She might indeed spend some time with the King, and could come to have some influence: certainly some of Sobhuza's Queens became major figures in the land; but many of them were likely to have to live out their lives in a distant royal Kraal, perhaps in the company of several other queens, under the watchful eye of royal guards whose main duty was to safeguard the King's honour.

While I was enjoying myself at the Ncwala, down at Manzini Jeremy and Wendy's spirits were at a low ebb. They had been blackballed from the Manzini Club on account of their 'liberal' views, which, in all truth, were merely a reflection of official government policy. Jeremy did not compromise on such matters, whereas all too many people in government service paid only the merest lip service to the official line on racial integration. One such was Jeremy's DC, Frank Fleck, who had given him no social support and who, astonishingly, only resigned from the club in protest at Jeremy's expulsion when ordered to do so by the Resident Commissioner. Frank Fleck could never escape from his South African roots.

On the subject of South African attitudes I had an example of these at their most pernicious at a dinner party in the Mankaiana area to which I was invited. One of the guests told a story how his father had outwitted one of his 'boys' (African labourers). I had met the father, who in a condescending way had told me that 'he knew the old native' and 'had learned how to handle him'. He apparently suspected that one of said 'natives' was stealing his calves. He therefore took the suspect with him down to his other farm, which was in the lowveld, a malaria area, and 'forgot' to give him paludrine, the standard antidote. As a result, the suspect died of malaria within a fortnight. Everyone around the table, barring myself and our hostess, thought the story screamingly funny;

yet these same South African Swazilanders could be charming, hospitable and were often deeply religious. Looking back, why did I not take the matter further? Presumably I had become sufficiently pragmatic to know to fight only the battles I could win. It would have been impossible in this case to prove homicidal intent or even negligence, as everyone would have closed ranks behind the farmer. Additionally, all this had happened in another District; so technically it was none of my business; but even at more than forty years' distance, I still have a nagging feeling about my inaction in this matter. "All that is needed for evil to flourish is for good men to do nothing."

However, there was soon another, much more clear-cut problem to occupy me. There was a minor outbreak of typhoid in Mankaiana. The Medical Officer, Manzini, whose jurisdiction included Mankaiana, seemed disinclined to do anything, despite my entreaties. I therefore phoned his superior, the Director of Medical Services in Mbabane and he promptly sent someone down to give TAB inoculations to the whole village. Apparently the medical people at Manzini resented my meddling in what they considered to be their preserve. There was also murmuring against me by several of the local Europeans because I did not arrange for Europeans to be inoculated separately. Most of the local Europeans focused on the Transvaal towns of Ermelo and Piet Retief and had not yet accepted that Swaziland would never be incorporated into the Republic. The injections were given according to strict best practice, so the Europeans' objections were on purely racial grounds. By contrast, the Swazis appeared to appreciate the government's swift response, particularly the prisoners up at the gaol, whose morale for some reason seemed to be considerably boosted. I suppose it was the spectacle of everyone being treated the same.

One of my most enjoyable days at Mankaiana was spent taking local chiefs and Swazi agricultural staff, field officers and cattle guards to the government's cattle breeding research station at Mpisi. I had earlier gone to an Open Day at the local cattle breeders' association near Goedgegun, a European only organisation, and had been much impressed by five Nguni bulls from Mpisi, the result of only fifteen years of selective breeding. If such a level of improvement could be sustained, I felt the Nguni breed could become a major force throughout Southern Africa. Improving the quality of its cattle would bring all manner of benefits to Swaziland.

A Nguni bull.

Better conversion of fodder into beef would mean more meat could be produced from any given area of land. If eight good bullocks sell for a higher total price than ten poor ones, the Swazi farmer would make more money and the eight would put less strain on the pasture which, rather than degenerate (which tended to be the ongoing norm in many areas), would recover its fertility, so that the next year, because it had not been overgrazed, the same pasture would perhaps be able to support nine beasts and the year after that ten or even twelve. This was the land use and economic argument for improving stock quality. However, I suspected that for most Swazis pride of ownership would be the effective spur for them to strive to breed cattle that had better conformation and were better food converters. The Swazi were great talkers and if one could start them talking about stock quality, rather than stock numbers, this would be a breakthrough. The problem was the Swazi attitude to cattle as wealth. It was just as unnatural for them to think about cattle quality as it was for Europeans to think about the quality of the banknotes they were carrying. If the Swazi national court fined a man one cow, that is what he had to pay; there was no consideration of the quality – a cow was a cow. It was the same with the payment of *lobola* - bride price; it was purely a matter of numbers. I do not know whether this trip changed people's attitudes; but it was a very jolly outing. The staff at Mpisi, both European and Swazi, had obvious pride in their work, were delighted to show off their achievements and did us proud.

As so often happened after a day spent with rural Swazis I came home from this trip with my batteries recharged.

Of course, at times the sun could be too hot, the dust too oppressive and even the Swazis could be trying, but not nearly as infuriating as some of the Europeans or, particularly, the Treasury people at the Secretariat. I had been conducting a running battle with the latter, who were exacting the maximum repayments of my car and tropical clothing advances while at the same time delaying payment of my pay rise and trying to mark down my travelling expenses from Cape Town to a quarter of my claim, even though I had claimed on a shortest distance basis so as not to charge for my sightseeing. It took extensive quotation from Queen's Regulations and much written argument before I prevailed and obtained my just entitlement. I was dealing, of course, with a junior, not the departmental head. Bob Martin, the Secretary for Finance and Development, had a considerable intellect and was able to look beyond the horizon, in contrast to some of his juniors whose vision appeared not to extend further than the edge of their desks. One of the stories about Bob concerned the head of a specialist government department, whose lifestyle suggested his salary was supplemented from other sources. He was driving Bob to a meeting in his new Mercedes. (In independent Kenya they invented a name for such people in government service and the aid agencies – in Swahili most tribal names are prefixed with 'wa', hence waKikuyu, waKamba etc. The new tribe were the 'wa Benzi' – the people who drove around in Mercedes Benz limousines). Bob Martin asked if the new car was satisfactory – "Oh yes, very." "Everything works OK?" "Yes." "Even the electrics?"

"Spot on." "Including the mileometer?" "Yes, indeed." "That's funny, because it reads less than half the mileage you have claimed as official government mileage since you got the car. You'd better look at your mileage claim again and correct the errors!" Thus, in his quiet way Bob gave a touch of the reins to someone who was otherwise good at his job. Tragically Bob Martin was murdered a year later in his house by a drunken armed robber.

Back at Mankaiana it was soon time to pack up and move out of the Residency in advance of the new DC's arrival. He was a 'retread', transferred to Swaziland on Uganda's independence and was moving to Mankaiana direct from UK leave until Mr Fannin was fit enough to return. So it was back to the dreaded Mankaiana hotel for a few days. It is often said that the Second World War, so traumatic and tragic for many, formed the highlight of a number of people's lives. This was probably the case with Miss Constance Adams, the hotel proprietor, who had a distinguished war record ferrying new military aircraft from America to Britain. After the war she came back, with her mother, to the little hotel. This could only have given her a very meagre livelihood and the dullest of lifestyles. I suspect she was saved from financial ruin by the 1961 abolition of the laws prohibiting the sale of intoxicating liquor to Africans. By 1963 the bottle store was probably the only money-making part of her business.

While I was preparing to move to Hlatikulu the constitutional conference opened on January 20th, 1963 in London. It coincided with the UK's coldest winter for a hundred years. The Thames froze over and there were bonfires and parties on the ice, evocative of Stuart times. The weather posed problems for the Swazi National Council delegates. They had intended to turn up to the first session of the conference in Swazi national dress to emphasize Swazi identity and tradition. Such attire, however, was totally unsuitable for the weather conditions, since it consisted principally of two pieces of brightly printed cotton cloth, the one slung over the shoulders and the other round the waist, much in the fashion of Scottish highland dress before it was glamourized by the Scottish romantic revival. For the sake of warmth the SNC delegation supplemented traditional costume with the bulk purchase of Scottish tartan rugs, in which they cocooned themselves, except for photo opportunities. By this serviceable compromise the delegation preserved their Swazi identity and avoided pneumonia. However, compromise was not much in evidence when it came to the business of the conference. This dragged on for two weeks without agreement between the rival factions, basically the 'new politicians' on the one side and the Swazi National Council on the other, with the Europeans somewhere in the middle. Neither of the two extremes was prepared to give ground. Duncan Sandys, the Secretary of State, invited Sobhuza to fly to London to join the talks in an attempt to break the deadlock, but he refused. Sandys therefore declared in exasperation that he would have to impose a constitution and sent the delegates home.

Ten days before my move, Ray Rawlins, my future DC, and Judy, his wife, invited me up to Hlatikulu for a look around, followed by lunch and an afternoon of tennis at the club. A family I met at tennis were having a drinks party that evening and invited me as well; and the Andersons had me to supper at Goedgegun on my way home. It was a thoroughly enjoyable day, a contrast to my usual Saturday relaxation, which, as like as not, was a ride out in the veld on the District horse. Of course, I could go off somewhere for the weekend and sometimes had done so, but I did not like to absent myself too much as there was no-one to leave in charge and these were slightly uncertain times. The Constitutional Conference had focused attention on the transition to independence. Everything was up in the air and people of all political persuasions were starting to jockey for position. There was always the chance of violence breaking out, whether planned or sparked off spontaneously because of someone's stupidity.

Although Mankaiana was a splendid posting during working hours, off duty it was, in truth, a dull place for a bachelor. The next few days back in the hotel after my visit to Hlatikulu made me realise how ready I was to leave.

My sojourn had turned out to be nearly three months. If I had known on arrival that I was to be there that long I would have used my time more fruitfully. The experience taught me a good lesson, namely, wherever you are, or whatever job you are given, assume it is for ever.

So I determined that when I arrived at Hlatikulu I would act as if I would be there for the rest of my service and not hold back for fear of failing to finish what I started. There should be plenty of opportunities in Hlatikulu to put my new resolve into practice.

Chapter 6

# Hlatikulu

While the Constitutional Conference was grinding towards deadlock amid the winter's snow at Church House, Westminster, I was moving to Hlatikulu (the name means 'big forest', but the forest had long since disappeared, used up for fuel and building). I was taking over from Edward Zwane, the territory's first Swazi District Officer and I had the great advantage of being able to overlap him for two weeks before he left for Mbabane. This enabled him to show me around the District, giving me an opportunity to learn about Swazi ways from someone on the inside track and not any sort of person either, but someone of outstanding ability.

Older than many of the Swazi administrative officers who were to be pressed into senior posts in a hurry ahead of independence, Edward had served a long and hard apprenticeship, coming into the administrative service after several years as interpreter at the High Court. He was impeccably connected. His late father, Amos Zwane, had been Sobhuza's personal physician and was said to have had an amazing knowledge of African medicine.

Dr Ambrose Zwane, the leader of the NNLC, was Edward's half brother. Anna, Edward's wife, had her own contacts; she was a home crafts education officer, a job which took her into all manner of households; and on their own home front Anna and Edward had a lively family. Edward's reputation for all-round ability was already established and he was known to be absolutely fair to everyone, irrespective of race or status. Combine these qualities with an impressive presence, a lightness of touch and a ready humour and you had a very good District Officer. We became friends before he left for Mbabane and thereafter he was someone whose advice I could always tap. He was to be inexplicably murdered shortly before independence.

Another plus point for Hlatikulu was having my friend Chris Anderson as the other District Officer, running the sub-office at Goedgegun, eighteen miles down the hill towards the Transvaal border. Chris and Val, his English wife, were by now proud parents of a baby daughter. They tended to home in on Hlatikulu for their social life as there was not much in that department for them in Afrikaner dominated Goedgegun.

Ray Rawlins, my District Commissioner, was the son of a British career diplomat. Ray had served briefly in the Indian Army and had then transferred to the Colonial Service and had several years in the Seychelles before coming to Swaziland. His wife, Judy, was a South African whose family owned the *Natal Mercury*, one of the 'big three' English language newspapers in South Africa. (*Natal Mercury*, *Cape Times* and *Rand Daily Mail*). Whereas the Great Trek of the Afrikaners out of Cape Province in the early Nineteenth Century to escape British dominance had meant that the white population of the Orange Free State and the Transvaal, at least in the rural areas, was predominantly Afrikaner, Natal had tended to be settled by British immigrants. Judy was typical of people in many of the well-established Natal families who were often more British than the British themselves. They sent their sons (and Chris Anderson was such a one) to schools like Michaelhouse and St Andrew's, Grahamstown, modelled on Eton and the other 'Butterfly Club' British schools, and their daughters went to private boarding schools in the Roedean mould. Ray and Judy, therefore, projected a very British image and their private money enabled them to do so in some style.

Image was important to 'Mr Rawlins', as he expected to be called by junior officers. It also went down well with him for Chris and me to call him 'Sir' in front of other people and likewise for us to open his car door for him when we were out and about with him on official business. John Sturgess, the visiting magistrate, took the mickey out of Chris and myself for these obsequiesnesses and sometimes could be seen mimicking us from the safety of the verandah outside the Court Office. John could have been a court jester in another age and he certainly livened up the Hlatikulu scene.

Sometimes Ray Rawlins stretched the image a little. "When I was in Rome with my father, the Ambassador . . ." was a frequent introduction to some reminiscence. His father had indeed served in Rome and he had indeed been an Ambassador, but not at Rome or anywhere equally prestigious: actually La Paz, Bolivia. However, I had learnt at an early age not to pay too much heed to people's little foibles. My first form master at Charterhouse, one E. A. 'Murky' Malaher, surveying his new class over his glasses at the start of the school year, had addressed us thus in his strangely affected voice, "Ey expect yew hev your peculiarities; well, ey hev main." Peculiarities notwithstanding, he was an excellent teacher.

Ray Rawlins' strengths far outweighed his little peculiarities. He was a fair man, fair to people of all races and from all strata of society. This was respected by the Swazis who knew him, but perhaps not very many did, since he did not go around the District as much as he might. From my perspective this was a plus point. It meant that Chris and I had the chance to do all sorts of interesting things which, in another District, the DC might have reserved for himself. Not only did Mr Rawlins delegate, but he backed us up, at least in public, in more or less whatever we did - in my book one of the prime essentials of leadership. If Mr Rawlins was to be criticised it should have been for his failure or reluctance to give his subordinates structured training. Certainly we learned from experience and we were given plenty of experience from which to learn; but sometimes experience is a cumbersome teacher.

This, however, is a minor quibble and Rawlins' approach, set side by side with over-supervision and the unnecessary clipping of wings (not unknown elsewhere in the territory) won hands down. Ray and Judy Rawlins were generous hosts and their residence was the base for open and sophisticated hospitality, embracing Swazis as well as Europeans, which made it the social hub of the district. Both of them were good tennis players and, thanks to several other able players, tennis at the club was always good value. Edward Zwane had helped found the Amadube multiracial tennis club in Mbabane and he was an established member of the Hlatikulu tennis fraternity.

Even without a strong lead from the DC and his lady Hlatikulu would have been a sociable place. Perched on a hill with lovely views, it enjoyed all the advantages of the highveld climate, with the fleshpots of Durban and the Natal seaside resorts within an easy day's driving due south and the luxurious mountain resorts of the Natal Drakensbergs a similar distance to the south-west. It was not surprising, therefore, that it had attracted an interesting European population. From a social perspective the contrast between Mankaiana, the smallest district in Swaziland, and Hlatikulu, the largest, could not have been more marked. Compared to District sizes in Kenya or Tanganyika, Hlatikulu District was tiny. Nevertheless, because of its relative size in Swaziland terms, a generous sprinkling of the various branches of the government service were stationed there - agriculture, veterinary, public works and education, not to mention a well-established government hospital. There was also a pleasant little hotel catering for tourists, mostly from South Africa, who were attracted by the cool climate, the scenery and the 'quaintness' of a lifestyle uninhibited by apartheid. Many South Africans came to non-racial Swaziland as if visiting a zoo. A small number, but increasing as the enforcement of apartheid became ever more stringent, came to sample the forbidden fruits of sex across the colour barrier.

The village had shops to provide basic requirements, certainly enough for a bachelor like myself. For more ambitious purchases people tended to go through to Ermelo or Piet Retief in the Transvaal, or even down to Durban. The Hlatikulu club was not merely somewhere to play tennis, but a general focus for social activities. Its chairman was Colonel Loringh van Beeck, the aristocratic retired Dutch cavalryman and former ADC to Queen Juliana, whose liberal racial views had ensured that the club had promptly opened its doors to Hlatikulu's first African doctor, Sidney Shongwe and the first African DO, Edward Zwane, as soon as they arrived. The Colonel and his lively wife, Nettie, had settled in Hlatikulu a few years after the end of the Second World War. He also presided over the local branch of the war veteran's association, the MOTHs (Memorable Order of Tin Hats!), whose members were drawn from all over southern and eastern Swaziland. Most had served in the North African and Italian campaigns; a few had fought in the First World War.

Sidney was a handsome and charming Zulu. He was one of a number of professionals who came to Swaziland in the late 1950s and early 1960s, both Africans and Europeans, to escape the stultifying apartheid system in their native South Africa. Sidney and his wife June fitted easily into any social scene on account of their charm and happy personalities. Edward and Anna Zwane were cast in the same mould, and both couples were generally welcomed by Hlatikulu's European population. Most of these new professionals coming to Swaziland from South Africa tended to be centred around Mbabane and Manzini. Courtesy of South Africa's racist policies, we were receiving an injection of professional people just when it was most needed. Better late than never for, in comparison with places like Ghana or Nigeria, Swaziland was woefully short of indigenous graduates.

It is easy to see how senior government servants, led by Marwick, Long and Fairlie, regarded the educated Africans from the professions as the most likely candidates to be the country's future political and social leaders. They did not want a repetition in Swaziland of Curzon's terrible error in India where, as Viceroy at the turn of the century he ignored the growing Indian middle class in favour of the traditional rulers, the maharajahs, thereby propelling those whom he spurned into the arms of the radical Congress Party. To be fair to Marwick, Long and Fairlie, one can hardly overestimate their achievement in breaking down Swaziland's social barriers between the races through their personal initiative and example and their encouragement to other Europeans to follow their lead. After all, it had only been in March 1962 that the anti-discrimination proclamation had been enacted. However, as so often happens in politics, the pendulum swung too far; they over-corrected by failing to accept that there were also people of ability within the ranks of the traditional authority.

The house which I was allocated was a cleverly designed modern dwelling of some size built on the side of a small hill, which took full advantage of its situation. Bellrigg (originally Bull-rigg, 'bull's hill') my parents' home in Galloway, where my sister Gill and I had grown up, stood on a hillock as its name implies and had lovely views in all directions. I suspect that having once enjoyed such a situation, one looks for a repeat elsewhere. So it was natural that I should feel instantly at home in my Hlatikulu house.

Abednego arrived, having negotiated a change of school and we set about creating a ménage which, if not equal to my married neighbours' establishments, would at least enable me to return hospitality. Since it was a modern house, with no ancient outbuildings to harbour vermin, the characterless cat was undisturbed by rats and mice. Happily Abednego's devotion to it never wavered. Soon he had another arrival to care for. This was a horse that was recovering from illness. He had been examined for me by Chris and a nursing sister at the hospital, who also knew about horses, and they recommended he would give me a good ride once he was fully fit. Because the horse still needed a few weeks' rest the price was very reasonable. We fenced part of the spare ground at the bottom of the garden as a paddock for him and constructed a little stable of wattle poles and branches as a shelter from sun and rain. He soon put on condition and clearly had a good nature and seemed appreciative of care and good grub.

While I was busy and happy settling into Hlatikuku poor old Jeremy, down at Manzini, found himself front-page news in the *South African Sunday Times*. His blackballing from the Manzini Club had provided the journalists with a parallel to the recent expulsion of the Mayor of Durban from the Durban Club; and the whole sorry saga of Jeremy's Manzini problems was given a second airing, reopening wounds which had barely started to heal. Their unpopularity amongst the majority of the European Community must have been very hard for Jeremy and Wendy, for both were gregarious and had been used to a full social life in the UK. Jeremy had reached the point of exploring other career options and was considering resigning. His ability and worth were well proven by his subsequent fine careers, first in law and then in the Diplomatic Service. As I write this narrative forty-one years later, his basic instinct to be something of a stormy petrel has surfaced once again, in that he was one of the fifty-two signatories of an open letter in *The Times* (27.4.04), all members of the so-called 'Camel Corps' (retired distinguished Foreign Office arabists) criticising the failure of the American dominated coalition to plan in advance for the post-Saddam era in Iraq. Certainly Jeremy, having held senior positions in the British Embassy in Ankara as well as two years' special leave with the Standard Chartered Bank in Istanbul and then a stint as Ambassador to Somalia, was well qualified to have an informed opinion on Iraq. He has always had the ability to see issues very clearly and then to express his views. In pre-independence Swaziland this did not go down well with the inward-looking European community of Manzini.

Left to right: Edward Zwane, Ray Rawlins and myself.

During our short overlap period Edward Zwane was able to pull back the curtain on Swazi life for me in a way that few Europeans could have managed. One day, out in the District, we chanced upon a lady *isangoma* (soothsayer), distinctive by her braided hair caked with red ochre, the uniform of her trade. We fell into conversation and Edward suggested she tell me something about myself. I had come from far off, *"peshaya"* (from overseas), she said – correct, but not very difficult; I did not exactly look like a local – any Afrikaner would have surmised the same with, probably, the unattractive term *rooinek* thrown in for good measure. But she then launched into a catalogue of less obvious information; my parents were both alive, I had a sister who was fair-haired like myself, although both our parents were dark. I would be seeing the three of them within several months. All these things were correct, including the family visit which we had only just started to organise. At this stage no one in Swaziland knew of our plans, nor indeed did anyone know of my parents' hair colour. How on earth could she know these things? As we drove on Edward and I fell to talking about isangomas. They are soothsayers; but the truths they foretell are not necessarily as innocuous as the details we had just heard about my family. The experience of Mnt Gija Dlamini who lived in the middleveld north-east of Pigg's Peak, was a case in point. As a young man he had been accosted by an isangoma at a beer drink who told him that after that day he would never walk again. While riding home that night Gija was thrown by his horse and broke his leg; complications set in, the leg failed to mend, the other leg became infected and, true to the isangoma's warning, Gija never walked again. I was to come across him two years later when I was posted to Pigg's Peak.

Although their predictions may come to pass isangomas are not to be confused with witchdoctors (*abathakathi*) who cast spells and curses and concoct 'medicine' to make bad things happen to people. You go to the traditional healer or soothsayer to get well or to gain insight into the future; you go to the witchdoctor to bring misfortune on someone, to cause him or her to fall ill or die. Often the effect of the curse is psychological; the person knows of the curse and simply wastes away or commits suicide. The witchdoctor's trade can be particularly sinister when it comes to procuring the ingredients for his potions; many are similar to those used by the witches in Shakespeare's *Macbeth*; others are more personal to the *mthakathi*'s intended victim, for instance, hair or menstrual blood.

"For a child in Swaziland 'the bogeyman in the dark' is no idle fantasy".

For the most deadly preparations human organs are required, usually from children. Thus for a child growing up in Swaziland, the 'bogeyman in the dark' is no idle fantasy, he is an ever present danger. Ritual murder was, and still is, particularly rife in Lesotho (previously Basutoland); but it is also endemic throughout Southern Africa. In Swaziland in the 1960s there was the legend of the *solinye* (single eye), a large black car with one headlight which was said to be driven around at night looking to pick up children to sell to witchdoctors who would then murder them and use their organs for *muti* (medicine). Edward confirmed the currency of this story and suggested that although only the occasional case of ritual murder came to court (the Mbabane Office messenger being a case in point) there was much more of it going on than people imagined and, like most of the nastiest crimes everywhere, it was committed right across the social spectrum. Much later I was to learn of a case which bore out this point.

The Swazi/Zulu/Xhosa language illustrates the extent that witchcraft and demonology are bound up in the culture of the Nguni peoples. Their language has a special prefix, *na* – which is *only* used to point out demons, e.g. *nango* (there he is – the demon); *nasi* (here it is - the demon); *naziya* (there they are over there – the demons) etc. The little vocabulary I carried around with me contained only a few hundred words, but it listed nineteen *na* words for pointing out demons.

On another trip Edward and I talked about the disappearance of the majority of Swaziland's wild game. He recalled how, as a boy, the old men used to talk about the huge herds of wildebeest, zebra and impala that had roamed the bushveld; lions were not uncommon, the smaller antelopes were plentiful in the middleveld and leopards abounded, especially on the rocky *koppies* (hillocks). With the proliferation of hunting rifles and the growth of the population the game had been nearly wiped out in two generations. But it had been reported in the local paper a few weeks earlier that a lion had been seen in the bushveld and leopards seemed able to survive almost anywhere and, although naturally secretive, were spotted occasionally throughout Southern Africa. While I had been at Mbabane an employee of the Havelock Asbestos Mine, driving up the main street of the village early one morning, had come face to face with a fine male leopard. It had probably been scavenging in the dustbins like the urban foxes in London. However, Swaziland's herds of impala, wildebeest and zebra had not entirely disappeared, as my trip the previous October had shown.

Hippos appeared from time to time in the bushveld rivers and laid waste the riverine crops, especially vegetables. They travelled long distances at night, so no one could predict when and where they would appear. A one-night visit from a herd of hippos could cost a Swazi farmer his season's crop. Therein lies the rub; game and agriculture do not easily coexist, hence the need for game reserves and eco-tourism if African game is not to disappear entirely.

The lumbering hippo, often cast as a figure of fun, is not to be trifled with. It can run amazingly fast for such an ungainly animal and also make good speed in the water. When I went on a visit to St Lucia Bay Game Reserve in Northern Natal the warden took me out in a boat to watch hippos and pelicans and he told me how, the previous weekend, he had done the same for a honeymoon couple. Without warning a bull hippo had charged the boat, capsizing it and throwing the three of them into the water. The young husband had panicked and struck out for the shore without any thought for his new bride. She was rescued by the warden, who helped her to swim quietly to safety while the bull vented his spleen on the boat. Once salvaged the boat proved repairable; not so, it seemed, the couple's week-old marriage! I was to remember this story two years later when, stopping off in Kenya en route for UK leave, I contrived to capsize my friend Bill Deverell's 505 dinghy amongst a herd of hippos during a race on Lake Naivasha. Happily, those hippos were used to dinghy sailors and they allowed Bill and me to right the boat and continue the race without interference. Whereas hippos tended to be shot only when they were a nuisance, their distant relatives, the rhinos, had been hunted almost to extinction on account of their horns, which were prized as phallic symbols by Africans and Europeans alike. Alternatively, the horns were ground up into powder for use as aphrodisiacs.

On a brief trip to Hluhluwe Game Reserve in Natal, I had been able to track white rhinos on foot, accompanied by a Zulu ranger with a rifle. Such a trip, of course, would have been impossible for Edward because of his race. Anything worthwhile in South Africa tended to be *net vir blankes* (whites only). The rhinos in question were 'white' or square-lipped rhino, one of the successes of South African game conservation. White rhinos are not white; the name comes from their habit of covering themselves with the dust, which in their natural habitat tends to be very light coloured. That is one explanation. Another, which I think is more plausible, is that the early Dutch settlers called them 'square lipped', the word they used being *wijd* which the

English settlers coming later mistook for 'white' Their numbers had dwindled to under thirty throughout Southern Africa in the 1940s, but by the 1960s herds were starting to re-establish themselves, thanks to the work done by the South African Game Department at Hluhluwe and the neighbouring reserve at Umfolozi. Black rhinos had also been in danger, but never to the same extent, for they had a much wider distribution than the white and were also better equipped to look after themselves, having good eyesight, whereas the white rhino can hardly see at all and tends to rely instead on its hearing and sense of smell. Their Asian relative, the Nepalese rhino, had not fared so well. In the 1930s a friend of my parents recounted having been on a rhino hunt as the guest of the King of Nepal. When he asked the King if he was worried the rhinos might become extinct, the King replied, "No, I think they will just see me out"!

The Octoped.

It was said to be fairly safe to stalk white rhinos on foot because of their poor eyesight. They might catch your scent and have a general idea of your position, but had difficulty picking you out amongst the thorn bushes. Although they had acute hearing this could be turned to the stalker's advantage. If a white rhino came too close and looked as if it had worked out where you were, the trick was to throw a stone to one side of it. This would cause it to veer off to where the stone had landed, guided by its hearing, rather than its sight.

Notwithstanding the known reputation of the stone stratagem, my heart gave a flutter the first time one of the huge creatures lumbered towards the guide and myself. We had only tiny thorn bushes for cover and a few small stones in our hands to create a diversion. There was, of course, the rifle; but the thought struck me that the guide would not be popular if he killed one of the game department's precious white rhinos merely to protect a rooinek. Perhaps he might leave the shot a little late or even not use the rifle at all, for no one in Pretoria would have worried about the death of a young Briton, intent on taking close-up photos, who could easily be made out to have brought the accident upon himself. There were, after all, plenty of well-documented accounts of game park visitors' extraordinarily stupid behaviour, which would give credibility to any cock and bull explanation for my demise. Such were the thoughts flashing through my excited mind the first time one of these great beasts looked me straight in the face, trying to decide whether I was a man or a bush. I took my photo, grateful for the Leica's silent shutter; then the guide threw his stone and the rhino crashed off after it. To my shame that first photo showed definite signs of camera shake!

During the course of a memorable afternoon, my Zulu friend - and I certainly regarded him as my friend after that first, judicious stone throw – found several more white rhinos for me to observe, including a massive cow and her bull calf, which was still suckling despite being almost as big as its mother.

Edward told me the Swazi/Zulu creation story about the rhinoceros. When God (Nkulunkulu – The Great, Great One) created the world he made the animals one by one. One hot day after lunch he was working on the rhino. Having fashioned its huge frame he then set about with needle and thread sewing on its tough hide coat. Half way through he fell asleep, the needle fell to the ground and the rhino accidentally swallowed it with a mouthful of grass. The story explains two things – first, why the rhino's skin hangs in untidy folds around him (because the stitching was never finished) and, secondly, why a rhino will habitually root about in its dung (looking for the needle so he can give it back to Nkulunkulu and allow him to complete his work).

Thinks "Is that a man or a bush?"

The story has echoes of the Indian legends, which Kipling reproduced in his *Just So* stories and, indeed, of a Malay creation story, told to me by my father. That also concerned the way God (in this case Allah) made the animals one by one. Presently he sent for the cat *Mitchi gumu* ('Mr Schoolmaster'), whom he had recently created, and said to it, "Today I have made a new animal called a tiger; I want you to take it away and teach it everything you know." *Mitchi Gumu* looked at the tiger and saw that it was a large and formidable creature, so he decided there was one thing he would not teach it: how to climb trees. The legend explains three phenomena: first, why, alone of the cat family, tigers do not have retractable claws; secondly, why tigers have a congenital hatred of cats and will resolutely seek them out and kill them, and thirdly, why cats bury their droppings: to conceal their whereabouts from tigers.

There is another Muslim animal story concerning The Flood, I am told, which was presumably censored out of the Pentateuch by early Mosaic scholars. To prevent complications in an overcrowded vessel, no procreation was allowed in Noah's Ark. All male animals had to surrender their genitals on boarding, with the understanding that they would receive them back when they disembarked. When the time for this arrived there was a slight mix-up and the donkey received the camel's genitalia and the camel the donkey's. This explains why the male donkey is so exceptionally well hung and the camel quite the reverse. It might also explain (although this is a purely personal view) why donkeys always seem rather pleased with themselves, whereas camels are so persistently disagreeable!

Proverbs, too, seem to transcend national and continental boundaries. There were masses of guinea fowl in Hluhluwe, as in most bushveld regions. The Swazi proverb about them is *"Ayikho mpangele equandele enye"* – 'you don't find one guinea fowl scratching up grubs for another'. It was a good proverb to chuck into homilies to rural communities about fifty/fifty community development schemes – people have to do something for themselves and not expect government to do it all. It is not a million miles away from the Lancastrian 'you never see kitten bring owt to cat'.

The two weeks of metaphorically sitting at Edward Zwane's feet, picking up all manner of knowledge, came to an end far too quickly and I soon found myself extremely busy. In addition, my Swazi language exam was looming and I was having lessons most evenings, so it was a relief when my teacher's efforts were rewarded and I was safely over this hurdle. That summer the Ngwenyama had really surpassed himself in providing rain so I had plenty of practice driving in mud. This included learning the rally driver's trick, especially useful on hills, of violently swinging the steering wheel from side to side while the passenger bounced on the back seat. This procedure, if properly synchronised, enabled a car's wheels to bite on even the most slippery of surfaces.

Land Rover stuck in a river.

Meanwhile I was learning something about cotton, which was a popular crop amongst European farmers in the lower regions of the District. There was an almost limitless market for Swaziland cotton, which was all hand picked and therefore sold better on the world market than the largely machine picked American crop. The Department of Agriculture was trying to promote cotton as a cash crop amongst the Swazis in the lower rainfall regions to give them a fallback if their maize crop failed. Maize was much more likely to fail in the bushveld than in the higher rainfall regions. The three main causes of maize failure were stalk-borer beetle, drought and witchweed (*isona*). Stalk-borer could be controlled effectively with insecticide, but drought and witchweed were much more difficult. Witchweed was endemic in Swaziland and was almost impossible to stamp out although thorough weeding could stop it from spreading. It kills maize almost completely. Fortunately witchweed only comes up in January and February, so it can be avoided by planting in August, September, or even October, which is perfectly feasible in the higher regions. However, in the bushveld, where the annual rainfall is often less than twenty inches, people normally had to wait until November before there was enough moisture in the ground for them to be able to plant. Most lowveld Swazi farmers were thus forced either to grow their maize in the witchweed months and risk loss from isona, or plant early and risk total failure from drought. Either way they needed an alternative crop, especially as irrigation is difficult except on a massive scale, because only the largest rivers in the bushveld flow through the summer.

The world over, of course, everyone is searching for the miracle crop. Apparently when Sir Julian Huxley and his wife were passing through Swaziland in 1961, they paid a call on the Ngwenyama, who asked Sir Julian if there was any plant that grew all over the world irrespective of soil conditions. "Yes," replied Huxley famously, "bracken."

Failing a miracle crop, which would make their fortunes overnight, most Swazi farmers were reluctant to abandon the practices of their fathers, keeping cattle and goats, mindless of their quality and growing the staple food, maize. In areas where cotton was a viable proposition the Agriculture Department's message to Swazi farmers was to substitute cotton for some of their maize so as to spread their risk; but such a proposition was as difficult to get across to the Swazi farmers as the concept of thinking of cattle in terms of quality, rather than numbers. To their credit the agricultural field officers kept plugging their advice, reinforced by demonstration plots which allowed local Swazis to see for themselves what could be done with cotton and in places the message was getting through.

Erosion – the result of ploughing in the river valley.

A little while after Edward had left we learned that Sir John Maud, the High Commissioner and Ambassador to South Africa (the functions were combined) was coming to visit Hlatikulu as part of his farewell tour of the High Commission territories before retiring from the

Diplomatic Service to be Master of University College, Oxford. We had to arrange a suitable function for his farewell to the south of Swaziland.

One fine morning before he left Edward had shown me a spot just outside Hlatikulu, which he felt would be the ideal place for a luxury hotel. It was a large level open space, set in the middle of some Crown Land only a short distance off the main road, which ran northwards out of the village. The view from this spot stretched far further than the compass of most local Swazis' daily lives, to the hills on Swaziland's western and eastern boundaries, with the middleveld and bushveld laid out in between. Edward was right, this would indeed be a superb place for a hotel. I wondered: could we hold the farewell on this site? I went and had another look at it and then put the suggestion to Mr Rawlins. He readily agreed and said, as it was my idea, I had better take on the responsibility of putting the whole thing into practice. I conferred with the office staff. We decided to construct a simple fenced arena on the site using wattle poles cut from the nearby Crown Land. As a focal point there would be a large dais on the slightly higher ground at one end, with its roof thatched with wattle branches, so as to provide shade for Sir John and local dignitaries. The dais would allow an uninterrupted view of proceedings against the backdrop of the amazing vista, which Edward and I had admired a few weeks earlier. All the work could be done by the prisoners, so the cost would be negligible. The arena would have to be sufficiently large to accommodate the numbers who were expected and to give everyone a good view. The site also had enough hard flat ground all around to provide parking. The vehicles involved would be innumerable pick-ups and large ageing Buicks and Chevrolets, the preferred transport of most well-off rural Swazis, not to mention buses crammed to overflowing, hung about externally with people perched on the roofs and clinging to the sides and tailgates. These were expected in profusion from all parts of the south, for we understood that word had gone out from Lobamba to the local chiefs that the Ngwenyama wanted a big turnout. Although Sir John (soon to be created Baron Redcliffe-Maud) was retiring into academia, it was likely, because of his varied and distinguished career, that he would remain something of an *éminence grise* and would always have political influence. This was shown some years later by his role in the reorganisation of English local government (*The Redcliffe Maud Report*). Thus the Ngwenyama was keen, since the Constitutional White Paper was still in the melting pot, that Sir John should carry home with him a clear reminder of the predominance of the Swazi traditional authority. For similar reasons a considerable representation was expected from the European community. Against this background, with all groupings competing to display their political clout, I rather wondered if the NNLC might use the occasion to stage a demonstration; but we never had any wind of this, nor did anything materialise.

Our plan was to add to the inevitable speeches a programme of songs by local schoolchildren and a performance by a troup of Sibhaca dancers. The Bhaca people had been comprehensively defeated by the Swazi in the unchronicled days before the Great Trek. They had migrated south, settling around the foothills of the Southern Drakenbergs, near East Griqualand, Chris Anderson's home country. The Bhaca's highly energetic style of dancing spread widely throughout southern Africa and in due course Sibhaca dancing contests became one of the features of the inter-mine competitions on the Rand.

All the construction and other arrangements were completed in good time and when Mr Rawlins and I went up to the arena on the morning of the big day everything looked most promising. The prisoners, with a little help from the PWD, had made an excellent job of the railing for the arena and the construction and thatching of the dais. As we stood there and gazed northwards in the morning sun the view took our breath away. Layer upon layer of hills glowed in the pink of the morning, etched against the pale blue sky and the air had that translucent quality which you sometimes find in the West Highlands of Scotland. Then, with the hint of a shiver, I reflected that the only time I had ever seen so far with such clarity had indeed been in Scotland and on that occasion the locals had sucked their teeth, pronounced the clarity an ill omen and correctly predicted heavy rain by midday. Happily, however, this was not Scotland; this was Swaziland in the dry season.

Not far away a group of long-tailed widow birds were flapping around in their disorganised fashion. They were generally known by their Zulu name, *Sakabula* birds. The Swazi, however, had separate names for the male and female, whose appearance, especially in the breeding season, is markedly different. Females and immature young males are the archetype LBJ (little brown job) of birdwatchers' parlance; but the adult male, in breeding plumage, is totally different. He is a magnificent sight, jet black with red chevrons on his wings and is resplendent with an enormous shiny black tail. This gives the male an overall length of nearly two feet, compared to the female's seven inches. When I was just arrived in Swaziland at the end of the previous winter, just as on this day near the start of the next winter, some of the males were in their wonderful breeding plumage, some not. A jocular Swazi had tried to tell me that the males without tails were ones that had been caught and had their tails plucked for use in Swazi traditional dress. *Roberts' Birds of South Africa* soon put me right.

The Swazi names for them were *Jojo* for the male and *Shikane* for the female. One of the praises of Sobhuza, mentioned by Hilda Kuper (p15) is translated as follows:

> *"Black bewildering widow bird*
> *You grew plumes in winter*
> *When other widow birds are bare".*

In other words he was a man for all seasons, a particularly apt simile, as one of Sobhuza's greatest attributes was his ability to switch from one mode to another, traditional to modern and then back again.

The sight of all those long black tails disturbed me. It was meant to be the start of winter, the dry season, so why did so many of the Jojos still have their long tails, the plumage of summer, i.e. the rainy season? It had been a very wet summer, was it possible that we had still not seen the last of the rains? And what about the amazing clarity? Was the comparison with the West Highlands relevant after all? Rawlins' voice, at its most enthusiastic, jerked me out of such negative musings: "What a view!" he exclaimed. "You've done well here, this was a grand idea of yours; we'll really give Sir John an afternoon to remember!" One could forgive a man anything, I reflected, who was so generous in his praise of a subordinate.

Sibhaca dancing.

To be realistic the occasion did indeed bode well. As we were speaking the Sibhaca dancers arrived in their pristine finery and sprung into an impromptu rehearsal – they were magnificent. People were now trickling onto the site and gave the dancers a round of applause. Amongst the arrivals, however, I spotted several sellers of Swazi beer. "Let's hope," I thought to myself, "the dancers haven't peaked too early." Then a phrase of my father's came to mind. It was totally uncharacteristic of him since he was one of the mildest-mannered of men and was used by him very sparingly and only in male company - "Nil desperandum, f**k it!" That was the spirit of leadership (or in my case subordinateship) not to let one's anxieties show. And, in truth, the prospect was becoming more dazzling by the minute, the lovely weather, the stunning view, the fantastic dancers and all those pretty widow birds with their long floppy tails. What wonderful memories Sir John would have to take back to his new home at the Master's Lodge at University College, Oxford.

Then I noticed it; a tiny cloud on the western horizon; and at that moment a Hammerkop stork (the *Tekwane*, a bird of ill omen to the Swazi) rose from the long grass with a raucous cry. It flapped around us, ugly and sinister, croaking without ceasing, before dropping down again in the same clump of grass whence it had arisen. Within a minute the little white cloud had been joined by others, darker and more threatening. "It's going to rain," I said to Mr Rawlins. "It had better bloody well not," he said, with uncharacteristic vehemence, adding, with just a hint of panic in his voice, "for goodness sake, it can't rain, *it's the dry season!*" I hoped he was right; after all, he had lived in the territory for years, he should know. But I had that nagging feeling, which creeps upon you when you sense that Dame Fortune's smile is changing to a frown.

By the time four and a half thousand Swazi and a large turnout from the European community had taken their places in the arena ahead of Sir John and Lady Maud's arrival the temperature had dropped thirty-five degrees Fahrenheit to a little above freezing, visibility was down to three hundred yards and the rain was incessant. The ambassadorial Rolls Royce emerged from the gloom and Rawlins, opening car doors for a change instead of having them opened for him, escorted the Ambassador and High Commissioner and his lady to the dais.

Despite his full dress uniform, complete with plumed hat, Sir John was soon showing signs of cold. Rawlins gave a brief speech of welcome and then the local schoolchildren, bedraggled in the downpour, performed their songs. They managed splendidly, singing a mixture of traditional Swazi melodies but ended, bizarrely, with *Auld Lang Syne*, rendered as 'Old Long Sin'. Now it was the turn of the Sibhaca dancers to strut their stuff. As I had half feared, in the time since their earlier, spectacular rehearsal, they had been bracing themselves against the elements with the aid of Swazi beer. In the cold and rain the beer had passed quickly through their systems so that, when it was the group's turn to perform many of them were temporarily absent, relieving themselves in the veld. It was a depleted and dishevelled bunch that took to the arena, with the rain hanging heavy on the fringes of their ankle-bands and the red ochre from their hair trickling down their faces. However, after a shaky start, they snapped into their rhythm and stomped around the arena to the frenzied Sibhaca beat. Every time their feet struck the ground, instead of the thunder of pounding on the baked earth, there was a sucking noise and showers of mud flew up onto their snow-white anklets. Soon the mud was splattered over the rest of their finery. When their programme was completed the dancers retired to prolonged clapping caused, at least in part, by the audience's need to regenerate their circulation. Sir John then rose to deliver his speech, which, like Rawlins' introduction, was translated as he went along by Abbey Mamba, the Chief Clerk.

By now the wattle thatching over the dais, designed as a shield against sun, was leaking. At the first drops Chris Anderson and John Sturgis, the Magistrate, sitting either side of me, dug me in the ribs, pointing jocularly at the dripping thatch. They had already nicknamed the arena and dais respectively 'Miller's Folly' and 'The Not so-Grandstand'. Soon the party under the roof were little better off than everyone else out in the open. Despite the rain pouring down the plumes of his hat and the increasing saturation of his tunic, the Ambassador and High Commissioner gave not the slightest indication of discomfort and delivered his speech with aplomb and humour. He was not for nothing renowned as a great showman. Finally, there was a brief speech by the senior chief present and the official party were able to move to the next stage of the programme, back at the Rawlins' house, where tea was to be served. Beneath the surface mud the ground was still hard and most of the vehicles moved off in good order, although some of the buses needed to be pushed the first few yards or even towed by police Land Rovers. All the great and the good of the District, Swazi and European, together with several Coloureds had been put on the tea invitation list. Numbers had not been thought a problem, as there should have been ample room for guests to spread out over the garden, which had been manicured for the occasion even beyond its normal excellence. With no sign of the rain abating everything and everyone had to be crammed indoors, so that the DC's Residency, normally so spick and span, started to resemble a Highland bothy invaded by a flock of sheep in a storm as copiously depicted by Landseer and his imitators. Steam rose from our clothing and there was an all-pervading smell of wet wool.

Most of the guests left after a quick cup of tea, anxious to reach home before the roads became impassable. We were then able to change out of our saturated clothing before a small drinks party and dinner where Sir John was the life and soul of the evening. He and Lady Maud left the next morning after attending Matins at the Hlatikulu Anglican church. Sir John thanked us all effusively, saying it had been a memorable visit. I dare say, in due course, a description of his visit to Hlatikulu found its way into High Table reminiscences at University College, Oxford, concluding, perhaps with words from Pliny's *Historia Naturalis* – not the shortened tag that everyone knows but, as befits an academic, the full quote: *"Unde etiam vulgare Graeciae dictum 'semper aliquid novi Africam adferre'"* – "Whence it is commonly said amongst the Greeks that 'Africa always offers something new'".

With the visit over it would not have been unreasonable for me to have received a tongue-lashing for the way it had turned out. Sir John's good humour had certainly helped; nevertheless many DCs in Ray Rawlins' shoes would have set about me in no uncertain fashion. However, one of Rawlins' most endearing qualities was the way he backed up his subordinates, even when things went wrong. He simply accepted the shambles as part of the quirky pattern of life in Swaziland.

Despite our increasing conviction that real trouble might be in the offing, life at Hlatikulu went on at its normal pace. My diary shows tennis matches on successive Saturdays, first at the Club against the local Swazi team and secondly, more surprisingly, since I was not a local resident, for the Goedgegun team against Big Bend. Both, in their different ways, were highly enjoyable and the match against Big Bend was shortly to stand me in good stead. The two matches illustrated the vagaries of the climate. At Hlatikulu, despite it being highveld, we played in stifling heat, whereas the following weekend at Goedgegun, which, being middleveld, ought to have been hot, we were frozen. I think it was this sort of variation of temperature, encountered in Swaziland on a daily basis, that caused the relatively high incidence of minor illness amongst expatriates, who generally enjoyed better health in other territories where the climate, although ostensibly more hostile, was not given to such extreme local variation. I suppose, in Swaziland, one's system never had the chance to acclimatise to any settled temperature.

It was the variety of terrain and temperature that was to play a part in my being given a new Swazi name, which, for my time at Hlatikulu District, supplanted the name of 'Malindzane', which I had been given at Mbabane. From the moment of my arrival at Hlatikulu I had sensed a certain hostility towards me from Abbey Mamba, the Chief Clerk. He was older than me and doubtless felt that Edward Zwane should have been followed as DO by another Swazi, ideally himself. One day Abbey and I went to visit a tax camp in an area so inaccessible that we had to park the Land Rover and cover the last four miles on foot. We had dropped perhaps two and a half thousand feet in the short drive from Hlatikulu and now as we plodded down the narrow rocky valley it was stiflingly hot. I decided to establish my position in the office hierarchy by walking Abbey off his feet, knowing he would be too proud to ask me to slow down. He was a large man, heavily built and carried more than a little surplus weight. After a short while Abbey's big round face was glistening with perspiration; by the time we arrived at the camp he was drenched in sweat and almost at his last gasp, but he had kept up. After we had done our business I suggested we were in no particular hurry to get home. He readily agreed and chatted happily as we ambled back to the Land Rover; and he was friendly and helpful to me ever afterwards. From then on, until I moved north again, my Swazi name was 'Twasi', meaning roughly 'Seven League Boots' – at least I think that is what it meant, but you could never be too sure with the names the Swazi gave to us Europeans. Of course, it was not just the Swazi who gave people nicknames. Mark Patey, the DC at Stegi, was 'Huff Puff' to us irreverent DOs. When, several days later, he and Rawlins came out from the DC's office after an ultra-serious private session on the deteriorating security scene, John Sturgis, seeing the sudden emergence of the two DCs who were probably the most pompous men in the administration, whatever their other excellent qualities, exclaimed for all and sundry to hear, "Ah, Gog and Magog." That made three of us who had got a new name in the same week!

The result of Gog and Magog's confabulation was a meeting of DCs and DOs at Manzini, under the able chairmanship of Frank Fleck, Jeremy's unsupportive DC. Frank had a considerable presence and was admirable in many ways; he just could not rid himself of his South African attitudes.

It was a constructive and wide-ranging meeting, focusing on how best we could prepare the Swazi people for independence. What had been provided up to the present had been *pax britannica*, the stock in trade of British colonialism, law and order (an end to tribal fighting and exploitation) usually the reason for our being invited there in the first place, coupled with a non-venal system of administration, which protected individuals' rights. None of this should be undervalued. The peoples of many of our former colonies only appreciated what we had given them after we had gone and all too often the gift did not long survive our going. However, it was not enough to give people new ideas and new mechanisms, i.e. democracy and universal franchise. We also needed to help them to understand how to use these things and what to expect from them.

Chris Anderson supplied an analogy from a friend's farm. They had bought a machine to slice turnips for the sheep. It was a simple contraption with a hopper into which you put the turnips and a slicer to cut them up. One man loaded the hopper, another turned a handle to operate the slicer. One of the Xhosa farm workers put in a turnip but did not remove his hand. The blade took off two of his fingers. When he came back in the afternoon having been patched up at Cedarville hospital, the others crowded round him. "*Kuenzeke kanjani?*" they asked. "How did it happen?" "*Angazi*" – "I don't know." "*Ndizifake lapha*" – "I just put them in there," he replied, and he pointed into the bottom of the hopper with his remaining fingers and promptly lost them too. He understood the idea of the machine, to chop up turnips quickly and effortlessly; but he had not grasped how the mechanism worked. Unless we educated the new electorate both in the concepts of democracy as well as the mechanisms of the elective process the Swazis would be at the mercy of the extremist politicians, each trying to outdo the other in their scramble to be top dog when independence arrived. The days of the old laissez-faire attitudes were numbered. We had to change the way we worked – PDQ – (Pretty Damned Quick).

I was asked to take the minutes of the meeting. I went to some trouble to make a coherent document out of the record of the day's proceedings, despite the inevitable interjections and non-sequiturs, which threaten the clarity of any large working group's deliberations. The conclusions of that day were basically three:

1. In order to educate the Swazi in democratic principles and thus to counter the influence of undesirables, administrative officers should spend much more time out among the people and much less time in their offices dealing with paperwork and relatively trivial matters.

2. To make this possible we needed District Assistants who could deal with the bulk of the routine deskwork.

3. To provide continuity of personnel there should be an end to the perpetual transfers of administrative officers. Every time someone went on long leave it seemed to produce a chain reaction of postings throughout the District administration. For instance, in the past seven months there had been three different DOs at Stegi. We proposed that Districts should provide their overseas leave cover from their own staff. Assuming our proposal for District Assistants was implemented this would be feasible and would achieve our aim. In addition, the proposal would have the advantage of enabling up-and-coming DOs to broaden their experience by having a spell in charge during their DCs' leave.

Frank Fleck accepted my draft minutes without alteration and Ray Rawlins told me that Marwick had said that he was taking the document just as it stood to put before the Secretary of State when he went to London the following month. (This was necessary, as the financial implications of our proposals would mean an increase in Swaziland's annual grant-in-aid.) It was typical of Ray Rawlins' kindness and management style that he told me of the RC's comments; it is always rewarding to feel that one has had a hand in something of consequence. To our delight the following year's grant-in-aid made allowance for the appointment of District Assistants and some further overall increase in the level of staffing within the District Administration, so our day's work at Manzini brought real benefits, not least to me personally for, although I was to have a total of six postings in my first tour, in my second I was to have only one!

Peter Simkin had gone on home leave to the UK while I was at Mankaina. It was from John Sturgis, Hlatikulu district's visiting magistrate and coiner of the mocking epithets about my preparations for the Mauds' visit, that I heard of Peter's encounter on his way back from leave. One Monday morning before starting court, John burst into my office. "John," he said, "I've just met Simkin's air hostess – she's stunning." "What air hostess?" I asked, giving him the pleasure of telling the whole romantic tale complete with embellishments in his inimitable style. On the top of his form John was the most amusing person on earth. Shortly after qualifying as a barrister in the UK he had come to Swaziland as a stipendiary magistrate and after several years had married Jeannette Kelly, a glamorous widow who ran her late husband's fruit farm at Ezulwini, down the hill from Mbabane. John combined his domestic duties with his work, which usually brought him to Hlatikulu for two or three days a week. There was a courthouse in Goedgegun, Chris Anderson's station, as well as at Hlatikulu itself. When sitting, John would stay at the Hlatikulu hotel. His visits brought a whiff of levity as well as an update on the social scene in the capital, for Jeannette was very much part of the Government House set.

Many people had been surprised at Jeannette's choice of second husband, for John was very different from Peter Kelly. Peter had been supremely good looking and possessed that easy charm which seems to come so naturally to many Irishmen, the sort who, in his youth, would have effortlessly attracted all the prettiest girls, to the alarm of their mothers. In 1930s parlance he would have been described as a 'remittance man'; certainly the little fruit farm by itself could not have provided for the family's needs, let alone the boarding school education of their three sons, so there must have been private money.

Tragically, Kelly, a popular figure in the European community, was killed when his car skidded off the dirt road between Mbabane and Pigg's Peak, leaving Jeannette with sole responsibility for the boys and the farm. Jeannette and John had been married several years by the time I arrived in Swaziland and the boys were away at schools in South Africa except during the holidays. Unlike Peter Kelly, John was no looker - quite short, thickset, like a bull terrier, with a fighting dog's hard stare. I think Jeannette was attracted by his sharp mind, wit and originality.

Like many people with the reputation for being amusing John sometimes tried too hard and trod the borderline between humour and bad taste, or even boorishness. I remember an example of this from one evening when I was at dinner with them. Amongst the small company were a middle-aged European couple and their pretty daughter. So old fashioned were the couple they could have stepped straight from the pages of Jane Austen. After dinner the conversation turned to party games and Jeannette asked if anyone had come across any new games. "Well, I heard of one the other day," ventured John. "Oh, do tell us, Mr Sturgis," urged the Jane Austen lady. "You need a rectangular table like this," John explained, "and you divide into two teams seated opposite each other. One team puts on jackboots and the other team is issued with axes. The aim is to hack off your opposite number's legs before he kicks you to death." "Oh no," said the Austen lady, "I don't think that sounds at all suitable." She and her husband beat an early retreat, taking their pretty daughter with them.

More often it was not John's absurd suggestions, but his dogs that broke up proceedings. John's dogs reflected his quirky personality. They were brindled Staffordshire bull terriers of vicious temperament. Both bore scars around the head, ears, muzzle, neck, chest and flanks, the legacies of their past attempts to kill each other, for this was their dominating passion and, it seemed, their only purpose in life. The house was divided into each dog's territory, with a *cordon sanitaire* in between. This arrangement was observed scrupulously by the whole household, mainly out of simple self-interest. None, and certainly not the servants, wished to risk life and limb trying to separate the two dogs once they were locked in combat; but the system broke down from time to time, usually when there were guests in the house. There would then ensue a cacophony like the soundtrack of a dinosaur movie and the two growling, roaring creatures would thrash around the drawing room, their jaws fixed in each other's throats, overturning everything in their path as they wrestled with unimaginable power. It was like the battle of the warrior, with confused noise and garments rolled in blood. John would pitch into the fray, bellowing dementedly to the dogs to stop and to everyone else present to help prize the brutes apart. Jeannette usually contributed by throwing buckets of water over the combatants. When it was all over and the dogs were finally separated and dragged off snarling, snapping and bleeding to their respective ends of the house and the debris removed, it was difficult to recapture the former relaxed mood of the evening. For myself, I would simply be grateful to have retained my full complement of fingers and not to have had my suit utterly shredded; as for Jeannette, she just regarded it all as part of the rich warp and weft of being Mrs John Sturgis.

To be fair, such incidents occurred rarely and normally an invitation to dinner with John and Jeannette was a guarantee of good food, fine wine and sparkling conversation. John and Jeannette did not have children of their own, as John was sterile. That, he would hasten to inform almost all and sundry, was a totally different thing from being impotent and, as if to underline the point, he and Jeannette once returned from a romantic weekend in South Africa with John nursing a broken wrist and Jeannette three cracked ribs, all the result of falling out of bed in the course of a night of passion. Such was John Sturgis, our visiting magistrate and my informant of the romantic tale concerning Peter Simkin and his air hostess.

Apparently, on Peter's return flight from overseas leave the plane had developed engine trouble and had put down at Khartoum. There the passengers and crew had been stranded for three days - Diana was one of the air hostesses. Soon afterwards Diana had flown to Swaziland to visit Peter. A short while later they announced their engagement and forthcoming marriage. Both Diana's parents were of British origin and lived in Argentina, where they were pillars of the Anglo-Argentinian community. Three out of their four children, their son John and Diana and Marcella, the older two daughters, had been sent to British boarding schools. Soon after the wedding Diana's father received a KBE for services to Anglo-Argentinian relations and it should be noted that when the Falklands War erupted some fifteen years later, the family were treated with kindness and respect by the Argentinians, amongst whom they lived.

The wedding was held in Mbabane. In marked contrast to present-day fashion it was a model of simplicity and sincerity, focusing on the proper purpose of the event. There was no Wedding Organiser, no fleet of hired vintage cars or horse-drawn carriages, no exotic flowers jetted in from the four corners of the earth, no wedding cake in the shape of a Swazi hut, surrounded by icing sugar models of bare-breasted Swazi maidens or whatever might have been deemed locally appropriate, no video operator, no society photographer and no one from *Hello* magazine. The bride and groom arrived at the church looking bright and happy, not hung-over and shamefaced from the excesses of their respective hen and stag nights; nor had they indulged in the present custom of living together for years before finally opting for marriage to try and kick-start a relationship that had lost its sparkle. It was all fresh and enthusiastic and (dare I say it, using an outmoded word?) romantic.

One of the pleasantest aspects of expatriate life is the way people rally round and help each other. This was certainly so at Peter and Diana's wedding. Ian Butler, who had recently joined the administration after service in the Pacific, provided and drove his large smart black car as the bridal vehicle, friends brought and arranged the flowers, other people, marshalled by the Mbabane office messenger, supervised the parking; the Swazi Inn surpassed itself to serve up delicious food and Nkulunkulu (The Lord God Almighty) laid on one of those sparkling, fresh highveld winter days, when one feels like shouting to the heavens at the joy of being alive.

Peter, Diana and Ian Butler.

So far as there was a photographer, it was me, very ill qualified for the role; but I came at the task determined to apply two principles – first, not to make a nuisance of myself, but to be as inconspicuous as possible and try to snatch my photos unnoticed so that people did not become self-conscious or, worse still, irritable; secondly, to photograph people as they were, as part of the occasion, rather than to pose them and record situations that were created simply for the camera. However, it was not these rules that produced quite a reasonable set of photographs, but sheer luck. How often is success really the result of luck? (Napoleon, famously, requiring his marshals to be lucky and Wellington acknowledging his luck by describing Waterloo as "A damned nice thing – the nearest run thing you ever saw in your life", the luck being that Blucher had arrived when he did and not half an hour later.) Anyway, a streak of luck ran for this amateur photographer that afternoon and was very welcome. My luck was twofold; first there was an incredible clarity to the air that day, which gave the photographs an extra bite and also helped keep people smiling and, secondly, and most important, all the principals turned out to be extraordinarily photogenic. Both Peter and Julian Faux, his best man, were good looking fellows, but their looks were enhanced a notch or two when processed through a camera. Diana was a lovely bride and she had just the right bone structure to look consistently stunning in photographs.

If Diana should have been a photographic model, Valerie Diesel, her matron of honour, had before marriage and a career in journalism, indeed been just that. To cap it all, Diana's parents, Weston and Marjorie Greaves, were as glamorous a fifty-year-old couple as one could find, the sort who always looked a million dollars whatever they wore.

Wedding guests including June Shongue (second from left), Pat Forsyth Thompson (fourth from left) and Tom Sililo (back right).

After the marriage service it was off to the reception at the Swazi Inn, perched on the edge of the Mbabane escarpment, looking right down the Ezulwini valley past Lobamba and Lozitha to Manzini and the middleveld, with the hills either side of the valley gradually turning purple in the late afternoon sun. The speeches were amusing but not over long, the champagne was excellent and, as the sun set to the west of the valley behind the twin peaks known as Sheba's Breasts, bride and bridegroom set off for their honeymoon in the Drakenbergs and the rest of us dispersed to dinner parties arranged by kind Mbabane-based fellow guests. Contrary to the expectations of some of his peers, Peter had not organised a crocodile-hunting honeymoon. This suggested that, for all her charm and winning smile, Diana had a will of her own. She certainly had the gift of repartee. I had not met her before the wedding and in the line-up I greeted her with: "Going by how you're dressed, you must be Diana," to which she replied, quick as a flash, "Going by that remark, you must be John Miller."

Lucky old Peter, I thought, as I drove back to Hlatikulu at the end of a delightful weekend. Little did I realise that Cupid was to involve an aeroplane in an equally unexpected fashion on my behalf eighteen months later. But in the meantime the political pot was starting to bubble.

Chapter 7

# A Gathering Storm

It was not long before we saw the first signs of the political unrest, which had long been predicted by Chris Anderson. There was trouble in the Mbabane gaol and the ringleaders were dispersed around the territory, including several to our gaol at Hlatikulu. On my next gaol inspection one of the new arrivals complained that he was being starved. I had him weighed and compared his weight with that on arrival. He had put on half a stone in two weeks. This revelation rather took the wind out of his sails. He then tried to stir up a prisoners' strike in protest at my unsympathetic treatment of his complaint, but nothing transpired. I had been able to procure some improvements in conditions at the gaol and this may have counted in my favour amongst the other prisoners to mitigate the offence I had given, so the rumour had it, of telling the agitator that gaol was not meant to be a hotel. That sort of statement, of course, cut right across time-honoured Swazi tradition and could have caused the average decent criminal to regard me with grave suspicion. A more likely reason for the failure of the agitator's strike call was probably the southern Swazis' dislike, prisoners included, of being told what to do by people from Mbabane, whoever they might be.

Strikes, however, were all the fashion. I had been able to lay my hands on a Swazi students' newsletter which was trying to whip up enthusiasm for school strikes in protest against the government, against the Ngwenyama and his chiefs, against the way the NNLC delegates were ignored by Duncan Sandys at the Constitutional Conference, and, more routinely, against the employment of Zulu and Basuto teachers, an old chestnut. Zulus, in particular, tended to be unpopular because they had always rather regarded the Swazis as a second-rate tribe, witness the fact, mentioned earlier, that one of the traditional praises chanted about Somhlolo, Sobhuza I, the Ngwenyama's great-great-grandfather, was that he had the courage to accept an invitation to visit Shaka, the great Zulu King and had looked him in the eye – i.e. refused to accept his superiority. Basutos were disliked simply because they were different.

School sports at Hlatikulu.

Following the failure of the Swaziland Constitutional Conference in London, Duncan Sandys, the Secretary of State, ('Shifting Sands' to some) sent his Minister of State, Lord Lansdowne, to Swaziland to canvass local opinion. The 8th Marquess of Lansdowne, 29th Baron of Kerry and Lixnaw, Earl of Kerry and Viscount Clanmaurice, Viscount FitzMaurice and Baron Dunkeron, Earl of Shelburne, Earl of Wycombe and Viscount Calne, was nobody's fool. He had served throughout the 1939 – 45 war, latterly with the rank of Major with the Free French forces and had been awarded the Croix de Guerre and the Legion d'Honneur by de Gaulle. He then became Private Secretary to Duff Cooper, the British Ambassador to Paris and in the 1950s had been Lord in Waiting to the Queen. At a reception at the Residency in Mbabane he asked me, pointing to a member of the European Advisory Council, "Who's that fellow? I bet he sleeps with African women!" He was dead right. Lansdowne's Private Secretary, a Wykhamist, stayed with me at Hlatikulu and, apart from leaving the shower tray inches deep in talcum powder, was an admirable fellow and highly intelligent.

By now the NNLC and particularly Mnt Dumisa Dlamini, the party's youth leader, saw that their opportunity lay in promoting labour unrest. Sensing this threat, Sobhuza appointed one of his sons, Masitsela Dlamini, as his chief labour representative. Hilda Kuper's comment was as follows: "Prince Masitsela had grown up at Lobamba and was known for his respect for custom. He had been employed as a clerk-typist at the Lobamba Appeal Court and then as a clerk in the Mbabane Post Office, where the treatment he received gave him an experience of racial prejudice, especially humiliating for a young prince trained in courtesy and conscious of his royal birth. He was, however, without knowledge or experience of modern labour organizations and the history of workers' movements in other countries." (*Sobhuza II Ngwenyama and King of Swaziland* p235). In short, in the political climate of 1963 Masitsela was no match for Dumisa.

It was not long before Dumisa was down our way and soon he had the workers at the sugar estates near Big Bend out on strike, marching round the town shouting "Africa!" at fifteen-second intervals. The police arrived in large numbers, but kept their cool. John Sturgis, our magistrate, always the ready wit, remarked it was a marvel the police did not stage a counter-demonstration by marching round shouting "South Africa!" in token of the political sympathies of most of their officers.

The strike was really just the NNLC flexing its muscles, even though the nominal aim was to secure higher wages for the workers in the cane fields. I had to concede that personally I would not be happy to cut cane all day in the heat of the bushveld for the equivalent of £3.50 a month, but the company was making a loss so it was hard to see how there could be much in the way of wage rises. Having made his mark in the south Dumisa moved on to Mbabane, leaving the Big Bend strikers to settle with the company as best they could, with a little help from the government's embryo labour department. Many people considered Dumisa lucky to be at liberty. He had been accused of raping a fellow politician's daughter and the case had only collapsed because of the prosecution's bungling.

Almost as soon as Dumisa was back in Mbabane, the capital had its first taste of trouble. This was ostensibly sparked off by a minor functionary officiously applying the letter of the law, rather than taking the broader view. The culprit was a government health inspector who had come down with a heavy hand on some of the Mbabane market women selling *mputhu* (traditional sour milk and maize porridge) without the requisite licence. The women's viewpoint was that mputhu had been sold without a licence for generations and they considered the sudden necessity to pay for a licence was an unjustified imposition; why should they now all at once have to conform to regulations and pay for licences? Their cause was first taken up, to little effect, by the moderate, non-racial Swaziland Democratic Party; but then Dumisa muscled in on the act. Within minutes of his arrival at the market a crowd had gathered and in no time the affair had turned into a demonstration. Julian Faux, now the DC in succession to Mr Elliot, called in the police who ordered the crowd to disperse. The demonstrators were slow to do so and instead started to sing political songs. Dumisa was arrested with some others and charged with a breach of the peace. Several political activists tried to make capital out of the arrests and led a band of around four hundred supporters to the Residency the next day, protesting about the arrests and also about the new proposed constitution. As the Resident Commissioner was in London, it was the Government Secretary, Athel Long, who came out to meet the demonstrators. He was well experienced in dealing, elsewhere, with peoples much more bellicose and excitable than the Swazis and was well prepared. The police were on the scene in force armed with tear gas, which they used when the crowd refused to disperse. So ended what could have been Swaziland's Amritsar. Fortunately the people on the ground had cool-enough heads and sufficient common humanity not to emulate Brigadier General Rex Dyer and create martyrs.

A few days later, as complete contrast to these events, a delegation from the Swazi National Council came to Hlatikulu to discuss the possibilities of developing the Hot Springs at Siphofaneni in the north of the district. The Siphofaneni Springs were on Swazi Area (land held in trust for the nation by the Ngwenyama) hence the dominant involvement of the Swazi National Council in any proposals for change.

Dealing with such an issue at such a time might seem akin to fiddling while Rome burned, but Hlatikulu District had a life of its own, however trivial, and we might as well get on with it. All three members of the delegation had been part of the Swazi National Council team for the Constitutional Conference and they were soon to travel again to London in an attempt to persuade the Secretary of State to amend his White Paper. Being who they were, they might have considered that they should have been received by the DC, not his underling; but if they were offended, it was not apparent. The least I could do, I felt, was to give them lunch in my house. The Andersons kindly lent me their excellent Swazi maid, Maria, for the day, and she was able to lay on a fitting repast in some style. My invitation caused a few raised eyebrows amongst the local Europeans who thought it extraordinary that I should entertain 'those people' in my own home. It was, after all, little more than a year since the passing of the anti-discrimination legislation. Quite apart from any other considerations the lunch party was an excellent opportunity to discuss new ideas for the Springs in a relaxed way, out of the dust of the bushveld, sitting by my dining room window overlooking the rolling hills. My minutes of our discussion and the synopsis of the ideas that emerged never, it seemed, made it to the top of the In Tray at the Swazi National Office at Lobamba. Certainly there was no movement on the matter before I left Swaziland. When a casino was subsequently built at the territory's other hot springs, the 'Cuddle Puddle' at Ezulwini, it turned that whole area rather seedy, despite the casino itself being well run. When I remarked to a local European that we only seemed able to pass on to the Swazi the worst aspects of our culture, he replied, "Perhaps that's what they like!"

Maria, Chris and Val Anderson's
excellent maid.

The SNC delegates and I continued to chew the fat after lunch and the conversation naturally turned to the political situation. I mentioned my connections with Bechuanaland, Arthur Douglas the Government Secretary, and my companions on the *Athlone Castle*, David Findlay

Swazi tradition, central to the nation's identity.

Princess Gcinaphi at her wedding, 1963.

Part of the bride's traditional trousseau: wooden
pillow (uncamelo), blanket and sleeping mat.

The *Umhlanga*. The girls restore the reed screening around the

*Ndlovukazi*'s kraal and then dance before the *Ngwenyama*.

A local Agricultural Field Officer with a vegetable grower.

A Ground Hornbill. Rather a surprise to see what looks like a Norfolk Black Turkey striding through the bushveld.

A Yellow-billed Hornbill blending splendidly with its environment.

Flamingos on a salt pan – a tempting target for a fish eagle.

A baby crocodile, with my wrist-watch for scale.

and Jonathan Harlow. We spoke about Seretse Khama's success in harnessing the personal support he enjoyed by virtue of having been born the traditional chief of the Bamangwato and how this status helped him to launch his own political party. That party was now sweeping all before it in Bechuanaland's peaceful preparation for independence.

The comparison with the Swaziland scene was obvious to all. I am sure that my guests had their own sources of information in Bechuanaland, but none of them disputed the assessment I had received from Jonathan, nor challenged the conclusions suggested by Seretse's example. I did not think it proper to ask my guests why Sobhuza had neither attended the Constitutional Conference in London, nor at least travelled there to try to resolve the deadlock when the conference stalled. I would doubtless have been given the official line about the King's health. I have to admit that at the time I thought Sobhuza was gravely mistaken in keeping a low profile at this juncture; later I realised it was another instance of his innate caution and patience. He did not want to rush into a situation that restricted his room for manoeuvre.

In May 1963 Duncan Sandys unveiled his imposed Constitution in the form of a White Paper. This upgraded the Resident Commissioner to the rank of Queen's Commissioner, a term deemed more appropriate for the run-up to independence than Governor, but carrying the same status. The Queen's Commissioner would be responsible directly to the Secretary of State without the previous need to filter everything through the High Commissioner in South Africa. The White Paper also provided for a Legislative Council (Legco) which would consist of the Queen's Commissioner, a Speaker, four official members nominated by the Queen's Commissioner, together with twenty-four elected members, of whom eight were to be Swazis appointed by the Ngwenyama in Council, four members elected from the European Roll, four Europeans elected by the National Roll and eight persons of any race, also elected on the National Roll. Finally, up to three other persons could be nominated by the Queen's Commissioner. Executive powers were to remain with the Queen's Commissioner, 'assisted by' an Executive Council (Exco) comprising three ex-officio government officers and five Legco members, again all appointed by the Commissioner. There was also power for the Queen's Commissioner to by-pass the Exco in important matters. Most members of the administration felt this constitution would be a suitably gentle first step towards internal self-government; but, excepting officials, the White Paper satisfied no one.

The NNLC and the other political parties feared that they were in danger of being squeezed out, most Europeans saw the Constitution as 'the beginning of the end' and the traditionalists argued that the Ngwenyama in Council should have been given greater powers in relation to land and mineral rights. Although he was nominally given these rights, the White Paper proposed that they could be overridden by a decision of the Legco. On these and other matters Sobhuza sought variation and, without consultation with Marwick, he prepared to send a delegation to London to request changes. The NNLC and other parties stepped up their activity and most of the European community went about in a state of shock and despondency.

It was the administration's job to explain the workings of the proposed new Constitution to people on the ground and this meant visiting the Swazi *tindkundhla* (regional meetings) as well as embryo advisory bodies, local associations, trade associations, farmers associations and the like.

One such association was the Lowveld Farmers Association at Big Bend, the scene of the recent strikes. Someone had to go down and address them and in view of the pleasant day I had spent with some of their members at the tennis match at Goedgegun, I volunteered and Rawlins agreed. I did not expect a comfortable time at the meeting since the politics of most of the association's European-only members were South Africa orientated. My expectation was proved right. Many of the audience were appalled at the very idea of Africans having any say in the Legco whatsoever. I was stunned by such attitudes – what did they expect when the policy of a measured progression towards independence had been clearly set out by Britain as the Colonial power? I suppose they still nurtured hopes of incorporation in South Africa and a South Africa that would be ruled by a white (preferably Nationalist Party) government forever. I wanted to yell at them, "Don't be such idiots, give a little now rather than have them take everything from you later!" Instead I tried to reason with them and suggested that the general alarm over the White Paper was overdone; and I went out of my way to stress how much control remained with the Queen's Commissioner. It was not an easy meeting, but I think the Lowveld farmers left disabused of most of their worst fears. I reminded them how essential the association's members and their like were to the viability of the country and I suggested that the government, of whatever make-up, would always know that law and order was the prerequisite for revenue creation because businesses would only continue to exist if they were considered a sound investment by their backers. Thus the financial imperative would put a brake on any hotheads in elected governments in the future. This, in fact, was what was to transpire in the early years after independence when Swaziland had inward investment on a scale that was the envy of much of Africa. However, I rather overdid the mollification of one persistent questioner by saying, "Look, you don't need to be so anxious; for the moment the Queen's Commissioner will be retaining ultimate power and the Legco will in reality be little more than a talking shop." I heard later that a Swazi Democratic Party member, who had kept a low profile at the meeting, lodged a complaint to the Queen's Commissioner about the phrase 'a talking shop'. Athel Long, the Chief Secretary, summoned Rawlins to explain and, as ever, Rawlins stuck by his DO; the complainant was rebuffed and no rebuke came my way.

The political parties, particularly the NNLC with Dumisa Dlamini and the youth wing of the party in the van, set out to target labour relations as their way of striking a blow at the soft underbelly, as they saw it, of white-dominated Swaziland. They had already shown the power of mass protest at Mbabane and had used the strike weapon at Big Bend. They now instigated a strike at the Havelock Asbestos Mine near Pigg's Peak, at that time the fifth highest producing asbestos mine in the world. In due course all the 1400 workers heeded the strike call, many under duress, and the strike lasted for over a month. At Hlatikulu we kept a wary eye on the potential strike targets, the prison and the major schools. Local European farmers were fearful and not a few, during these anxious weeks, would have been prepared to sell up if offered a half decent price.

As Chris and I, and sometimes Rawlins too, went out and about in the District explaining the new Constitution, we found rumour and alarm. I nearly spread further confusion at one Nkundla meeting. There, for the benefit of those in the gathering who had read about systems of government in the newly independent African countries as well as in Europe, I tried to compare the Exco with a Cabinet. My interpreter rendered this as *"iyExco ifana ibokisi"* - 'the Exco is just like a box.' I was able to correct this mistake, but one wonders how many mistranslations went unnoticed every day in a difficult tonal language.

Local matters also kept us gossiping and occupied. Chris had decided to leave the service and was off home to East Griqualand in August, convinced that there would be a better future there for his family than in Swaziland. His successor was announced, a 'retread' from Tanganyika named Ian Aers. Rawlins was in no way delighted by the prospect of this change. This newcomer had apparently been a District Commissioner with a District bigger than the whole of Swaziland, and five DOs working for him. Was such a man going to settle happily as a DO, working for Rawlins? It seemed a crazy plan. He was Rawlins' age, so he certainly would not grant Rawlins the deference which Chris and I accorded him and which, no doubt, was the reason for his good opinion of us and his willingness to give us a more or less free rein provided we kept our noses clean. It was sufficient for him that to all outward appearances he was very much in charge, as evidenced by our calling him 'Sir' and 'Mr Rawlins' and opening his car door for him and like obeisances. From what we had heard Ian Aers, the retread, would do none of these things. What was needed was someone of Chris Anderson's age (i.e. 30 or so).

About this time there was a setback to my efforts to establish a vegetable garden. I had employed a part-time gardener to prepare and fence the virgin ground at the foot of the front lawn and then to tend the newly sown vegetables once they came through. With the young crop beginning to look promising, his main task, apart from checking the bird and animal defences, was to keep everything watered. One day he obviously decided to cut out the tedium by inventing his own flood irrigation system, which resulted in all the seedlings being swept down the hillside. As a rule, with notable exceptions, Swazi men were not natural gardeners, house servants or tradesmen, nor were they good with machinery; and it tended to be said of them (adapting the World War II slogan 'Give us the tools and we'll finish the job') 'Give them the job and they'll finish the tools'! Like the menfolk of other pastoral tribes, their minds tended to be on higher things. Perhaps the Swazis were not so set in their traditional ways and attitudes as the nomadic pastoralists in East Africa, like the Karamojong or the Masai, but even they, as a story from my Kenyan friend, Bill Deverell, demonstrates, were not totally unreceptive to the idea of a different lifestyle.

The story concerned a geologist who was working out on the Serengeti near the Kenyan/Tanzanian border. He became friendly with the local Masai sub-chief and offered to take him on a weekend visit to Mombasa to show him 'the other world'. The trip was an extraordinary eye-opener for the Masai. Within the space of thirty-six hours, for the first time he travelled in a train, saw the Indian Ocean stretching forever till it met the sky, waded in its waves and felt the salt on his legs, saw ships, multi-storey buildings, countless smart shops and rode up and down their escalators and lifts, ate in 'European-style' restaurants, went to a cinema and stayed in a large smart hotel with his own en suite bathroom, etc. etc. There was no end to the range of his new experiences. When the weekend was over and his geologist friend finally dropped him at his grass hut the chief thanked him profusely, "You have indeed shown me another world," he said. "What," asked the geologist, "amongst all the things you saw, impressed you most?" "Oh," replied the Masai quickly, his face aglow, "the women; they were amazing!" We are none of us so different under the skin.

During this time of uneasy expectancy I was lured into becoming involved in an entertainment such as I had read about in lampoons on colonial life. It was the performance of a play, or rather two short plays, in the Hlatikulu Club, followed by a *braivleis* (barbecue) on the club stoep in aid of a local missionary society. It was not really a play, more a play reading, but in costume 'with acting'. I felt it would have been more effective had we dispensed with the acting and the costumes and read our lines behind a sort of safety curtain made up in the form of a giant Bush radio – the brown bakelite best-seller of the post-war years. That way something could have been left to the imagination. I knew better than to make this suggestion; the producer would have had a fit. So we duly did our stuff, embracing fondly and then disengaging in order to read the next line, dropping our scripts as we bounded from one side of the stage to the other or, in the case of one or two of the older cast members, losing their way in the midst of amorous scenes when their glasses steamed up. In the interval an elderly South African lady, mother of one of the hospital doctors, accompanied herself on the piano and gave a rendering of music hall favourites, climaxing with 'Danny Boy'. When the final curtain fell and the audience had duly applauded, perhaps more from gratitude that it was all over than delight at our skills, and the female leads had received their bunches of garden flowers to more applause, we all went off for a barbecue. Thus, for a hundred years or more, had the outposts of Empire sustained themselves. Perhaps television, which the South African government banned lest the Africans be corrupted, was not such a bad thing after all. Swaziland, likewise, had no television and the only radio we could receive was the South African Broadcasting Corporation offering biased news, Nationalist Party propaganda, interspersed with *boeremusik* the Afrikaner equivalent of country and western. Swaziland Radio was to be launched in embryo fashion several months later.

As a contrast to these village preoccupations I had a short weekend with my sugar-planting friends Doug and Elsa Starling at Mhlume in the bushveld near the north eastern corner of Swaziland. They were concessionaires on this major undertaking run by the Commonwealth Development Corporation and the entire cane crop was irrigated as at Big Bend. The two concerns used the country's largest rivers, the Usutu and the Komati, to provide the water. This was capital-intensive agriculture on a corporate scale, the other end of the spectrum from the peasant agriculture being pursued by individual progressive Swazi farmers with the help of their local Field Officer. I had learned at the Devonshire Course how the two great civilisations of biblical times, Mesopotamia and Egypt, had been based on irrigation from the Euphrates and the Nile respectively and how both eventually failed because of salinity, the build up of salt deposits which gradually turned the land sour. How, I asked Doug, were they going to prevent this happening in Swaziland? The technique they were using, apparently, was to limit the irrigation to quick rushes of water from holding dams when required, rather than allowing a continual trickle to seep through the soil – 'flood irrigation' no less; but sugar cane was sterner stuff than my lettuce and runner beans seedlings which had been washed down the hill the week before and the Mhlume engineers were perhaps a little more sophisticated than my part-time Swazi gardener.

Polo at Mhlume: horse and groom immaculately
turned out.

A young kudu.

Doug and Elsa were an attractive couple. Doug, from Natal, was an accomplished polo player and Elsa, from the UK, had taken to life in the Swaziland bushveld as if born to it. We had lunch on the stoep in the shade. Just a few feet away was a bird-bath and beside it a bird table, piled with mealie-meal. These were obviously favourite haunts for the local bird population. I remember a proliferation of finches and Cape Sparrows, but ruling the roost dominantly and very appropriately were starlings – not the humdrum birds we see in flocks in the UK, but Cape Glossy Starlings, bigger than the European variety, longer in the body and resplendent in British Racing Green plumage. When they flocked to the tables nothing much else had a look in. Likewise Doug and Elsa seemed very much in command of their well-run enterprise when we rode around their sugar kingdom. It was no surprise, a year later, when they moved to even bigger and better things across the Transvaal border. In the cool of the evening they took me to the CDC ranch, which practised game preservation alongside cattle farming. This seemed to work well without any of the cross-infection from game to the cattle, which many ranchers used as the reason, or pretext, for shooting out the game. We saw, in a short time, a number of impala, wildebeest and zebra, as well as several kudu.

Nowadays, of course, there are a few small private game reserves in South Africa, as elsewhere, doing good business for their owners, providing jobs for people in areas of low employment and preserving a little part of Africa's heritage into the bargain. One such had already been opened in Swaziland at Mlilwane in the Ezulwini valley below Mbabane, run by Ted Reilly and his wife. It was there, fifteen months later, that I was to learn something about ostriches.

But in the meantime the situation was hotting up in Mbabane and Pigg's Peak and there was even the possibility of unrest in Hlatikulu.

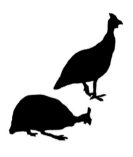

Chapter 8

# Alarms and Excursions

While I was being occupied by such inconsequential things, up at
Havelock the strikers showed no signs of reaching any settlement
with the management. Large numbers of police were transferred up
there to protect law and order, leaving Mbabane and Manzini, the
main urban centres, dangerously exposed. Marwick was in London,
discussing implementation of the new Constitution. He had rendered
long and distinguished service to Swaziland, but in his last years he
seemed to rely more and more on Athel Long and Mike Fairlie,
rather than follow the promptings of his own experience, which
might have led him to challenge the Colonial Office's 'one pattern
fits all' approach to the run-up of Swaziland's independence. The
truth, I think, was that he was tired and he started to lose patience
with Sobhuza and the Swazi National Council, with whom he had
for so long enjoyed excellent relations and ties of genuine mutual
respect. By the time I came to Swaziland in 1962 there were few
government servants who knew Sobhuza well, certainly not the
influential Long and Fairlie; nor did Marwick or Purcell, the
Secretary for Swazi affairs, often meet with Sobhuza. This was
unfortunate at an important time for Swaziland when events were
moving fast. Sobhuza considered he had been betrayed by his old
friend because of Marwick's perceived encouragement of the new

politicians; Marwick thought Sobhuza was obstructing progress. Each felt bitterness towards the other, as happens when old friendships collapse.

Marwick had been due to leave Swaziland in June 1963 on reaching the Colonial Service retirement age of 55, but he had been persuaded to stay on to implement the new Constitution. He was hardworking by nature; but by now this admirable trait had become obsessive and today we would have dubbed him a workaholic. There was the danger that when a situation arose that called for reserves of energy and judgement he would have nothing left on which to draw.

Such a crisis came as soon as Sir Brian (as he had just become) returned from London in early June. On 8th June the Swaziland Democratic Party, anxious to compete with the NNLC and broaden their support base, called a mass meeting of domestic servants in Mbabane. The Mbabane market sellers, already stirred up over the porridge incident a month before, became involved and the NNLC muscled in on a widening eruption of discontent.

Whereas we were living in peace and quiet at Hlatikulu, we received reports of all sorts of trouble elsewhere. Up at Pigg's Peak the Havelock mine strikers were threatening the other Swazi workers, pressuring them to join the strike. Emboldened by his success, Dumisa called for a general strike on 10th June. This was something that had been rumoured to be in the offing for over a year. The next day Dumisa led a demonstration of 3,000 men and women to Government House (as the Queen's Commissioner's Residence was now called). Marwick agreed to talk to fifteen representatives of the demonstrators, but no agreement was reached.

By now over a thousand demonstrators were marching up and down the streets of Mbabane more or less unchecked, since the police, being so heavily committed at Havelock, were hopelessly overstretched. Gangs roamed the town threatening both shop staff and office workers. Most government departments sent their African civil servants home so that they could protect their families and be spared intimidation; European staff kept things going. The Controller of Posts and Telegraphs, for instance, worked the Mbabane telephone exchange. In the residential areas of Mbabane the gangs threatened any domestic servants who had not responded to the strike call. Most families, European and African, told their servants to go home and keep their heads down.

There were riots in the Mbabane gaol and two gaol break attempts in which a total of ten prisoners escaped. One prisoner was shot, but not fatally. A number of white residents formed a special guard, later to be superceded by Special Constables and Mbabane was described as 'a town in a state of siege'.

There was another strike at Big Bend and a riot in Mankaiana prison. The two prisoners who masterminded that riot were transferred to us at Hlatikulu. I felt they must be dangerous men to have been able to stir up my nice Mankaiana prisoners who planted the trees, looked after the zoo and the district horses, kept the village neat and tidy, collected the rubbish and were so grateful to be given typhoid injections. We therefore segregated the new arrivals so that they could not create further trouble. Workers started coming out on strike in Manzini and we learned that there were plans for strikes in Goedgegun and Hlatikulu within several days.

All these developments notwithstanding, I wrote in a letter home on 11th June, "Tonight it is raining hard here. This is almost unknown for the time of year and perhaps the rain will cool a few hot heads. There is no question of there being any violence of a serious nature. There is nothing going on here in Hlatikulu and I will be surprised if we do have trouble, unless the school goes on strike." What I wrote in my next paragraph showed that for all the attempts I made to appear mature and serious, I was still a kid at heart – a cross, perhaps, between 'Sanders of the River' and 'Biggles', for I wrote, "I wish I were in Mbabane – down here I'm missing all the fun."

Up in Mbabane, however, it was not the stuff of schoolboy adventure, but a potentially serious situation. The Security Committee had told Sir Brian, first, that the police were badly overstretched and could not contain any further escalation of the trouble and secondly, that there was a real danger that the South African Government would send in troops and police under pretext of protecting South African nationals and South African-owned property. This expectation was probably founded on fairly reliable intelligence. On the whole the administration's security committee had a good idea of what was happening in South Africa.

Marwick promptly went down to see Sobhuza and asked him to call up his *impis* (traditional age regiments) to support the police. Sobhuza refused. According to Hilda Kuper he told Marwick that if he acceded to the request he "would have embroiled his people in civil war. The British had provoked the situation through their support of the parties; and had then rushed through legislation under which they arrested leaders they themselves had encouraged, thereby inciting the masses to violence", (*Sobhuza II, Ngwenyama and King of Swaziland*).

Marwick was shocked and deeply hurt to be so flatly rejected in his hour of need by his old friend. He probably had not appreciated how far he had neglected to maintain their friendship because of the influence on him of several members of the administration, as well as others in the 'Residency set' where his wife Riva, now delighted to be styled Lady Marwick, held court. In truth, Sir Brian, knowing the Ngwenyama so well, should never have expected him to agree to such an appeal for help, for Sobhuza had a very different temperament from Montrose ('Bonnie Dundee'), who famously wrote:

> *"He either fears his fate too much*
> *Or his deserts are small*
> *That puts it not unto the touch*
> *To win or lose it all"*

(James Graham, Marquis of Montrose, 1612 – 1650,
lines written on the window of his jail the night before
his execution).

Unlike Montrose, Sobhuza was a survivor and one who was very unwilling to put anything "unto the touch" until he was sure of the outcome.

Gordon Highlanders at Havelock.
*(Photo courtesy of Swaziland Administration, 1963)*

What a week it had been for Brian Marwick - the announcement of his Knighthood to mark the peak of his career and now, six days later, after being rebuffed by Sobhuza, he was suffering the ultimate humiliation for any colonial administrator, having to telephone the Colonial Office, admit that he had lost control and ask for troops to restore order. The next day 37 police were flown in from Bechuanaland and the following day, 13th June, a battalion of British infantry, the Gordon Highlanders, arrived from Kenya. The giant planes that brought them circled Mbabane and Manzini before landing at Matsapha airport. The strikers and agitators looked up in awe at a sight such as they had never seen before. Then there was the further spectacle of a fleet of open trucks trundling up to Mbabane, crammed with Highlanders in full combat gear with bayonets fixed, Bren guns mounted on the truck cabs, looking like they meant business.

At the time I did not recognize the significance of what happened next. Seeing the Gordons' arrival, Swazis, strikers and non-strikers alike, flocked to Lobamba, the royal headquarters. Dr Zwane and

Dumisa asked the King to call out his regiments against the British troops. As with Marwick's request, Sobhuza refused. Instead, he addressed his people in the Sibaya, the ceremonial cattle kraal. He urged the strikers to go back to work pending investigation of their grievances, and told everyone to keep the peace; and he invoked the *mlamuli* – the symbol of protection (from the verb *lamula* – to make peace between people). It was noteworthy that although many Swazis might have experimented with the new politics, when the chips were down they went to the Ngwenyama. And, significantly, most of them did his bidding.

Shortly afterwards, unusually for the time of year, heavy rain started to fall and continued for 36 hours. The Gordon Highlanders, meanwhile, waited in the schools where they were billeted in Mbabane and Manzini, dry and out of sight. In contrast, soaked to the skin, shivering in the cold that accompanied the rain, splattered with mud as the dust turned to quagmire, hungry and thirsty, the strikers and demonstrators started to drift home. Not a shot was fired by the British troops and within a few days all was back to normal. If Sir Brian lost face in London by calling for help, the local Swazis, as well as Europeans, were impressed that a British Government was prepared to send troops with such speed to protect the integrity of the territory. Most people had absorbed the South African propaganda that the British had become spineless and did not care any longer about their remaining colonies and would never do anything which might cause Washington or Moscow to frown. Suez had cast a long shadow. To boot, the Colonial Office must have been well pleased with the outcome of the situation and the sensitive way it had been handled. I do not think that the Ngwenyama's part in it all was fully understood, either inside or outside Swaziland, and very little credit was accorded to Jupiter Pluvius. Many Swazis, of course, would say that rainmaking was one of the Ngwenyama's powers and that he had turned on the tap at just the right moment.

In Hlatikulu the best sayings of the week to my mind were (a) by a very senior Swazi who asked me, referring to Dr Ambrose Zwane and Mnt Dumisa Dlamini, "Have those two coons been arrested yet?" and

(b) from the local postmaster's wife before the troops arrived, addressed to the assembled company in the bar of the hotel, "It's no good putting your trust in governments, you must put your trust in God." Two of the strike leaders, who had been arrested for inciting violence and intimidation, were sent down to us to keep them out of the way. One told me whilst I was doing gaol inspection that he would give me three minutes to leave the country when the NNLC would come to power a year later. I told him that he, as an aspiring politician, should know the old saying that a week, let alone a year, was a long time in politics. My diary note, made before the troops arrived, read, "These blighters certainly have their tails up"; but, true to the adage, by the next inspection a week later they had changed their tune.

Operations rooms had been set up at each District Headquarters, in wireless contact with Mbabane. A large number of Special Constables were sworn in (we had 49 in Hlatikulu) – regrettably nearly all were Europeans as hardly any Swazi volunteered, and one can understand why. In our district several Swazi malcontents in government service came close to showing their true colours; but in the end they were too prudent to do anything, with the exception of one minor official who tried to spread the rumour that Dr Banda and 30 Malawi policemen, plus some American troops, had arrived to help the strikers. Three days after the Gordons flew in we had reports of an illegal meeting at Goedgegun and charged down with the police loaded up with tear smoke, together with lots of Special Constables. It was a false alarm. The previous day the strikers at Big Bend had attempted to fire the sugar cane, but they were thwarted by rain and the company's fire brigade.

As the dust settled one could look back and assess how it had all worked out. As always in times of trouble there were winners and losers. The winners, first and foremost, were the Swazi people. Like most Ngoni tribes in Southern Africa the Swazis are naturally gentle, kind and courteous, not excitable, nor given to excesses of violence. What had been so remarkable about Shaka, the great Zulu conqueror, was the way he was able to turn the peaceable Zulus into a fearsome war machine. Sobhuza was the other hero. What might have happened had he responded either to Marwick's or Zwane's request and turned out his warriors for one of their respective causes? The Swaziland police force did well and showed steadiness and reliability, not to mention loyalty. Life must have been difficult for young Swazi constables and junior NCOs, many of whose age-mates in their regiment, the Malindzane (my regiment!) were amongst the rioters and demonstrators. Truth be told, once the troops arrived, Marwick never put a foot wrong. He had the good sense to keep the troops hidden away in their billets. Often better to carry a big stick than to use it; but there must have been hotheads urging him to send in the military 'to teach the strikers a lesson'. Instead he was wise enough to let the situation start to solve itself. Then six days after their arrival, the troops began to be used for cordon and search operations in support of the police. The Gordons proved to be highly effective and totally professional in this work, enabling the police to identify, arrest and charge the leaders of the intimidation with the minimum fuss and bother. The Gordons' public relations amongst the Swazis was imaginative, sensitive and very successful and they soon became well liked by all sections of the community. Give or take a little initial alarm, the European population at Havelock and Pigg's Peak (where they had to endure a much longer period of unrest than elsewhere) behaved with good humour and moderation. Dr Nquku, leader of the Swaziland Progressive Party, Simon Nxumalo, leader of the multiracial Swaziland Democratic Party and George Msibi, of the Mbandzeni National Convention, all responded to the Ngwenyama's mlamuli by disassociating themselves from the strikers. In effect they put conscience before expediency and lost support as a result.

Julian Faux, the DC at Mbabane, gained himself a reputation as a latter day Horatius when, two days after the Gordons arrived, there was a half-hearted attempt by some NNLC supporters to stage another demonstration in Mbabane. They marched down towards the centre of town from Msunduza Township where many of them lived. Julian, accompanied by a small detachment of police, was waiting on the bridge over the Mbabane River and persuaded them to turn round and go back to their homes. A few days earlier at the height of the unrest, John Harrison, the DC at Pigg's Peak, had not been so fortunate. He had confronted a large demonstration of Havelock Mine strikers and they had ignored him. It was probably just a question of timing. Had he known that the weather was going to break and that within a very short time the strikers would, like their Mbabane counterparts, be wet and cold and dispirited by the news of the troops' arrival, he might have had more success. Unfairly, he was never given much credit for there having been so little violence and damage to property in his District throughout the prolonged Havelock strike. Several days afterwards the Secretariat (I use the term advisedly as I do not know who gave the insensitive order) sent Mark Patey, the Stegi DC, who had previously served at Pigg's Peak, to talk to the Havelock strikers. The sorry body of bedraggled and exhausted men he addressed was very different from the optimistic and enthusiastic crowd who had confronted John several days earlier. Mark spoke to the strikers and they agreed to return to their homes and the trickle back to work began. This was made easier for them by the arrest of ringleaders. There would doubtless have been the same result had John been allowed to deal with the situation himself instead of Mark being brought onto the scene.

To people outside Pigg's Peak, however, the word was that Patey and Faux had succeeded where Harrison had failed. Luck, it seems, often plays a part where reputations are concerned. Perhaps, however, it should be noted that John, a Royal Naval Officer in the war, was a fairly independent spirit and he may have previously ruffled a few feathers at the Secretariat. This might explain the way he was treated. Certainly, a few months later, when I was taking the minutes of a meeting between Marwick and Long and the District Commissioners, there was a peremptory message from Pigg's Peak that John Harrison was busy in the District and would not be coming. Such high-handedness did not go down well.

For us in Hlatikulu District life resumed its normal course. There was, however, a perceptible touchiness on the part of some of the middle-ranking Swazi staff, not so much in the administration as in the service departments. At a meeting of the local staff housing advisory committee, which I was chairing, the main agenda item was the examination of plans and specifications for some new houses for clerical grade officers. One Swazi member of the committee took grave exception to the proposed houses having been designed with stable external doors. "We are being treated like animals!" he expostulated. I explained that stable doors had become very fashionable in new house design in Europe as well as in South Africa. If, for instance, one went to the expensive European suburbs of Johannesburg or Cape Town, many of the modern houses had such doors because of the advantages they offered. In hot weather you could open the top half of the door to let the air in, while the bottom half could be kept shut to stop children or dogs running out, but if the committee wanted, they could request standard one-piece doors. There would be no problem since stable doors were more expensive than one-piece doors, owing to the extra work and duplication of door furniture, which the stable doors entailed. I cannot remember which way the vote went, but the banal matter stuck in my memory because it so well demonstrated the underlying sensitivity that lingered for some time after the unrest.

Two years before, Peter Simkin had been less fortunate than I in his dealings with this housing committee. Someone had complained that one of the staff houses was excessively overshadowed by a huge blue gum tree. Always quick to act, Peter arranged for the tree to be cut down. Unfortunately it fell the wrong way and flattened the house – luckily no one was inside. What made matters worse was that, a few days earlier, a PWD road grader, which Peter had brought in to improve a local road, had fallen down a donga and had to be written off. Rawlins reportedly told Marwick that he wondered if he could afford Peter any longer. Marwick's Private Secretary was going on leave, so Marwick took Peter on for the time the PS was going to be away; and he appreciated Peter so much that he kept him as PS till the end of Peter's tour, fifteen months later.

Another instance of the new sensitivity, which was stirred up by the unrest, involved Abbey Mamba, the Chief Clerk. It was established practice that the DO and Chief Clerk did a two-day tour of the eastern area of the District, 'the round tour', dealing with any court cases at minor stations and attending *tinkundla*. The DO, as allowed by government regulations, could claim expenses for staying at the Big Bend Hotel, which was conveniently placed in the middle of the area covered by the tour. The Chief Clerk, being on a lower grade in the service, was only entitled to claim for cheaper accommodation. So when Edward Zwane was DO, he stayed at the Big Bend Hotel (despite this at first raising one or two eyebrows amongst white fellow guests). Then, for the one trip we had together in the overlap period, both he and I stayed at the Big Bend Hotel. When Edward left, it was back to the old practice of the DO (now a European) going to the smart hotel and the Chief Clerk (a Swazi) having to make do with something inferior. Abbey who, it had to be said, liked his comforts, raised the matter quite diplomatically but argued that the established practice gave off the wrong signals. I responded that this was not a matter of racism, but of professional precedence. For instance, in the British Army a commissioned officer was entitled to first class rail travel, but a non-commissioned officer was not. So if the subaltern happened to be black and the sergeant white, it would be the black man travelling first class and the white man travelling standard class. The same, in due course, would be happening in Swaziland. My knee-jerk reaction was that Abbey was swinging the lead, but on reflection it seemed he had a point. Two of the most nefarious phrases in the English language, I suspect, are "It is the regulation" and "It is a matter of principle". The regulation was probably made by some idiot generations earlier with no one thereafter having the gumption to change it; and the 'principle', as like as not, could be no more than self-interest or prejudice.

The more I thought about it, the more I felt that we should change the practice. In matters of race, people in the district administration, more than anyone, had to be seen to be beyond reproach. One could suggest this when putting the matter to Mr Rawlins – "Could I please have a word with you, Sir, on a confidential matter?" – i.e. one set the right tone beforehand. Also one could, and I did, suggest that there would be efficiency gains by acceding to Abbey's request. We were understaffed and it would help if the DO and Chief Clerk stayed at the same hotel, enabling them to work together before and after dinner, if need be, and talk shop while dining. If this was casuistry there were worse things, would not Mr Rawlins agree, like outsiders accusing us of not practising the multiracialism we were so keen to preach; and plenty of people down there in the bushveld would be all too keen to have a go at us, did he not think? "Might we be in danger of creating a precedent?" Rawlins asked. "No," I replied, with the certainty of youth, "a precedent is only binding where the circumstances of the two cases match exactly. It would be easy for us to distinguish our particular case from others elsewhere." "Yes," he agreed. "I suppose that's so." Abbey and I were home and dry. Once convinced, Ray Rawlins was not afraid to act and be prepared to justify what he had done. Abbey got his fortnightly jaunt to the posh Big Bend Hotel and, at the cost of only a few extra rand a year, Swaziland was set on the path to getting a local civil servant who would grow in all-round competence and judgement thanks to a concession to him at a time when he probably needed to be shown that he was valued. Had we slapped him down, he could have chased after false gods in his frustration.

Perhaps going down this sort of road was taking the easy way out (the peppery Brigadier General Dyer would certainly have thought so); but was not taking the easy way out just what retreat from Empire was all about? Surely the aim was to leave with the maximum goodwill, having prepared the country to run efficiently and humanely, thanks to the careful tutoring and encouragement of those who were going to take over.

When I visited Swaziland with my family in 1982, Abbey was Deputy General Manager of 'Tibiyo' (Tibiyo Taka Ngwane), a key development agency based at Lobamba, having earlier been a DC; from what I could gather after spending a morning with him, he knew his stuff and was a fulfilled and happy man.

Fairly soon after the unrest had subsided, Ray Rawlins brought back from a special meeting of the Central Intelligence Committee a resumé of all that had happened. However, people back home who relied for their information on the tabloids were not so accurately informed. We had a reporter sent out from the *News of the World*. When I was at school, the *News of the World* was banned because of its photos of what in those staid days were thought to be shockingly scantily clad young women, not to mention the paper's racy innuendo about the private lives of public figures, usually also illustrated by further photos of scantily clad women. To enable his copy to fight its way into print in amongst such titillation, the paper's reporter doubtless concluded that he had to spice up the reality of the Swaziland scene. His purple prose related how the 'kilted Highlanders' – (usually battle fatigues) 'patrolled the jungle' – (nearest jungle 1000 miles north-west) 'in their tanks' – (they were infantry) 'while the Swazi warriors in feathered headdresses and leopard skin loincloths' – (more likely in the cold weather to be old army greatcoats and felt bush-hats) 'looked on in awe' - (token picture) 'together with their bare-breasted womenfolk' - (lots of pictures) 'all to the accompaniment of the roaring of lions' - (the only lions were 80 miles away in the Kruger Game Reserve in South Africa). I gathered that the intrepid reporter rarely left the Swazi Inn in Mbabane and that his vision of what had happened was filtered through the bottom of a whisky glass!

If the chap from the *News of the World* had really wanted to see a lion he should have gone down the road to Masundvwini (The Place of Palms). Here Ngwenyama yemaSwati, Sobhuza II, the Lion of Swaziland, was keeping a low profile, but working away. Several months earlier he had sent his delegates to all the tinkundla to confirm that the bulk of the Swazi population was solidly behind him. This intelligence had allowed him to assess the strikes in their proper perspective and not panic. Now, at last, he was ready to act.

He now sent his delegation to the Secretary of State in London to request a variation of the White Paper. Its members were the three SNC members who had come down to discuss with me the future of the Hot Springs at Siphofaneni in April and had then lunched with me afterwards: Mnt Makhosini Dlamini, later to become Swaziland's first Prime Minister, Polycarp Dlamini, Secretary of the Swazi Nation and Abednego Khuseni Hlophe, Sobhuza's Private Secretary. All, incidentally, were active Christians. Marwick was not advised of this mission and felt that Sobhuza had gone behind his back. He was probably still feeling sore that the Ngwenyama had refused him help over the strikes. Now he had suffered this further slight. He warned the Commonwealth Office that these delegates were 'the wrong people' and no one should listen to them. He also stated that: "Sobhuza no longer enjoyed the support of his people."

As a result, when Sobhuza's three emissaries arrived in London, they found most official doors closed to them. They were, however, invited to speak at a meeting of one of the student bodies in Oxford. After their address a young man stood up and appeared to confirm Marwick's warning. "I am also a Swazi," he said. "These men have no right to speak for the majority of the people. They represent the uneducated reactionaries. They are nobodies." Then another man from the audience spoke and said, "I have worked in the Secretariat in Swaziland and I know these men. They are important men and not uneducated and, whether you like it or not, the facts are as they have reported." This speaker turned out to be John Stebbing, who had been Government Secretary in Swaziland in the 1950s. Apart from this affirmation, and a pleasant visit to the recently retired High Commissioner, Sir John Maud, now Master of University College, Oxford, the delegates found themselves ignored. When, with the greatest difficulty, they finally secured an audience with Duncan Sandys, the Commonwealth Secretary, they were simply told that he was "not changing a paragraph of the White Paper, not even a sentence".

The delegation returned at once to Swaziland, not a little displeased at the way they had been received. I think that the earlier delegation's decision to wear traditional dress for the opening of the Constitutional Conference at the beginning of the year had created an impression in the UK, especially in British Government circles, that Sobhuza and his people were folk from bygone times, quaint and colourful, but not to be taken seriously. They had tried to look distinctive; but to many people they just looked backward. Thanks to Marwick's warning to the Commonwealth Office this latest delegation was treated as if they indeed were 'the wrong people' and no one gave them any credibility.

Sobhuza immediately prepared to try again. Duncan Sandys had delivered his rebuff to the delegation on 29th July. Makhosini immediately telephoned the King and the next day, 30th July, The Swazi National Council agreed a resolution to petition the Queen to delay enactment of the White Paper until the British Parliament had a chance to further examine the matter. The Petition sought variance of the proposed Constitution on three issues: on the way elections were to be conducted, on the Constitution and particularly on the role of the Ngwenyama and land issues, requesting that land and minerals should be vested in the Ngwenyama in Council. The petition cut little ice in Westminster, Marwick's epithet branding the King and his Council as 'the wrong people' had stuck in the minds of members of the Conservative Government. 'Shifting Sandys' was not shifting his stand on the Constitution and it was duly promulgated with elections set for June 1964.

There was now a clear-cut difference of views between Sir Brian Marwick and Sobhuza. Sir Brian was holding to his assertion, made to such good effect to the Commonwealth Office, that Sobhuza did not represent the views of his people. Sobhuza for his part insisted that the people were behind him. He asked Marwick to help to organise a referendum to decide the issue. Sir Brian refused, saying that the Constitution was already drafted. Sobhuza told him in that case he would carry out the plebiscite on his own. Marwick warned him that if he went ahead and there was trouble he would hold Sobhuza responsible. Sobhuza made no response, but if Marwick imagined he had faced Sobhuza down he was mistaken. Sobhuza just took his time and worked away at his plans.

Around this time Hendrik Verwoerd, the South African President, was putting pressure on Swaziland and the other High Commission territories, Basutoland and Bechuanaland, by unilaterally limiting freedom of aircraft flights between them and by imposing stricter border controls on those travelling between South Africa and the territories by vehicle or on foot. This meant that we had to issue Swaziland passports to people who had habitually travelled unimpeded between the Republic and Swaziland and we embarked on a crash programme to beat the deadline. There was a particular need for passports in Gollel, the little town at the south-easternmost corner of the District, where many local Swazis crossed over into the Republic every day to work. We went down there and over two days issued passports to nearly two hundred people. There was much grumbling at the ending of more or less unrestricted passage between Swaziland and the Republic. Personally I welcomed the change. For too long many people in Swaziland had behaved as if the Swaziland Protectorate were part of South Africa; now the new restrictions emphasized Swaziland's separate identity.

While we were scurrying around issuing passports there were rumours that Hendrik Verwoerd was having a go at Swaziland through another stratagem. In a paper issued by the State Information Office he wrote regarding the High Commission Territories, "I am now making an offer to Great Britain – I might almost call it a challenge – to allow us to put the essentials of our policies before the inhabitants of these territories. Let us demonstrate to them what our policies really are, that our feelings towards them are now friendly, how we would view their future and how we could co-operate. We should have an opportunity of presenting our case to them. It means a new and a better deal than that which they are getting or can get – not through ill will on the part of the United Kingdom, but merely because the United Kingdom is not in a geographical position to do for the High Commission territories what the Republic of South Africa can do for them". (*The Road to Freedom for Basutoland, Bechuanaland and Swaziland*, South African Government Fact Paper 107-1963 11-18). The Swazis had long considered that a large chunk of the Eastern Transvaal should be part of Swaziland and the chiefs from that area habitually attended the Incwala and other traditional Swazi ceremonies. Verwoerd, as part of his blandishment, offered to incorporate this area of the Transvaal into Swaziland as well as to buy out white farmers in Swaziland and establish South African industries on the Swaziland border. What Verwoerd did not spell out was the extent to which Swaziland would have to forfeit its autonomy as the price for all these preferred benefits.

Unsurprisingly the British Government made no overt response to Verwoerd's offer, but rumours abounded that Sobhuza was discussing the matter with the South African Government, using as intermediary Carl Todd, the European Advisory Council member who, in addition to his Swaziland interests, had a law practice in Johannesburg. Personally, I felt that although Sobhuza may have sniffed the bait, he steered well clear of the trap. However, it is interesting that in July 1964, by which time Sobhuza was in a much stronger position than ever before to do a deal with Pretoria, he deemed it necessary to call a meeting of the nation to scotch the rumours. His 'authentic statement' on the matter was published in *The Times of Swaziland* (24th July, 1964). His language was typical of his style:

"Do you remember", he began, "when you and I were young? There were in this country hyenas, which pulled kids out of the huts. Sometimes the hyenas would howl from a distance and the unwary would think it was too far to bother about, only to find that all of a sudden it had broken into the hut and snatched its prey. Today we have hyenas that walk on two legs. They are to be heard howling and yelling around homesteads, frightening our children out of their wits so that some of them desert their homes in an effort to escape, only to find themselves landing right into the snarling teeth of the hyena that is ready to draw them to its masters. And the child will not be able to run one way or the other as he is now in the clutches of this formidable animal.

If you set snares for game, closing all possible openings except one, you then set a bait attractive to the victim – so, for a bird the rich white ant, or similar tempting decoys. It is only guinea fowl which shows true caution; when it sees something enticing it stops to consider the motive behind this unknown friend's generous act and leaves without eating of the gift.

Prosperity that suddenly springs from nowhere and shoots up overnight like mushrooms must be looked at with the same suspicion".

As to the accusation that he had accepted a bribe of £25,000 to hand the country over to South Africa, he asked, "Is this country and its inhabitants worth only that amount?" He stated he had challenged the author of the rumour to come into the open " if he had anything to say. If no one comes forward this would be an indication that his story is a lie. No one took up my challenge". He went on:

"I do not remember the Swazi nation meeting in the royal kraal to give me the mandate for the annexation or incorporation of Swaziland into the Republic. I cannot endorse or act on issues for which I have received no mandate from the Swazi nation. I am like a rubber stamp. What is surprising is that while all the nations are clamouring for freedom we, the Swazi nation, should wish to go from one domination to another."

The unseasonal rain, which killed off the unrest in June 1993, did not seem to know how to stop. A letter home during July recorded solid rain all that week and snow on the Transvaal hills forty miles to the south. The letter was written in bed, whence I had retired immediately after supper, not because of illness but to try to escape the bitter cold. The Deputy Inspector General of Colonial Police had been visiting Swaziland and only managed to reach us in Hlatikulu in a four-wheel drive Land Rover with the utmost difficulty and a day late, because of the deep mud and swollen river crossings. Apparently, before every trip he enquired of the countries he was visiting as to what weather to expect and what clothes to bring. He said he always took what was recommended and was invariably caught out and found himself wrongly attired. Before coming to Swaziland he had been informed that the last thing he would need in late July was rainproof clothing, yet it rained continuously throughout his visit. We told him that the weather he was encountering with us was totally unusual for the season. "That's what they all say," he replied, "everywhere I go." I hope people also told him that the Swaziland Police Force had acquitted itself with distinction when put to the test during the strikes and unrest. I initially had my doubts about them because of the political orientation of some of their South African born officers; but I could not fault the force's behaviour when the chips were down.

Several weeks after they arrived in Swaziland the Gordon Highlanders sent a company down to Hlatikulu to show the flag. The Company Commander, a Major Brown, turned out to be the son of a friend of my parents in Galloway, Mrs Brown of Walton Park. I invited him and his two subalterns to dinner at the bungalow one evening. I had brought back two chickens that had been given to me in the bushveld and these formed the main course. Swazi chickens tend to roam far and wide and are thus strongly muscled and lean fleshed. These two must have been particularly high mileage birds, for one of the subalterns, when struggling to cut up his helping of roast chicken asked, with more wit than good manners, "How do you tell the difference between the flesh and the bone?" "It's easy," I replied, masking my irritation with this cocky young fellow (he was perhaps two years my junior!) "put your fork into it, if it goes in easily it's probably bone." The Gordons, having come to Swaziland in a hurry, did not stay long, being needed back in Kenya. They were replaced by the South Lancashire regiment.

It was not only the administrative service that was receiving 'retreads' from East Africa. Other government departments were recruiting them too. People were already beginning to query the calibre of one of the new arrivals, a government vet, recently transferred from Tanganyika, when Ian Aers, also, of course, from Tanganyika, recognised him as someone he had put in gaol several years earlier for paying his two boxer dogs as government cattle guards. The fellow had quickly become a habitué of the Tavern Hotel bar in Mbabane and had made a point of chatting up the owner, Lew Sargent, who had been a Spitfire pilot in the war and was a well-known figure in the territory. When the retread vet found himself leaving the Government Service only a short while after his arrival, he asked Lew for a keepsake to remind him of the happy hours he had spent in theTavern. "Of course, choose anything you like," replied Lew, affably. "Well," said the vet, "can I have one of those mugs?" pointing to a pair of Battle of Britain commemorative mugs. These had been given to Lew by his fellow pilots on their unit's disbandment at the end of the war and he was loath to part with them, but, having made the offer, felt bound by it. The vet thanked Lew effusively. However, a week after the vet's departure, Lew saw the mug displayed for sale in the window of the Mbabane second-hand shop. I never heard of anyone who spoke of this vet doing any good to their animals, but thanks to the stories of the boxer dogs and the Battle of Britain mug, his short spell in Swaziland is stuck in people's memory, even forty years on. It is sobering for me to reflect that the same system that had chosen him also recruited me!

I too was to be on the move for, suddenly, after he had been in Hlatikulu two days at the start of his proposed induction into the District before taking over at Goedgegun, Ian Aers, the retread from Tanganyika, was not going to be DO at Goedgegun after all. The DO was to be me, as Rawlins had originally requested when Chris had announced his resignation. So, on Chris and Val's departure, Abednego and I moved down to Goedgegun. I handed over my post at Hlatikulu to Edward Zwane, who was coming back for a second stint there. Rawlins, Chris and I had been a happy team. I expected the same of Rawlins, Edward and myself; and so it transpired.

Chapter 9

# Goedgegun

It was easy to settle into Goedgegun. Chris Anderson and I had worked quite closely together and I had also done odd stints filling in when he had been on local leave and once when he was off sick. As a result I had met the office staff and knew who they were and they had some idea of what to expect from me, coupled with the reports they no doubt had received from their colleagues up the hill in Hlatikulu. Chris would be a hard act to follow; he was rightly well liked and I could never match his linguistic skills. But I had already learned that there was no point in trying to be a carbon copy of one's predecessor, however excellent he might be. One just had to be oneself, Polonius style: "To thine own self be true".

Goedgegun, as the only stand-alone posting for a District Officer, was considered something of a plum and I was lucky to be given it with only eleven months' service under my belt. In addition, the house was suitable for my parents' and Gill's impending visit and there was a good stable and excellent paddock for 'Horsa' my horse. He was by now in fine fettle and we quickly took advantage of the good riding country surrounding my new home. The excellent Maria, Chris and Val's capable Swazi maid, who had come up to Hlatikulu to help me out at the time of the SNC delegation's visit, agreed to stay on and was looking forward to having a full house when the family arrived. The downside of this new arrangement was that Abednego now had too little to do and he probably resented having to play second fiddle to Maria. Horsa, of which he seemed fond, and the garden, which interested him less, became his main responsibilities; but I sensed after a while that he might be drifting into bad company. However, his devotion to the characterless cat continued unabated, until its sad demise a few weeks after we moved.

Goedgegun was a larger place than Hlatikulu, with a much higher proportion of Europeans. These were mostly people in employment, with relatively few retired folk and nearly all the Europeans were of South African rather than British stock, many of them Afrikaners. One of the latter was 'Oom' Ben Esterhuizen, the owner of the local drug store, next to the bicycle shop. He was the father of Henni Esterhuizen, the territory's Director of Education whose son Richard grew up to become the well-known film star, Richard E. Grant. Richard took the Grant name from his step-mother, Ann-Marie Grant. Having established his reputation as a film actor, he made his debut as a director with the film *Wa-Wa* (2005) in which he also played the major role. *Wa-Wa*, incidentally, was the word used by Africans and, supposedly, Americans to describe the way British expatriates spoke. The film was set in Swaziland in the late 1960s, and included actual footage taken of the independence celebrations. It gives a good idea of the beauty of the Swaziland scenery and the grace and charm of the Swazi people.

'Oom' Ben was quite a character in his own right. One of the stories about him, which may be apocryphal but had wide currency, concerned the large public weighing machine he kept in the shop. As like as not customers would hop on the scales in the course of their visit to the store; when the customer was a young married woman 'Oom' Ben would privily catch a glimpse of the reading and write it down and when he detected a rising trend in a young lady's weight he would draw the most likely conclusion and quietly direct a sales pitch at her, directing her attention to the wide range of products he stocked for the benefit of the mother-to-be and her unborn child.

Another local character, who impinged much more on my daily life, was August Language, an acerbic little man who ran a successful legal practice in the town. The Transvaal border was only a few miles away and much of the hill grazing land was owned by absentee South African sheep farmers. This situation generated a sizeable proportion of the work of the local court, with these farmers bringing cases against Swazi squatters and other alleged miscreants from the neighbouring Swazi areas. The attorney acting for the landlords was usually August Language. I was not the first DO at Goedgegun whose heart sank when he went into court and saw that Language was appearing. Socially, and even in court as far as he dared, he was openly critical of the Swaziland administration and hostile to the successive DOs who had to deal with him. It was not only DOs and magistrates who found August Language a trial. Mike Fairlie in *No Time Like the Past*, recalls the first time that Language appeared before Sir Walter Harragin (the High Court Judge who had carried out the Seretse enquiry in 1949). Harragin was hearing an appeal, sitting with assessors and the little Goedgegun attorney was up to his usual tricks. Fairlie recounts the following sequence: "Harragin leaned over to one of his assessors and whispered, 'Who's that cheeky little bugger?' He was told, 'Language, m'lud'. 'Damn the language,' replied the Judge, 'what's his name?'"

Fortunately the stipendiary magistrates heard the bulk of the court cases; but there were always some that fell to the DO when the magistrate, in my case John Sturgis, was engaged elsewhere.

Often it was not so much the legal business of the court that presented problems, but the subsequent enforcement of the Court's judgements. This was so in the case of an absentee landlord's claim against squatters on his land near Hluti, a little settlement lying in the middleveld east of Goedgegun, close to the South African border.

However much I personally disliked what had to be done, as in the Mankaiana eviction the previous year, the law had to be enforced and, once again, it was to the District administration that the court's officers turned. Since this emotive judgement came hard on the heels of the recent unrest, I made it clear that a little time would be needed if the desired evacuation were to be achieved without trouble, especially as the nearby Swazi areas were full to overflowing.

However, we were lucky. Thanks to the excellent Ndabazabantu and particularly Edward Zwane, a chief was found in Edward's half of the District (previously my half) who had spare land and would be happy to accept the squatters. Edward and I worked together to fashion a deal that we could offer the squatters. We had considerable sympathy for them; they had lived many years on the farm, which the owner rarely visited, and the action was probably only being taken against them at this time because the owner was said to be preparing to sell the land. The PWD would give some help, both with materials and construction of new kraals; lorries would be laid on to transport the households to their new area, as well as their smaller livestock and everything in the way of materials that could be salvaged from the old homesteads. The squatters' cattle would be herded across country. Finally, a large gang of prisoners would be available on moving day to lend a hand generally and then to pull down what remained of the squatters' former homes. Such was the deal we were able to put together; the next step was to persuade the squatters to accept it. There was much sitting and talking under shade trees, some to-ing and fro-ing by the squatters to discuss matters with their prospective new chief and much oiling of the wheels of the agreement by the Ndabazabantu and his assistants under Edward's and my joint supervision. In all this I found the squatters to be well mannered and receptive to reasoned argument. In their heart of hearts they had known that one day they would have to leave the Boer's land and they had heard of others who had been required to go without any help whatsoever. There was some attempt by local NNLC activists to make the issue a cause célèbre. The squatters obviously decided that the angry young men, although long on rhetoric, would be short on practical help. Moving day turned out to be quite a jolly occasion. A little kindness goes a long way. It is a cliché, of course, but clichés would not be clichés if they did not often turn out to be true.

Normally my visits to Hluti were uneventful. It was an inconsequential place with a police post, a small courtroom where minor cases were heard, either by the DO or the visiting magistrate; and there was a shop, a filling station and garage, a post office and a primary school. In the heat of a sleepy afternoon, driving on the dirt road from Goedgegun to Gollel, one could have missed Hluti altogether but for the fine avenue of Jacaranda trees that lined the road where it passed through the village. Sitting in the shade of the Jacarandas were usually a motley collection of women selling vegetables and other produce, with their donkeys tethered nearby and perhaps a few nondescript chickens in wicker coops or insecure cardboard boxes. Beside them a mangy dog could be nosing around, trying to snaffle something edible when no one was looking and on the unkempt verges would be a goat or two, nibbling up the scrub vegetation or straining for the lowest branches of the overhanging trees; and a Swazi pony might be hitched, cowboy style, to the rails outside the store waiting for its owner to finish his purchases inside.

Like many similar places in Southern Africa, Hluti could well have doubled as the set for a 19th century western. All this I had known for some time, so why, one particular morning, as I drove up to the police post, did I find myself humming the theme tune of the quintessential western, *High Noon*? And then I realised: the place was deserted, just like that little mid-west town on the day the bad men were coming to kill the sheriff at High Noon and everyone had retreated behind closed doors and shutters, leaving their law man to face the baddies by himself 'or die a coward, a craven coward in his bed'. However, it was not Gary Cooper who came out to greet me from the Swaziland equivalent of the Sheriff's Office, but the duty constable; nor was there a Grace Kelly figure in the back office loading her twelve-bore, ready to blast the last of the bad guys to kingdom come as soon as he drew a bead on her man.

"What's going on?" I asked. "Hau, Nkos', it's a serious business." Apparently the local chief had hired a celebrated witchdoctor from the Northern Transvaal to establish who was causing the successive deaths in his family and the 'smelling out' procedure was already under way, half a mile out into the veld.

Witchcraft was fairly commonplace in Swaziland, as in most parts of Southern Africa, but it was illegal, so it was incumbent on me to do something. With all the confidence of a twenty-five-year-old, twelve months wise in the service of the Swaziland administration, I told the constable to fetch his colleague and the police Land Rover and we drove out over the veld to see things for ourselves. I knew more or less what to expect having, as a boy, read Henry Rider Haggard's *King Solomon's Mines* with its dramatic account of the smelling out conducted by Gagul, the nefarious witchdoctor into whose clutches Alan Quatermain and his small group of Victorian 'good chaps' had stumbled; but unlike Haggard's hero, who knew that an eclipse of the moon was imminent, I had no cunning plan up my sleeve.

When we arrived we found a spectacle much like Rider Haggard had described. Seated on the grass in a big circle were some five hundred people, including the local chief, his family and ndunas and also a local European farmer, who had apparently done a separate deal with the witchdoctor to find out for him who was stealing his horses.

But there the similarity with Rider Haggard's narrative ended. Sheer farce was never far from the surface on most occasions in Swaziland and this was to prove no exception. Instead of being menaced by a modern-day 'Gagul' figure in the full ceremonial kit of his trade, we found the witchdoctor clad in an old army greatcoat taking a comfort break and relieving himself in the long grass. Having him at a disadvantage we lifted him up unceremoniously, still in the squatting position and still about his immediate business, plonked him into the back of the Land Rover and drove him down to a police cell in the village.

This snatch provoked a certain amount of muttering, not least on the part of the local chief, who had paid out good money as a *voorskoot* (prepayment) of the witchdoctor's fees, but also from the crowd who had come for the show and perhaps a good dose of *schadenfreude* into the bargain. Witchcraft was a forbidden fruit, viewed with a mixture of fascination and fear, and many more people were involved in it than one was led to believe. But there was really nothing to be said, for the law was clear.

However, the locals had the last laugh. When the police started putting the case together, no one could be found to testify against the witchdoctor except myself and the two constables and of course, all we had witnessed had been five hundred people sitting peaceably on the grass and a man from the Transvaal in an ex-army greatcoat relieving himself at a modest distance from the multitude. None of these things was indictable.

The whole saga could, I suppose, have been seen as an illustration of the aptness of my Swazi name, Malindzane, the name of the Swazi Age Regiment to which I would have belonged had I been a Swazi. The name might seem harmless enough, but amongst their seniors and particularly amongst the older regiments like the 'Londolozi', to which most of the Ngwenyama's counsellors belonged, the Malindzane were regarded as troublemakers, lacking experience or judgement and given to impatient and intemperate behaviour. However, for all that my actions at Hluti that day might have been considered typical 'Malindzane behaviour', no rebuke came to me from the Chief Justice, to whom my report was sent, nor from the Chief Secretary.

For myself I was not unhappy with the way the whole incident had resolved itself. While reading for my degree in French and German I had been impressed by the passage in the Prologue to Goethe's *Faust* where God in Heaven tells The Devil that the person who is always striving and 'having a go' can be granted redemption; perhaps my Lord and Redeemer had his hand in that incident at Hluti. Of course, I could have turned a blind eye to the smelling out; that would have been feeble; but a more 'gung-ho' method of arresting the witchdoctor, had it gone wrong, could have involved severe embarrassment, or even loss of life. Beyond that, a public trial of the witchdoctor would have involved obtaining corroboration of his status from the South African government, who were cordially hated by most Swazis. If the South African officials had refused to help a prosecution would have been hopeless, whereas if they had given us the necessary information, the Swaziland administration would have been depicted as being in cahoots with that white supremacist regime. Inevitably a trial would have implicated the local chief, irritating the Swazi National Council and possibly even King Sobhuza himself, as amounting to meddling in Swazi traditional affairs which were the preserve of the King and his Council. If found guilty, the witchdoctor would have had to serve a lengthy term in a Swazi gaol, where he might well have fermented trouble and sought to practise by proxy, causing problems to the Swaziland prison service. I have to admit that none of these considerations had been in my mind as I had driven up the hill with those two constables, but it had come fairly lucky for me.

Nothing, of course, is ideal; yet, as it turned out, the administration was seen to have responded to a challenge, and the local chief kept his role. However, he was left the poorer for the escapade and hopefully learned his lesson, and the European farmer emerged as something of a laughing stock, but otherwise suffered no sanctions. Thus neither the local Swazi nor the European community was upset and the witchdoctor would probably steer clear of Swaziland in the future. Most important, there had been no civil disturbance and no loss of life; and, as far as we knew, no one was endangered by being labelled the cause of the deaths in the chief's family where, whether by coincidence or otherwise, the spate of deaths ceased.

Muriel Miller.

Not long afterwards my parents and sister Gill arrived, coming by ship to Cape Town. After two days in the Mount Nelson Hotel they came up to Johannesburg by the Blue Train, which still ranks as one of the great luxury railway journeys of the world. They quickly settled into life at the Goedgegun bungalow.

My mother set to work to turn Maria into the Mrs Beeton of Southern Africa. Gill, a good horsewoman, explored the local countryside on my horse, now fully restored to fitness, and she also made friends with Edward and Anna Zwane up the hill in Hlatikulu. More generally the family were quickly gathered into the social life of the little community of Hlatikulu and,

179

Archie Miller.

with the use of my car, they could come and go as they chose. My father was taken on board by the local ex-servicemen's association, The MOTHS (Memorable Order of Tin Hats!).

A particular highlight for him was an afternoon spent with me, at the invitation of the local chiefs, attending a ceremony to mark the start of the building of a new house for the Ngwenyama at Shiselweni, one of the traditional sites of Swazi Royal Kraals. Sobhuza was charming to him and the two of them hit it off from the start. They were much of an age and had many character traits in common, courtesy, patience, shrewdness and a widespread interest in rural matters. In addition, my father was able to swap wartime memories from North Africa and Italy with some of the King's entourage. He had a grand afternoon and made a considerable impression –"a complete Scottish gentleman" as Mnt Makhungu, who was present, later described him to me. Makhungu never quite managed to disabuse himself of the idea I had aristocratic connections. The myth arose because of my home address, 'Bellrigg, Castle Douglas'. Move the comma on a word and you had a posh address, but all your mail would go the Isle of Man. More mundanely, my father devised a potato-planting scheme for Abednego - earlies, main crop and late crop - and took him through to Piet Relief to collect the seed potatoes. We lived like fighting cocks as Maria was keen to show off all the recipes she had learned from Val Anderson, as well as her new mastery of the Miller family favourites.

I had booked a week's local leave and we went to the Kruger Park,

180

gradually making our way from south to north, before exiting at Punda Milia, beside the great, green, greasy Limpopo. The Kruger, in early October, is a delight; the air is bright and clear; it is sunny with negligible humidity and the temperature never much exceeds 75° F, with the evenings cool enough to enjoy a log fire. You could feel you were truly in *Jock of the Bushveld* country by day; but after sunset, when you repaired to one of the lodges with their thatched rondavel family cottages, you were back in considerable comfort. It made a lovely family holiday. In our six days in the Park we saw a wide variety of species, both animals and birds, as well as enjoying the startling changes of topography. Many people go to the Park to look at birds, rather than the animals, or to study the flora. One can, of course, have a surfeit of anything and nineteen years later when we took our two children back to Swaziland and had a few days in the Kruger, our daughter Kate, then twelve, protested, while on animal count duty, "If I see another perishing impala, I'll scream!"

An impala.

181

They certainly abounded in huge numbers. Too many of a species in an area can become a real problem for nature, too, and on our trip in October 1963 we came across a large area where the elephant population had outgrown its habitat, resulting in a shattered landscape resembling photos of World War I battlefields, with not a tree left standing and great swathes of country rendered useless to practically every living creature, including the elephants themselves. Shortly after our visit, the Park authorities carried out an elephant cull in this area of the park to restore the balance of nature.

An elephant smashing up its habitat in the south of the Kruger Park.

Overcrowding in the South African game reserves was a minor local difficulty compared to the overcrowding in the African reserves and Bantustans. That was a problem on a grand scale, which could only be tackled by massive land redistribution, which the Nationalist white supremacist government refused to contemplate. By doing so, I felt they effectively set a term on white rule in South Africa. History has confirmed that view.

History has also shown, most startlingly in Zimbabwe since its independence, that redistribution *per se* is useless. The process has to be carried out fairly and with a regard to maintaining the productivity of the land, lest the result of redistribution is simply starvation. In other words, those taking over the redistributed land must have the energy and ability to farm it. Commonsense therefore suggests that the earlier the redistribution process can begin, the more chance it will have of being successful.

Gill (right) with Chris and Val Anderson and baby Fiona.

Our next trip, over a long weekend, was to East Griqualand, in the north of Cape Province, close to the Basutoland border, as guests of Chris and Val Anderson and Chris's charming parents. Like many emigré Scots farming families all over the world, the Andersons were running a model farming operation on land which less resourceful people might have found too challenging. It was a happy place, too. The Xhosa farm workers went around with a smile on their faces, never more so than on the morning after our arrival, when, knowing what we did not know, they prepared two horses for Gill and me to use. It came out later, following our extremely lively ride, that one of the staff had been slipping these two animals extra oats. Immediately upon being released by the grinning farm workers, our mounts had taken off with the speed of Pegasus for what seemed miles across the veld, until pulling up sweating and panting, with inches to spare, on the lip of a disused quarry. Some of the happy farm workers had been Chris's childhood companions in his mouse-hunting days and the jape with the horses had the flavour of their juvenile pranks of times long past. When we rode back to the stables, still pallid but unharmed, I hope Gill and I were seen to be taking it all in good part. The 'groom' asked, with a grin on his face, if we had enjoyed our ride. "Yes," I replied, "they are quite lively animals – well fed, I should imagine," pointing at a half empty bag of oats. "*Yebo Nkos*", replied the groom, his grin widening. All was well that ended well. However, I do not recall our opting for further horse riding that weekend.

Each morning we awoke to bright sunshine, with the trees and shrubs almost leaping out of the clarity of the mountain air and, on the lawn, hoopoes in their orange and black plumage flaunting their Grecian crests as they systematically drilled for worms with their curved beaks, calling to each other 'hu-pu-pu'. They were totally undisturbed by the rhythmic movements of a stately Xhosa matron sweeping the grass with a besom. The whole garden and policies were immaculate; but was manicuring the lawn to this extent really necessary? "Not really" said Chris, the work was in fact "make work" to give employment to someone who would otherwise have no income. Actually there was a fungus that came up on the lawn and its daily removal, lest the children eat it, was the overt purpose of the job. The fungus was not a major hazard like the ubiquitous putsi fly, which laid its miniscule and thus undetected eggs in damp clothing. When hatched out, the larvae (jiggers) burrowed into the wearer's flesh, causing festering sores. Babies' nappies were particular targets; the remedy was scrupulous ironing of all washing. Of course, if one bathed or even just briefly waded in African freshwater streams and lakes, except in the highest altitudes or the fastest flowing streams, there lurked another much more insidious hazard, the tiny bilharzia snail which infects its host's bloodstream, causing general lassitude and sometimes acute physical deterioration. Sub-clinical bilharzia, especially when combined with the effects of systematic smoking of cannabis or *dagga* (pronounced dacha – 'ch' as in 'loch') as the Swazi called it, accounted for the high incidence in Africa of people who were TFB (tired from birth), or TSW (three sheets in the wind). Anyone who considers cannabis harmless need go no further than the Atlas mountains in Morocco, or rural areas of Southern Africa, to see the long term effects of the endemic use of this so-called 'harmless recreational drug'. Malaria was not much of a problem in Southern Africa, except for a few parts of the lowveld. Generally, East and Southern Africa were much healthier places than they had been when Speke and Livingstone were discovering the interior of Central Africa and the Voortrekkers were pushing northwards to escape from the British administration in the Cape of Good Hope. It was the European settlers, moving into empty lands, who removed most of the hazards to man and beast which had kept much of Africa a barren wilderness until their arrival.

One could understand the descendants of these pioneers being reluctant to yield to the pan-africanist doctrine of 'Africa for the Africans'. The European settlers had not only controlled all the major human diseases, they had instituted good veterinary practices which made animal husbandry feasible by eliminating *rinderpest* (cattle plague, akin to the European 'murrain' of the Middle Ages) and suppressing tick-borne diseases, thanks to constant stock dipping.

People like the Andersons felt that if they were required one day to hand over their farms for African occupation, they should at least receive fair compensation for all the effort and capital which they had poured into the place, which had enabled it to provide a good life not only for its owners, but also for their African farm workers and their extended families. So far neither the Nationalist Government nor its post-apartheid successors have made a move to take over the Andersons' farm; but the spectre of compulsory purchase has been on their horizon for over forty years, as well as being a deterrent to potential purchasers, should they ever wish to sell.

On our way back through Natal we had arranged to call on a farming family my parents and Gill had met on the boat coming out to Cape Town. We arrived mid-morning and they gave us a brief tour of their excellent farm. After lunch the husband suggested that he and I should go out and test a .303 rifle, which he had just bought from another farmer. He put up a large turnip as a target – "About the size of a Freedom Fighter's head," he remarked. For all his charm, his perfect manners, to Africans, it appeared, as well as Europeans and his obviously enlightened employment practices, if push came to shove and his family or farm workers were threatened, he would shove with the best of them to protect those for whom he was responsible, nor would he easily give up the land he felt was rightly his.

Soon after our return from our brief visit to East Griqualand, I was again on the move, this time with my holidaying family in tow. Hugh Jones, Sir Brian Marwick's Private Secretary, was due for home leave and I was to stand in for him.

Chapter 10

# Private Secretary

The move to Mbabane meant that for my family the last two weeks of their visit turned out to be something of an anticlimax. They were rather stuck in my bungalow on the edge of the Government House grounds while I was tied to the coat-tails of the Queen's Commissioner, as Sir Brian Marwick was now styled. People, including the Marwicks, were kind to Gill and my parents; but the family missed the flexibility of our life in Goedegegun.

For my horse, Horsa, who had so visibly flourished on the sweet pasture of Goedgegun, the move to Mbabane was a miserable experience. I had arranged with Abednego for him to ride Horsa to Mbabane by easy stages with a break at his home in Mankaiana, together with other stops overnight, so that neither man nor beast was overtaxed by the long journey. I had provided the necessary funds for food and lodging for him and the horse, allowing the best part of a week for the trip. However, by the late afternoon of their expected arrival in Mbabane there was still no sign of them. Eventually, near to midnight, they pitched up, both in a dreadful state. Apparently, instead of setting off just after the rest of us, Abednego had dallied behind, probably in dubious company, until he had spent all the food and accommodation money. He then proceeded to do the whole journey in one day. Horsa, lame and with terrible saddle sores, took much longer to recover than Abednego; in the end, thanks to the vet and a long rest, he did recover and I was able to ride him again. However it turned out to be quite complicated to have a horse in Mbabane; he had to live several miles away and, since I had little prospect of a more rural posting and my overseas leave was coming up, I passed Horsa on to a friend of Makhungu where I knew he would have a good life. As for Abednego, I should have sacked him there and then. Instead, I gave him another chance, but the trust between us was broken and, in the end, after several months, he had to go.

Soon it was time to take the family down to Durban to catch the boat home and I settled into life as Her Majesty's Commissioner's Private Secretary. It turned out to be a disappointing assignment. Sir Brian had only a short time left before his postponed retirement and I think he was worn out. He showed the classic signs of exhaustion, tending to spend his time sitting in his office busying himself with paperwork, often quite inconsequential stuff. He had an eye for detail, which was in danger of becoming an obsession and most nights, after dinner, he would retire to his study, bring out the papers he had brought home and slog away at them into the small hours. When draft documents came to be discussed in committee, his comments tended towards nit-picking – "page 44, line 7, insert a comma after 'and', the clause that follows is parenthetic" – correct enough, but not the stuff by which a country is governed.

I probably did not have the confidence to interact with him successfully. For instance, when I learned that he was being asked by the fledgling Radio Service to give the territory's first ever Christmas Broadcast, I drafted a suggested text and took it into him. He said to leave it on his desk; he would look at it in due course. He made no further reference to my draft and I assumed he had either dismissed it as unsuitable or thought that this was something in which I should not be meddling. So it was a surprise, the day before the recording, which he was to accomplish with some style, that I found he was using my draft, with hardly a word altered. Later, when I remarked to him that his broadcast seemed to have been very well received, he merely said, "Oh good," or something equally non-committal; and that was that.

In a letter home I wrote: "This is a funny job and often there seems to be very little thanks to it. H.E. is not of a particularly effusive nature and keeps most things to himself. In contrast, the Chief Secretary, Athel Long, is delightful, most approachable and always sees the amusing side of things." Their differing styles helped me define my emerging management philosophy which eventually condensed into "Make life fun for those who work for you; show them that their job is important, and never forget to say 'please', 'thank you' and 'sorry' and when the going gets tough, say them all together". Years later I heard an American business studies guru expounding on a similar theme. "All we need to know about life we learn at nursery school – to say 'please', 'thank you' and 'sorry'; to clean up our own mess and to hold hands crossing the road."

As so often happened it was only when I was out and about amongst the Swazis that I was able to recharge my batteries. Accompanying Sir Brian to the Christmas service at the Leper Colony was one such occasion. This joyful place was run by Dr David Hynd, a Scots medical missionary in Swaziland since 1925. He had been an independent delegate to the Constitutional Conference in London ten months earlier. From the time the Leper Colony opened in 1948, some five hundred in-patients had passed through, often staying for long years; but by 1963 there were only forty-five residents left, thanks to the advanced treatments which Dr Hynd introduced, enabling most patients to go home with the disease halted in its tracks. The majority of these forty-five were no longer actually suffering from leprosy, but from its legacy. This amounted to varying levels of disability, most notably atrophied limbs and features. Often the leprosy had eaten away at people's ears and noses so extensively that you needed a conscious effort not to flinch when they first turned or lifted their face towards you.

The service, conducted by Dr Hynd and attended by the nursing staff and all the colony's patients and residents, was predominantly in siSwati, including hymns and carols, several of them well-rehearsed choral numbers, performed by different groups of patients. For the offertory, which was given to a local clinic, a bowl was placed before the altar and the whole congregation filed up to put in their contributions. Some also brought fruit and vegetables from their garden plots on the settlement. Next, the Christmas presents were carried in and handed around, including a pen of chickens for the local Red Cross representative, the joint gift of several of the 'cured' residents. One of the patients gave the doctor a *tikki* (sixpence – truly a widow's mite), all lovingly wrapped up with a greeting card. Some others had clubbed together to buy him a straw hat.

It was my second visit to the leper colony and confirmed my earlier impression that here was true goodness at work and the living-out of the Gospel message: 'In as much as you have done it for the least of these my brethren, you have done it unto Me'.

Over New Year, of all absurd things, I went down with chickenpox. There was a day or two of discomfort and then I felt fine; but I was banned from work lest I infect others in the Secretariat. People were extremely good to me. Lady Marwick, about whom I tended to be fairly equivocal, was the first person to call and Sir Brian came hard on her heels with a selection of light reading. They were followed by a succession of visitors, usually bearing delicious dishes to tempt my supposedly jaded appetite. I felt something of a fraud, as I was barely ill at all. Fortunately I was able to respond in some measure by offering my callers cake as well as the tea or coffee Maria was quick to serve them, for Miss Constance Adams of the Mankaiana Hotel had, with extraordinary kindness, sent me a large, exquisitely iced and utterly delicious Christmas cake. I was rather taken aback by this present. She was an enigma. There was no reason on earth for her to send me a Christmas present of any sort, let alone a gift of such magnificence over which she had obviously laboured for many hours; yet during my stay in her hotel there had been little obvious attempt to make me comfortable and when, a few weeks later she was to be entrusted with providing a farewell lunch for the Marwicks from the people of Mankaiana District, the meal was served two hours late. However, during the war, this same person had flown all those new American aircraft across the Atlantic and in so doing had played a significant part in the British war effort. I was reminded of Colonel Mike Evett, my erstwhile regimental second in command, who had served with the Chindits. The men who turned up trumps in the Burmese jungle, he said, were often the very last from whom one might have expected heroics.

Just before I went back to work after chickenpox, Peter and Diana suggested I join them and an army chap for a weekend trip to Ndumu, a very isolated game reserve at the north-easternmost tip of Natal, right up against the Mozambique border in the area where the Tonga people lived. It was only a few miles from Stegi but there was no road. To get there you had to go south towards Gollel and then cross over into Natal, go east to Ngwavuma and then strike north through very rocky country, a trip of some forty miles from the Swaziland border. Peter knew Ndumu from earlier visits. Conditions there were Spartan, just four simple rondavels, unfurnished except for camp beds; and we had to bring our own food and bedding. We would be hard pressed to fit the four of us and all our stuff into Peter's Volkswagen Beetle, so I offered my Peugeot 403, which was more spacious, with a good boot. "No", said Peter, "only a Land Rover or a Beetle can be relied upon to get through." Anyway, he had a mistrust of my cars, born of experience of the vehicle I had brought out from the UK, a Ford Capri, a model recently released onto the market. This car's design, with large tail fins and long overhangs, marked the apogée of Italian car designer influence on the British motor industry. I had taken delivery of it shortly before embarking for Africa and practically my first trip in it had been to the Oxford suburbs to see Marjery Perham, the doyen of Oxford African historians. She was Lugard's biographer and tended to cast a kindly eye over anyone going out to the 'dark continent'. During my visit her nice secretary dubbed the car a '*dolce vita* vehicle' and the name stuck. She was right; the Capri was totally unsuited to life in Swaziland, but it had two advantages. First, it was extremely comfortable for eating lunch out in the District. You could sit across the level boot lid, with your back resting against one of the tail fins and your feet up against other, with your picnic spread out on the flat expanse between you and the rear window. Secondly, it had a wonderfully efficient jack and spare tyre storage system. This I greatly appreciated as one had countless punctures from flints and rocks on the dirt roads. For these reasons I felt the car was not to be lightly cast away, but by the time I arrived at Hlatikulu I was ready to bite the bullet. The Capri must go before it fell to pieces. There would be no difficulty doing a part exchange, as the garage would soon find a ready buyer for it. Its *dolce vita* image would appeal to upwardly mobile young urban Swazis, working in the Republic, who liked to cut a dash but could not run to a big Chev or Buick, chaps rather like the young NNLC politico who had visited me in Mankaiana, with sharp Italian-style suits from the Indian tailors, square-cut ties and pointed shoes, tsotsi wannabees, probably down from the Rand on a spree. However, I needed my DC's approval to transfer my car loan to a different vehicle.

I had decided to go for a Volkswagen Beetle, like Peter's. They had the reputation of being tough as old boots and Peter got away with treating his more or less like a cross-country 4 x 4. Mr Rawlins, however, would have none of this; "a Beetle", he said, "was not a fitting vehicle for a District Officer". Occasionally I had given him a lift when his car was being serviced and he was quite happy to be seen in the *dolce vita* vehicle. Perhaps it took him back to his idyllic adolescence within the bosom of the diplomatic corps in Rome with his father, 'The Ambassador'. But the idea of arriving somewhere in a Volkswagen Beetle was unthinkable to him. Probably Rawlins also remembered Peter's little yellow car parked beside the office, letting down the tone of the place. Peter, who, he remembered, in the same week had written off a Government grader and also demolished a clerical officer's house by felling a big blue gum tree the wrong way. "What if this new chap, Miller, turned out equally unlucky? No, a Volkswagen was not to be recommended." If it seemed that Rawlins was being a little unreasonable by refusing to allow me to buy a Volkswagen Beetle, this was nothing compared to the unfairness of the way he blamed Peter for the destruction of the road grader and the government quarter for, although Peter had instigated both these undertakings, he had been at one remove from their execution. At the time of the accidents the road grader was being driven by its normal PWD driver and the tree felling was carried out by the government forester. In the latter case it was lucky that no one was in the house at the moment of its destruction. Its occupier at the time was Percy Pym Diamini, soon to qualify as the first Swazi dentist thanks to a government scholarship to Edinburgh; and he was to be appointed Minister of Education in 1972. It would have been sad if the blue gum had denied Swaziland the benefit of his talents.

The '*dolce vita*' car

Unreasonable or not, Rawlins was not budging on the question of the Beetle, so I had to shell out more than I wanted and bought a Peugeot 403 instead. I never saw the Capri again. It probably went up to 'Tsotsi-land'.

Peter's Beetle was more or less indestructible and more or less amphibious. Both qualities were to be tested on the trip to Ndumu. During our journey there was a vicious downpour, turning the hill streams into torrents so that every river crossing became a major hazard.

We thought one particularly swollen river was going to be our Waterloo when, as the raging water bore down on us, the engine started to splutter mid-stream; but the valiant little car just made it to the other bank before giving up the ghost. Luckily the rain stopped a few seconds later and we were able to dry the engine and proceed without further ado.

There were no other visitors to Ndumu that weekend, so we had David Pooley, the delightful game warden, to ourselves. He was well known in game conservation circles and spent much of his time at Ndumu doing research. He had also found time to record an LP, *Sounds of the Bushveld*, a comprehensive collection of bird song and animal noises. We had just enough time to unpack and eat our sandwich lunch before he whisked us off in the Land Rover to look at hippos wallowing around in a deep pool near the camp. I had always imagined that hippos led an almost ideal life, with no natural predators and the ability to be equally at home on land or in the water. Apparently this was not so; they were plagued by a sort of giant tsetse fly, hence their need to escape from the fly by spending so much time under water, with only their nostrils breaking the surface. Mature hippo bulls, David told us, each had their own herd of cows and their own territory. For months on end one could observe two bulls confronting one another on the borders of their respective territories, engaging in fantastic shadow-boxing, each secretly scared of the other, while their cows looked on. This continued until the day when a cow crossed over from one territory to the other, breaking the deadlock. The phoney war between the two bulls ended abruptly as they engaged in deadly combat. The fight could last for as long as a week until one bull finally emerged as the victor and the other was either killed or at best escaped with terrible injuries.

David drew our attention to a particular point of land, set about with fever trees, which juts out into one of the pans in the reserve. This, he said, used to be the place where the local Africans held human sacrifices. Apparently, when there was a drought and the local witchdoctor was asked to make rain, as far as he could he would delay until he sensed the drought was breaking, when he would order a great feast to be prepared. A beast or beasts would be killed and large chunks of the meat would be hung up on one of the trees on the point right on the water's edge. Then the people beat their drums and the crocodiles, attracted by the smell, would converge on the point and thrash about in a frenzy trying in vain to reach the meat. Eventually they gave up, slunk back into the water and hung around in the shallows off the point. Meanwhile, at the feast, a teenage girl would be chosen for sacrifice and put into a trance. The drums would start to beat again and the girl was led down to the water's edge. Once there, she would wade out into the water amongst the crocs, totally fearless, waving to the people and laughing as the hordes of crocodiles tore at her, seeming to feel no pain. She was soon dragged down and the churning water gradually fell calm, glazed over with her blood. Now the stillness would only be broken by the gentle wash from the crocodiles as they cruised over to the opposite shoreline, to rest in the shallows or sunbathe on the shore. "At last they are happy," the witchdoctor would announce, "and they will bring us rain." Apparently the ritual was repeated year after year and some of the old Africans in the nearby reserve would recount how they had seen all this in their youth.

Five months earlier I had compared the actual 'smelling out' I had encountered at Hluti with the fictional 'smelling out' conducted by Gagul in Rider Haggard's best-seller, *King Solomon's Mines*, written in 1885. Now, at Ndumu, I was once again finding parallels between current or recent practice amongst Ngoni peoples and Haggard's adventure story. In *King Solomon's Mines* the smelling out was followed by a dance at which the most beautiful dancer was chosen for slaughter as an offering to the ancestors, symbolised by the figures of stone; in that instance she was saved thanks to the intervention of Alan Quatermain and his band of Victorian heroes. Haggard's story has echoes, too, of the Swazi *Umhlanga*, or Reed Dance, where likewise a girl is chosen from among the dancers, not, however, to be a sacrifice, but as a new wife for the King.

People who know and love Africa will probably agree that part of the continent's fascination lies in the constant interweaving, perhaps more poignantly than elsewhere, of past and present, fact and fiction, myth and reality. Pliny was probably not the first, and certainly not the last, to highlight the continent for the benefit of those searching for something unusual.

As if to underline the point, when he came back for a drink with us before going home in the evening, David Pooley started telling us about his pride and joy, the white rhinos, and soon side-tracked into the local creation story about how the rhino got its coat, which was essentially the same as the Swazi legend that Edward Zwane had recounted to me nine months earlier.

David also talked about some of the birds we had seen. I was particularly interested in his remarks about the Fish Eagle. From my first sighting of this handsome bird on my second day in Africa I had been intrigued. Somewhat larger than an Osprey, with proportionately longer wings, its call and colouring make it instantly recognisable. Roberts describes its voice as "one of the characteristic sounds of Africa, a loud, challenging, yelping 'kow, kow, kow, kow, kow', uttered with its head thrown right back even while soaring". Grant (*Birds of the Southern Third of Africa*) describes its call as "a cheerful squealing call... like the laugh of one of the big gulls, only more piercing". Its Latin name is quoted by these two authorities as, respectively, *Haliaëtus vocifer* and *Cuncuma* (alternatively *Falco vocifer*) i.e. all the names stress its voice. The Fish Eagle's colouring is as distinctive as its call, brilliant white on the head, back, crest and tail, black wings and chestnut abdomen and shoulders. I think if I had to try and encapsulate the essence of Africa in two sounds, I would choose the voices of Swazi women and children calling to each other in the Swaziland twilight and, secondly, the cry of the Fish Eagle – "kow, kow, kow-kow-kow" "mew, mew, hi-mew-yah". I don't think you can do any justice to the sound with phonetics – you have to find a recording – or better still go and hear it for yourself.

David was able to tell us much more about the ways of the wonderful Fish Eagle. We had that evening seen one bird stoop at a fish with a rushing noise as it hurtled downwards, checking just before it hit the water. Sometimes, David said, Fish Eagles would continue their dive unchecked to claw up a fish from well below the surface. Having caught its fish with its talons, he said, the eagle would carry it off to a branch of a tall tree and there, as like as not, drop it and not bother to fly down to recover it. Rural Africans thus kept a close eye on any fish eagles when they saw them hunting and were quick to take advantage of the gratuitous supply of fresh fish they provided. It seems there are two possible explanations for the Eagles' behaviour. First, they seem to have a fondness for carrion, indicating, rather like humans who hang their meat and game, that they do not always like their food to be too fresh. Secondly, they appear to enjoy hunting and killing for pleasure. They will harry and rob other fish-eating birds and chase or kill other birds for sport. They seem to like chasing herons, particularly Goliath Herons; and they kill not only smaller waders, like coots, but bigger birds too, like cormorants and flamingos, again, it seems, just for the fun of it.

I was to see an example of this thirteen months later out on the Serengeti, in Tanzania, where I was watching flamingos feeding at one of the smaller salt pans. Suddenly there was a shadow moving across the water. Up in the sky was a fish eagle circling the pan. With a cacophony of beating wings and thrashing water, the flamingos took flight, shrieking in panic. Down came the fish eagle, straight as an arrow, right through the melée. By the time the flamingos were safely dispersed and the surface of the water was falling still again, the eagle was perched on a dead tree at the water's edge; floating in the middle of the pan was the corpse of a flamingo, killed just for the eagle's enjoyment.

We chatted for some while until David went off home, then we had our supper and turned in to the accompaniment of a frogs' chorus. The following morning we were up early so that we could be shown the precious rhinos, which we eventually spotted in the thick *mopane* thorn. And then it was time to go back to camp, have lunch, pack up and grind our way back over the rocky road to Ngwavuma and from there on to Swaziland to be ready for work the next day. It was one of the joys of Swaziland that we had resources like Ndumu within easy distance, so we could have a complete break and recharge our batteries without too much travelling.

We agreed to go back another weekend as soon as possible. In fact that turned out to be fully ten months later, by which time Diana and Peter were proud parents of a baby boy, whom they were never to allow to cramp their adventurous style.

Meanwhile, the year's Ncwala (annual fertility and rainmaking festival) passed off without incident and the Ngwenyama succeeded in demonstrating his continuing powers by producing rain, against the meteorologists' forecast, within the requisite twenty-four hours of the end of the ceremony. In fact, he rather overdid things, for there was a vicious thunderstorm, which set the roads awash and immobilised much of the territory's telephone system.

Such success augured well for Sobhuza's referendum, which took place two weeks later. Through this he sought to challenge the imposed Constitution and give the lie to Marwick's assertion to his London masters that the Ngwenyama no longer represented the views of his people. Some months had passed since Sobhuza had asked Sir Brian to organise a plebiscite on the Constitution and Sir Brian had refused, telling him, if he felt so strongly, to go ahead and carry out his own referendum. Sobhuza had not said much at the time, but had, characteristically, worked quietly until his plans were ready.

The referendum was officially billed as a vote on the acceptability of the new Constitution; but it was in effect a vote either for the Ngwenyama and his approach or for Marwick and his way. Symbols were used on the voting cards, a *Lion* (instantly recognisable as 'Ngwenyama yema Swati' – the Lion of Swaziland, signifying dissatisfaction with the Constitution, i.e. backing Sobhuza, and a *Reindeer* (to the average Swazi a totally unknown creature) signifying support for the Constitution, i.e. backing Marwick. (A picture of a reindeer hung in the offices of the Swazi National Council. Sobhuza was in the habit of referring to it "with its curving horns and no straight directions like the new political parties".)

It was expected in some quarters, and particularly amongst Marwick, Long and Fairlie's circle, that the referendum would be a chaotic farce and that few people would turn out. One heard remarks such as "Those people couldn't organise a booze-up in a brewery". But the Old Lion had taken his time and done his homework. 'Those people', working through the network of chiefs and tinkundla produced an orderly and relatively well-organised poll. I went out to have a look at the voting at three different polling stations. Of the three, only one could be said to offer a truly secret ballot, but there were no signs of coercion and good humour abounded.

The result of the referendum was 122,000 votes for the *Lion* and 154 for the *Reindeer*.

Sobhuza's success left Swaziland thunderstruck. Launching the Swazi National Council's own political party was the natural next step, following the earlier example of Seretse Khama in Bechuanaland.

The new party was named the *Imbokoto* or *Imbokodvo* – The Grinding Stone. Sobhuza insisted that the Imbokodvo was not a party, but a national movement: the full name should be *Imbokodvo lemabahlaba* – The Grinding Stone that brings together many colours - an easily understood description as the grinding stone was known in every house for breaking down separate grains of corn into a single paste or flour. An imbokodvo also featured in the Swazi legend of the miraculous hare Chakijane. Pursued by hunters and finding his escape blocked by a river he could not cross, the hare turned himself into an imbokodvo. The hunters were astonished at the hare's disappearance. One, in his frustration, picked up the imbokodvo yelling, "If I could get my hands on that Chakijane I'd kill him like this!" – and hurled the stone across the river. Thus landed safely on the other side, the grinding stone turned itself back into Chakijane, who shouted triumphantly, "Thank you for getting me across the river!" The symbolism is clear: the Imbokodvo would be the means whereby Swaziland would be carried over the river of independence into a new life as a sovereign state.

As the weeks went by I was enjoying my role as H.E.'s Private Secretary less and less. When it had first been mooted that I should fit into the vacant PS slot for the duration of Huw Jones' overseas leave, Ray Rawlins had suggested that I would find the job boring compared to being a DO. He advised me to request to be left at Goedgegun on the grounds of having already been shunted around enough in my first tour. He would back up my request. I thought I knew better and that a stint as Private Secretary would look good on my CV. So I had only myself to blame. However, I was looking forward to moving to Mbabane District Office in April.

This proposed appointment had been included in the round of

postings that had been announced under the new plan to reorganise the District Administration. The number of Districts was to be reduced by merging Mankaiana with Manzini and Mbabane with Pigg's Peak, with their headquarters at Manzini and Pigg's Peak respectively. I was delighted to be going as DO Mbabane, reporting to Julian Faux at Pigg's Peak. Julian was the youngest DC, progressive and not the sort to fuss you the whole time. I was to move when Huw Jones came back from overseas leave to return to his old post as Private Secretary.

Poor old Mr Fannin, now recovered from illness and back as DC Mankaiana, found he was to stay at Mankaiana, but as DO, reporting to the DC Manzini, despite having been a DC for seventeen years. He soon retired. Another casualty was Ray Rawlins, who was asked to retire early under the 'over 45 rule' (similar to the rule in the Armed Services whereby officers may be required to retire if they have not attained a certain rank by a specific age). I think this was a blow to his pride and we tried to give him a good send-off. His hobbies included collecting signatures and he had an impressive array of documents signed by some of the great figures of history. More prosaically he also collected beer mugs and tankards. Mindful of these interests, we decided to give him a solid silver beer tankard, engraved with all our signatures, as a farewell gift from his fellow officers. Since the suggestion was mine, I was charged with its implementation and, as often happens to the banker, the kitty fell seriously short, bearing out the old army adage, 'never volunteer'. However, Rawlins had been good to me and if this gift went even a little way towards making him feel appreciated, my loss was worth every penny.

In view of Swaziland's impending restoration of national sovereignty, three of the Districts were given traditional Swazi names. Pigg's Peak became 'Hhohho' and Hlatikulu 'Shiselweni', both named after Royal Kraals; and Stegi District was to be called 'Lubombo' after the mountain range, which formed the District's eastern boundary. Manzini ,'by the waterside', had already been changed from the Afrikaans 'Bremersdorp' some years earlier and its relatively new Swazi name was retained.

Moves to abandon old attitudes were mildly nudged forward by the visit of a senior UN official, a Mr Amachree, the Secretary of the UN Committee of 17 (Colonialism). He was a charming and very sensible Nigerian QC with a lawyer's sharp mind. Being both an African and from the UN, he could say things to 'the politicians' as well as to the Swazi National Council which they would never accept from government officials. I had the interesting task of preparing a paper for him on Swaziland's economic dependence on South Africa and I enjoyed helping take him out and about.

A letter written home at this time bears out Pope's pronouncement that 'gentle dullness ever loves a joke'. In an effort to enliven the dullness of my reports on my life as PS I included a joke that was going the rounds in Mbabane. An international prize was offered for a book about elephants. An Englishman submitted, *Shooting Elephants in Africa*; a Frenchman offered *The Love Life of Elephants*; and a Pole sent in *Elephants and the Polish Question*. Perhaps humour has moved on a little since that joke seemed so funny; but in those days before the spawning of political correctness, jokes about other nationalities were much in vogue. The Poles had long been the butt of German humour, like the Belgians at the hands of the French; Scots were forever the subjects of jokes by the English, usually concerning their alleged tight-fistedness and everyone had a go at the Irish.

So relaxed was the general attitude to racial stereotyping that Jo Grimond, Leader of the Liberal Party and MP for Orkney and Shetland, was able to pronounce and get away with his famous dictum about the Scots being, "next to the Poles, the most politically incompetent people on earth".

At last, 'the gentle dullness' of my life as PS was at an end. Huw Jones came back from leave and I was delighted to hand over the Private Office. Life would be a great deal more fulfilling back in the District Administration.

Not long after I moved to the Mbabane District Office the Marwicks started preparing to leave. They gave an excellent twenty-first birthday dance for their daughter Tessa, who was at Cape Town University, and the government service laid on a grand farewell party for them two days later.

In contrast to these two happy occasions, Sir Brian's leave-taking from the Ngwenyama was marred by bitterness. Hilda Kuper described the occasion as follows: "Before Marwick's return to England for his next appointment, Sobhuza invited him and his wife to Masundwini for a formal farewell. It was a small gathering – senior civil servants, a handful of old friends, and a few representatives of the Swazi National Council. Sobhuza did not know that Sir Brian had prepared a formal speech criticising the King for entering politics. On arrival Sir Brian handed a copy to the Ngwenyama who, when he had absorbed the contents, asked Sir Brian not to deliver it. But it was already in the hands of the Press. In it Sir Brian stated that the developments in economic, health and other fields 'owed little or nothing to the Swazi National Council, which for the most part was content to contemplate the imagined wrongs of the past and to be critical of the government's efforts to bring progress and stability to the people of Swaziland . . . I leave Swaziland dissatisfied with the results of my efforts to produce leaders amongst the Swazi people capable of supporting their King with sound, objective and fearless advice, or capable of removing from his shoulders the heavy burden which he has carried for so long', (*Times of Swaziland*, 24 April 1964).

Sobhuza made a short speech regretting that their long association should have such an unhappy end, but wishing him and his family well in the future. Though Sir Brian did not read his carefully written speech, he expressed its substance spontaneously and angrily to the distress of most of those present. This was not the occasion for public denunciation, it violated a fundamental code of Swazi manners which he, more than any other white should have appreciated. The Swazis, in particular, felt wounded and insulted by someone they had once trusted. The tea provided by the King was drunk perfunctorily and without pleasure. And the guests left silently and sadly."

It says much for Sobhuza's magnanimity that Sir Brian and Lady Marwick were invited to the Independence Celebrations in 1968 as the King's special guests.

Chapter 11

# On Familiar Ground Again

It felt good to be back in the Mbabane District Office where I had started twenty months earlier. Now, however, it was a stand-alone post and although I was responsible to Julian Faux up in Pigg's Peak, to a large extent I could set my own tone and do things in my own way. The staff were mostly good people and I was pleased that Mnt Makhungu Dlamini was still there as Chief Clerk. I liked him and his position in the royal hierarchy gave him an influence far beyond his government service job description.

The main change since I last worked in the Mbabane District Office had been the creation of Mbabane Town Council, with an office beside mine. It was independent of the District Administration, although we had to liaise over a variety of matters where our roles overlapped.

The Town Council's remit did not include the Msunduza Township, which was where most of the Africans lived. This now had an elected Advisory Committee, with whom I had to work. Its members were mostly relatively young and all were NNLC activists or sympathisers, for Msunduza was the party's main stronghold. At our first meeting they revealed a kneejerk antagonism to me and to all that my position represented. This hostility was soon exacerbated by the Town Council's announcement that most of the roads serving the mainly European areas of Mbabane would be tarmacked. I knew from experience that some of the dirt roads were very difficult in wet weather. Two months previously I and my house guests, one of whom was an elderly lady, had to walk one and a half miles through mud and torrential rain after our two cars slithered off the road on a hill following a major downpour while we had been at dinner in central Mbabane.

The Town Council had every right to use some of their income from rates to make life easier for their ratepayers. However, members of the Msunduza Committee saw things differently. To them the suburban road improvement programme typified the way the European dominated administration looked after its own, less than two thousand of them, while neglecting the six thousand or so Africans who lived in Msunduza with no tarred roads whatsoever nor, indeed, any other facilities.

It was little use for me to try to point out that the roads programme was being paid for from the rates (people in Msunduza paid no rates) nor that the few Africans who were senior or wealthy enough to have government or privately owned houses on the roads in question would benefit from the tarring programme along with their European neighbours. To most Msunduza residents it was simply a black and white issue.

By the time of the next Msunduza Committee meeting the members had pumped up their feelings of outrage and they sounded off in the fashion one would expect. When they had all had their say I briefly mentioned the matter of rates and then said that, basically, I agreed with them. They had better record a motion outlining their viewpoint and I would see what could be done. Next day, armed with a copy of the minutes of the meeting, I wrote to the Director of Public Works requesting that the road from Mbabane up the hill to Msunduza and then through the centre of the township be tarred at the same time as the suburban roads in Mbabane. The letter was copied to the Chief Secretary, the Secretary for Finance and Development, the Secretary for Local Government and Administration and, of course, to Julian Faux, my DC, with whom I had discussed how I wished to handle the matter. These copies were accompanied by a confidential memo, saying that if something could not be done along the lines of my request I could not warrant continuing law and order in the capital.

Good to be out in district work again.

Athel Long, the Chief Secretary, sent for me and asked me to explain myself. I did so and he listened carefully, finally conceding that I probably had a point and that we could not risk riots just before the territory's first elections. I also suggested that while we were about it we ought to replace the public toilet block in the centre of Msunduza, which was a health hazard, as well as an affront to human dignity. These toilets were ash based with no running water and offered no privacy to the people who used them, oozing raw sewage down the township's main street. This request was also conceded. I was then able, at a hastily convened meeting of the Msunduza Advisory Committee, to tell them that the government had agreed to their request for a tarred road and if they wanted a new public toilet block they just had to ask. I had learned in National Service that the best way of dealing with people who felt aggrieved was, somehow or other, to give them a sense of self-respect. It was the same with the representatives of the people of Msunduza. Their attitude changed as soon as they felt they could achieve something. Beneath all their political posturing they were grand chaps, hard working and progressive, and we developed a happy and largely fruitful relationship.

Meanwhile, I was coming up in the world. As DO Mbabane I now had a telephone in my bungalow. It was just as well for, with elections looming, I was out in the District from dawn to dusk, trying to explain the electoral process. The only time people could get hold of me was early in the morning, or late at night, at home. I was aiming, through a series of meetings, to explain or oversee the explanation of the voting procedure to at least half the total number of registered voters in my patch, covering all the polling divisions. At the halfway stage we had addressed 23% and were hoping for larger attendances as the election grew closer, to bring the total attendance to over 50%.

On May 12th, however, I was not out in the field for that was the day the new Queen's Commissioner, Francis Loyd, arrived. I had spent much of the previous day trying to persuade the NNLC leaders that it was not in their best interests to disrupt the Swearing-In ceremony. I think it was more a lack of enthusiasm on the part of their supporters that caused them to abandon any such plans, rather than my persuasiveness. Then, an hour or two before the swearing in I was told that Huw Jones had been taken to hospital with pleurisy and I was to stand in for him as Private Secretary, both for the ceremony and for the subsequent reception at Government House. This involved doing the introductions in the line-up. I have never been good at names, but as the guest list was more or less the same great and good who had come to Government House receptions during my time as Sir Brian's PS, I did not anticipate too many problems. The introductions were going fine until I was suddenly confronted by a woman I had never seen before in my life. Of this I was certain because her appearance, for a forty-year-old or so, was stunning, straight out of the pages of *Vogue South Africa*.

This was not a normal sight in Mbabane and I would not have forgotten such a person. Her shining hair was immaculately cut and she wore just the right amount of very modern make-up and a stylish dress, set off by the latest fashion in high heels. I had to ask her name. She looked surprised and told me. She was the Deputy Director of one of the government departments, but she had been completely transformed by what today is known as a 'makeover' (including a change of hair colour, style and length) so as to make herself unrecognisable. I apologised, saying something banal about being overcome by the whole palaver into which I had been thrust at the last moment. Apart from this faux pas I think the occasion went quite well. Our new Queen's Commissioner and his lady made a good impression. Mr Loyd was of medium height, dapper and alert and Mrs Loyd had that understated look and slight shyness which goes down very well in the county scene in the UK. (In fact she had grown up in Kenya.)

Mr Loyd had obviously been well briefed and asked pertinent questions. In the case of one particular member of the administration he instructed me to point him out well in advance of his reaching the head of the line-up. I speculated whether this particular officer was being sized up for promotion or downgrading! I ended the day feeling that Mr Loyd would bring a new style and new energy to the role of Queen's Commissioner and his wife

The new Queen's Commissioner and his wife, Mr and Mrs Francis Loyd, later Sir Frank Loyd and Lady Loyd.

*(Photo courtesy of Swaziland Administration, 1964)*

did not look the sort to surround herself with a coterie of favourites. In the course of the function I had to answer all sorts of questions from HE about people and events; it was good to have someone in that position who was so enquiring and had not arrived with his mind made up, with fixed ideas and opinions.

I was also relieved that the day had passed without disturbance or any additions to the number of NNLC activists in the Mbabane gaol. We already had one high profile guest there, none other than the charismatic, but wayward, Prince Dumisa Dlamini, who had caused so many problems the previous year. He was now serving a gaol sentence for inciting intimidation. He had that languid charm, which could change in an instant to frenzied activity, which a few years later so characterised Mick Jagger in his heyday. I had a sneaking admiration for him, not only because of his style, but particularly because of a discovery made a few days before the end of my time as Private Secretary. It had been revealed that Dumisa, in his prison cell, was regularly receiving a copy of the territory's 'top secret' Monthly Security Report! Furthermore, he was getting it about half an hour earlier than the Queen's Commissioner and the Chief Secretary!! It transpired that a middle-aged lady secretary sent out by the Colonial Office to join HE's Private Office, who was responsible for the duplicating and distribution of the report, was in the habit of accepting help from one of the Secretariat messengers. This charming young man, whose assistance the rather smug secretary accepted gratefully, had perfected the art of running off an extra copy of anything he thought might be interesting and was slipping the stuff down to Dumisa in the gaol. Thanks to Dumisa having masterminded this ruse, which was doubtless one of the tricks he had learned from his communist friends up in Dar-es-Salaam, the secretary was left with egg on her face. Anyone who could achieve that won my admiration!

On my first Mbabane gaol inspection I gave Dumisa a copy of Proust's *A la Recherche du Temps Perdu*, translated as 'Chronicles of Wasted Time', suggesting it might compensate for the recent ending of his regular supply of reading matter. He took the joke well and we were able to maintain a fairly light-hearted relationship thereafter – e.g. I, in my office, "Good morning Mntwanenkos, have you come to give me my marching orders?" He, "Not today Nkos,' but the time will come." "Not today then, that's a relief, so what can I do for you?" etc. A few years later, seeing the way the wind was blowing, Dumisa reached an accommodation with the Ngwenyama, abjectly asking his pardon. This was granted, but Dumisa could never keep out of trouble for long and his potential remained unfulfilled. Back in 1964 I had no illusions, however, that had the opportunity arisen, just as easily as joke with me, he could have given me twenty-four hours to leave the country or even had me strung up from a Marula tree.

Around this time Diana Simkin was safely delivered of a son and I was invited down to Goedegegun by Peter to inspect the newly arrived Michael Simkin, soon to become my godson. Now, forty years on, Michael is a highly successful maker of documentary films, with a lovely family of his own. As Diana had not yet been released from hospital, Marcella, her delightful sister, was running the house. She had come over from Argentina to help Diana in the weeks after the birth, but travelled early enough to have a good look at South Africa and Swaziland beforehand. For those of us who had come from the UK our first glimpse of African poverty, whether in South Africa or Swaziland, had been a considerable shock. Marcella, however, observed that the most startling examples of poverty she encountered were as nothing compared to what was commonplace back home in Argentina. The same went for malnutrition and even more so for disease. My father had made much the same comment with regard to what he had seen in rural districts of Southern Italy during the war.

Certainly, in the 1960s, if not now, you had to try pretty hard to be destitute and malnourished in fertile and well-watered little Swaziland where, if a grain of maize fell to the ground, it took root and grew; or if you sat under a tree its fruit dropped into your lap and your cattle, sheep and goats could usually scavenge enough to eat without any effort on your part. Into this rural idyll we were trying to inject modern methods of animal and crop husbandry, to develop a manufacturing and cash economy; and now we were seeking to establish the principles of democratic government. Why on earth, one might ask, were we doing all this and not leaving Swaziland to its old charming ways? The answer was simple. We could not let Swaziland become a vacuum. If it did not develop in pace with its larger neighbours they would, in due course, swallow it up and the gentle proud Swazis would become serfs in their own land. It was, after all, for this cause that the Swazi people had originally petitioned the British for protection and if we were to be criticised, it should be for too laissez-faire an approach to the first fifty years of our administration.

While I was down at Goedgegun inspecting young Michael they had a major veld fire, which was efficiently controlled and, through the technique of back-burning, eventually extinguished by the local prisoners. Not for the first time I wondered how the territory would cope if ever there was a fall in the crime rate or, worse still, if the gaols, instead of being peopled by traditional sorts of criminals, capable men who could turn their hand to anything, imprisoned for murder, brawling, cattle theft or other warrior-like activities, were, instead, filled by loads of tsotsis, effete city slickers, the product of the creeping westernisation of Swazi life, shifty types whose specialities were burglary, fraud, falsification of accounts, peddling narcotics or passing off stolen goods and who could not be trusted to make a decent job of any sort of work; if those sorts of people were to fill the gaols, how then could the place be kept running efficiently?

Back in Mbabane after a good weekend in Goedgegun I was again busy with election preparations and all the routine tasks that had to be fitted in round the edges. Additionally, there was the Queen's Birthday Parade to organise. Previously this task had fallen to the DC, Mbabane; but now that Mbabane District had been absorbed into the new Hhohho District and the DC was forty miles away in Pigg's Peak, the organisation of the parade fell to the DO Mbabane, i.e. to me. The task was not intrinsically difficult; what made it tricky was the variety of people on whom one had to rely. In the event, it all passed off well, rather better, I gathered, than some previous years and Mr Loyd had kind words to say about the organisation – changed times! There was one minor hitch and very nearly a major one too. The minor hitch was typical of Africa. At the height of the parade, when two thousand Swazi warriors in their finery, the boy scouts and girl guides and a detachment of be-medalled war veterans were all drawn up in revue order and the police band was playing, a stately Swazi lady in her working clothes with a huge bundle of firewood perched atop a folded blanket on her head, without hesitation, deviation or a hint of awkwardness, walked through the middle of the whole parade with her two cross-lurcher dogs at her heels. She presumably did this trip every day as part of her routine. No one moved a muscle to deter her; it was a reminder of the unchanging pace of the old Africa and I think people enjoyed the spectacle. That was the minor hitch.

The narrowly avoided major snarl-up involved the seating plan. This was something of a nightmare, as one had to make decisions about precedence and some people became very upset on such occasions if their status, or more frequently that of their husbands (for it was often the wives who were most touchy in these matters) was not recognised to the minutest degree by the position in which they were seated. I had sought to achieve a seating plan that put everyone in the correct place. People's names were typed in a carefully worked out order one beneath the other, on a long narrow strip. The idea was that the person marking the chairs started at the left hand end of the front row, cut off the top name on the list and stuck it to the seat, similarly the second name on the seat second from the left and so on until the end of the front row. He then continued with the second row, right to left, the third row left to right, etc. Carried out systematically, this procedure meant that with the sticking of the last name on the last chair of the last row, everyone on the guest list, from the Queen's Commissioner and his lady to the head teacher of the smallest primary school, would be seated in accordance with protocol. I thought the plan bomb-proof and left the office staff to label the chairs while I went to change into my 'ice cream suit', the white formal Colonial Service dress uniform, complete with gilt embroidered epaulettes and polished buttons and, of course, the solar topi and the ceremonial sword (the latter something of a hazard when getting in and out of a car).

When I came back thus attired expecting to find all the chairs correctly labelled, there was a circle of disturbed looking office staff and their friends surrounding a mound of name slips all jumbled up on the grass. Instead of fixing the slips as they went along, they had first cut all the names off the strips and then realised, too late, that they had created a random pyramid of name slips with not a clue as to which should go where! The simple methodical plan was out of the window. Time was running out so I simply dished out handfuls of name slips to the staff with rough directions where to put them, making sure that the major figures were seated in their rightful places. We were just ready in time before people started arriving. There were no complaints about breaches of protocol or, at least, not to me; and this time I managed to recognise the lady deputy director of department in her new hairstyle and finery, whom I had risked offending at the Government House reception a few days before!

The previous year, following the parade, some of the younger warriors, (the 'Malindzane' - my regiment) had gone off and started making trouble

A Warrior on the march.

in the town; this had been the beginning of the disturbances that led to the Gordon Highlanders being flown in from Kenya. This year there was no such aftermath, which was just as well with two thousand warriors on parade.

The territory's first elections were duly held under strict government surveillance with police and troops standing by. Inanimate symbols were used on the ballot papers to identify the candidates (no animals this time, unlike the earlier battle of the Lion and the Reindeer) and voting was done by using a nail (which was secured to the booth by a string) to spear a hole in the image of the voter's chosen candidate. The procedure caused a new term to be added to the Swazi language – *Ukuhlaba* – literally 'to stab', acquired a secondary meaning – 'to vote' and the term is used to this day.

We had about 2000 Swazi Warriors on parade for the
Queen's Birthday (1964).

In our training exercises during the run-up period we had used mock polling booths and ballot papers and we had stressed the need for people to identify and remember the names and particularly the symbols of their chosen candidates. On my rounds on polling day I came across a voter who clearly had not absorbed the message. I was asked by the polling officer what to do about one old lady who had been in the voting booth for over twenty minutes. She did not appear to be ill, but she showed no signs of coming out. I enquired of her if anything was amiss. She replied, "It hasn't come." "What hasn't come?" I asked. "The voice from the sky telling me who to vote for."

The election passed off peacefully and with good humour all round. The final figures showed that 60% of Europeans and 85% of Swazis who were registered to vote had done so. The results provided a landslide victory for the Imbokodvo, the King's party, both on the National roll as well as for their four sponsored candidates on the European roll. On the National roll the Imbokodvo took 85% of the vote, the NNLC 12.3% and the moderate, Swaziland Democratic Party (SDP) 1.4%. The two branches of the Swaziland Progressive party (SPP) (Nquku and Maseko) each had under 0.5%. The defeated parties tried to have the results reversed through a court action: but their suit was thrown out for lack of evidence. In the final outcome, therefore, even when the nominated members were added in, the Imbokodvo dominated the Legislative Council by a high majority.

It had been a hard-working ten weeks and I was ready for a little light relief. This was to come from an unexpected quarter.

Chapter 12

# Encounters

Not long after Julian and I had played our respective parts in organising Swaziland's first, tentative steps towards parliamentary government we became the beneficiaries of a by-product of the centuries old British parliamentary process and were able to cash in on an expenses-paid jaunt, thanks to the Commonwealth Parliamentary Association. I first showed an interest in a visit of a delegation of four Westminster parliamentarians when I learned that their itinerary included a two-day trip to the Kruger National Park in the Transvaal. Luckily the authorities approved my presumptuous suggestion that my knowledge of African wild life and the Kruger topography (which they accepted at my own estimation) qualified me to accompany Julian as co-host, guide and chauffeur to the party, for a trip that involved two days game watching in the Kruger, followed by a day visiting various commercial and industrial concerns in the Hhohho District, en route to their stay at Government House.

*Who's Who* provided some clues about the four members of the delegation, as follows: (1) Leader of the delegation – Cdr Sir Douglas Marshall RNVR, MP for Bodmin since 1945, interests shooting and fishing, member Royal Fowey Yacht Club, twice married, director of some twenty companies – Conservative. (2) John Mackie, educated at

Aberdeen Grammar School, farmer North East Scotland and Norfolk/Suffolk, MP Enfield East, married - Labour. (3) Dr Patrick Duffy, Lecturer, Department of Extra-mural studies Leeds University, Naval Officer during the war, bachelor, MP Colne Valley - Labour. Finally there was (4) The Lord Somers, 8th Baron, professional musician, sometime second music master Westonbirt and sometime music master Epsom College, interests music.

Number (4) put one in mind of Elspeth Huxley's amusing novel The *Merry Hippo* about a Royal Commission sent to the mythical Protectorate of Hapana and of the Deputy Leader of the Commission, Lord Bagpuize, an authority on Norfolk New Spot pigs, who had been put on the delegation by mistake, owing to the similarity of his name with someone else's when heard over a long distance telephone.

On our arrival at the Embassy in Pretoria to collect them, our prospective charges were still at lunch with the Ambassador, having been held up by Immigration at the airport. The immediate thought was that 'Lord Bagpuize' must have lost his passport, but apparently the problem had been the absence of the Chief Immigration Officer who had been at another airport. Presumably, in the jumpy atmosphere of South Africa at the time, no immigration official would take the risk of admitting four members of the dreaded British Parliament without the approval of the head of the service. The delay gave Julian and me a chance to study the delegates' luggage. Sir Douglas had large numbers of heavy leather suitcases, fairly well-travelled, middle- aged cameras and binoculars, a navy raincoat by Gieves and a panama hat; Mackie's luggage was mainly airline zip bags; Duffy's was sparse, but he seemed to have collected an unconscionable amount of literature and handouts on the trip so far, all bundled together with string. Lord Somers' impedimenta included *Roberts' Birds of South Africa*, a Kodak instamatic camera and a vast, crudely carved polished wood beast with a long neck, plaintive eyes and huge ears.

The doors opened and the delegation emerged. Sir Hugh Stephenson, the Ambassador, made effusive remarks that he would have asked us to lunch if he had known when we were coming, or thought, or something. (It was just as well we had not been invited, as it turned out, because when I had filled up with petrol on arrival in Pretoria I discovered that the fuel filler pipe to the petrol tank had sprung a leak which must have developed during the long and, in parts, dusty and bumpy drive from Swaziland that morning. I had spent the lunch hour having the pipe replaced and the whole car, plus my own luggage, fumigated).

The Ambassador introduced us. Sir Douglas had straight, shortish, grey hair, a small cherubic face set on a thick neck and one of those bodies which taper outwards, downwards, whether looked at frontways or sideways. His clothes were rather crumpled and he wore a Royal Fowey Yacht Club tie. Mackie was a big man, fifty-five or so, one of those socialists who tried to look like a Tory – suede shoes, cavalry twill trousers, fawn waistcoat and russet sports jacket. The appearance of Patrick Duffy was unremarkable; he was a small and ill-looking man, younger than the rest, whose clothes lacked any particular colour or cut. Somers was immediately distinguishable as he was basically the human lookalike of his carved animal – a tall spare figure in a grey striped suit, with the beast's long thin neck and vacant stare. I never could quite make him out. He was vague and charming, but from time to time he volunteered remarks, humbly and almost apologetically delivered, of considerable perspicacity. I suspect his ilk were more common among the leisured classes of the eighteenth and nineteenth centuries, people who had the time to work out original patterns of thought, thanks to being comfortably removed from the pressures of career or financial necessity. That notwithstanding, he shortly afterwards became Professor of Composition and Theory at the Royal College of Music, a post he held for ten years, not retiring until he was seventy.

From the start our travelling arrangements followed a set sequence. Julian and I took two delegates apiece; after two hours we would stop and change over so that, during every six hour period each delegate spent two hours travelling with each of the others. After the first switchover a remarkably constant pattern emerged. For the first hour after the change the new pairing would discuss how delighted they were to be shot of their previous companions and they swapped stories of the ways said previous travelling companions had managed to irritate them and how badly they had behaved. These exchanges created a certain conviviality within the pairings; but then they started to rub each other up the wrong way, becoming increasingly tetchy and sometimes downright aggressive. By the time we reached the last half hour before the next changeover, each pair had more or less reached verbal exhaustion and they started to disengage their locked antlers and withdraw into sullen silence, sometimes feigning interest in the flora and fauna they had allegedly come to see. To be fair, Somers should not be included in this stricture. He was only mildly critical of his companions and he had a genuine interest in the natural world. Come changeover time each pair would separate with obvious relief and the whole pattern would be played out all over again.

The intensity of these verbal encounters varied with the pairings. Sir Douglas and Mackie clearly disliked each other. Maxwell variously described Mackie as "A four letter fellow," "a farmer without a dog," (i.e. someone who farmed at one remove from his crops and his stock) and "a socialist who inherited his farm and then shirked out of the war to make his fortune".

Mackie baited Sir Douglas with complaints about the iniquity of successive Conservative governments and he had a particular bee in his bonnet that the Tories had failed to tackle the land tenure problem in our African colonies because of Tory prejudice in favour of any sort of aristocracy. Although I thought at the time that he was barking up the wrong tree, over the years I have come to consider that John Mackie had a point. Allowing hereditary chiefs to control the allocation of land, with the power to take it away from one person and reallocate it to another or appropriate it for themselves or their own families was the strongest disincentive to the emergence of a rural African middle class. A progressive farmer might invest money and effort in irrigating, fencing and fertilising his land, and then find that his tenure was rescinded and he was given, instead, some barren rocky outcrop miles from the nearest road or river. What progressive farmers needed was officially recognised long leases so that they could count on security of tenure for the duration of the lease and could plan accordingly. Conversely, European settlers, by being granted freehold tenure, had too long a right to their land. If, instead of freeholds European settlers had been granted protected leases, long enough to make it worthwhile developing the land, then perhaps we would not have today's problems of African land-hunger, resulting after independence in white settlers having their farms (as they consider it) stolen from them by the state. Leasehold tenure would have accorded with the traditional African view of land, that it is vested in the people and inalienable. As most Africans view it (the other side of the stolen land argument) freehold tenure is nothing more than land theft in the past. It is a huge, almost intractable problem which, in truth, has only really arisen because of the benefits brought by white rule – law and order, medical care and eradication of disease, which have allowed the African population to grow to levels which were unimaginable when the original white settlers moved onto empty land.

Patrick Duffy flew off the handle not so much on doctrinaire questions, but when he was in some way inconvenienced or when matters were not working out to his personal satisfaction. He was given to illogical outbursts brought on, perhaps, by stomach trouble. That notwithstanding, he was well received wherever we went and his observations were acute. He was younger than the rest, but did not look as if he would make old bones. Appearances were deceptive. He went on to have an excellent parliamentary career, earning a Knighthood for his efforts and continuing in the House of Commons until the age of seventy-two, and he lived into his eighties.

Lord Somers was different from the others. They were men of action. One could easily imagine Sir Douglas commanding a wartime destroyer and running a tight ship (perhaps a shade too tight with much attention to form and detail). Patrick Duffy had not only been in the Navy for the duration of the war, but the Fleet Air Arm to boot. Mackie was obviously a most able agriculturalist on top of his achievements at Westminster. Somers, however, was cast in a different mould, so it was not surprising that the others tended to use him as the butt of their humour. He was the one who would have gained most from the time in the Kruger, the only one who was really interested when I pointed out a bird or a beast; and he made frequent use of his copy of *Birds of South Africa.*

If I had to be shipwrecked on a desert island and was offered my pick of the delegation for my 'Man Friday' I think I would have chosen the 8th Baron, fully accepting that I would have to catch the fish and build the shelter and that when, at last, the ship arrived to rescue us, he would be somewhere in the interior chasing butterflies and we would be delayed until he reappeared; but I think he would have kept me sane.

Such was our frolic in the Kruger Park at the British taxpayer's expense. Three days of this sort of thing (including the day in Hhohho District) was long enough for Julian and myself. The Alice in Wonderland atmosphere only lasted so long before palling. If this was the case for us, how about Sir Douglas? This was his seventeenth CPA trip since 1945, almost one a year. I suppose it was a good way of having a free holiday, breaking up the tedium of life on the backbenches, but he must have tired of such jaunts, hence, perhaps, his tetchiness with his colleagues.

When it came to tetchiness, however, Sir Douglas was not in the same league as another aggressive male I was to encounter a few days later, an encounter I was lucky to survive. There was a very fine cock ostrich in the Mlilwane Game Reserve. This bird had gained a reputation for hostility to anyone who ventured too close to his harem. I wanted to take some close-up pictures of him and, as is often the way when someone has set his mind on something, I rather discounted the warnings.

The pictures were not just for my own amusement. The reserve, down the hill from Mbabane, was in my patch and I tried to make a point of knowing what was going on there, the better to advance the reserve's case to the neighbouring chiefs and their people, hoping to help them regard it as a resource for the whole country and a reminder of their heritage rather than a source of free meat for anyone wanting to try their hand at a spot of poaching. There was a job to be done in educating people, at all levels, that game should be cherished as a national resource and that people like Ted Reilly and his wife, the owners, who were prepared to put their own money into game conservation with no financial help from government, were to be valued and encouraged. The Reillys' public relations amongst the Swazis were excellent; but the administration had to play its part too. Not only should I know what was going on at Mlilwane, it was helpful to have photographs to illustrate what I was saying – hence my quest for pictures of the big ostrich.

Zebras at full gallop through the long summer grass of Mlilwane.

In the space of a couple of hours on a Sunday afternoon I saw zebra, kudu, red and grey duiker, impala, wildebeest, waterbuck, ostriches and springbok and I was lucky to see a demonstration of the latter's extraordinary behaviour which the South Africans call *pronking*. While running at full pelt a herd of springbok will suddenly break into a routine of interspersing every few strides with great vertical leaps into the air, a sort of jack-in-the-box action, all accomplished without slowdown or loss of rhythm, managing to touch their toes together in mid-air like a ballet dancer doing an entrechat but, in their case it is a four-footed movement rather than two. One wants to laugh aloud in amazement or at least shout 'Bravo!' like an appreciative audience at Covent Garden. Springbok pelts make very fine fireside rugs; seeing a herd of them in all their glory puts one right off the idea.

The ostrich that was nearly my nemesis.

After a while I espied the big cock ostrich, strutting about amongst his hens. I selected my camera equipment, stepped quietly out of the car and approached him slowly, taking care not to get behind him, for I knew about ostriches having a savage kick. He started to run towards me, allowing me two action shots. He then stopped in front of me, giving me the opportunity every wildlife photographer craves, the chance to fill the viewfinder with his subject without the aid of a telephoto lens. I had the camera up to my eye, focusing on his head and beak, still conscious that I was safely in front of him, when he made an extraordinary 'phut' noise. The same instant I felt a vicious punch in my kidneys. I had got it wrong – ostriches kicked *forwards*!

A second later there was another 'phut' and a kick in the stomach, which sent me spinning to the ground. I was extraordinarily fortunate; after the second kick the ostrich also sank to the ground with his knees bent, performing a swaying victory display, his wings spread out with the tips pointing downwards, waving from side to side and round and round like a swirling dervish. This gave me the chance to high tail it to the car. Once there I discovered that my light meter was in smithereens; it had taken the full force of the first kick and my Bolex cine camera, in its stout, ancient leather pouch round my waist had absorbed much of the force of the second kick. My equipment, but fortunately not my Leica, had taken a hammering, leaving me relatively unscathed. Had either kick landed directly instead of being deflected by my camera equipment, I would have been in a very bad way. Ted Reilly told me that ostriches, by virtue of the large single claws on their feet, are well able to disembowel a man with just one kick. A few days earlier, apparently, this same bird had kicked straight through the door of a new Mercedes. My urine ran red for three days and I had major bruises, but I suffered no long-term damage. It was, indeed, a lucky escape. Apart from anything else, whereas being killed by a lion might, in some quarters, be deemed mildly heroic, being killed by an ostrich could never be construed as anything but comical.

My escapade with the ostrich prompted Ted Reilly to tell me of another amateur photographer who, some months earlier, had also left his brains behind when he went off to take wildlife pictures. His particular quarry were the lesser and greater flamingos nesting on one of the salt pans in the Serengeti, in East Africa. He waded out and was having a wonderful time shooting away, surrounded by thousands of flamingos tracing extraordinary patterns in the air, often reflected in the water, when he started to notice irritation in his legs, caused (as he later learned) by the chemical interaction between the salts in the water and the flamingos' guano. By the time he had driven himself to the nearest hospital he was in a terrible state and, despite treatment, he lost both his legs.

Buffalo – not to be trifled with.

There were various stories about people being killed or injured by buffaloes, usually illustrating the buffalo's cunning. The one that stuck in my memory concerned a fellow up north trying to shoot a buffalo. He thought he was stalking the buffalo; actually it was stalking him. Suddenly it came at him from behind. He just managed to shin up the nearest tree without having time for a shot and dropped his rifle in the process. The tree was too small to give him proper sanctuary. By dint of sitting in the fork of the only two branches strong enough to bear his weight and holding his knees almost up to his chin, he could just keep his legs and feet above the buffalo's reach. The buffalo waited below. It appeared that the hunter eventually fainted from the effort of this prolonged discomfort in the heat of the day, so that his legs dropped down loose. When by an extraordinary chance someone found him, the buffalo was still in attendance and it had licked away the flesh of one of the man's legs right down to the bone. The currency of this and various other buffalo stories meant that most people realised buffaloes had to be treated with extreme caution.

The real old Africa hands were less 'gung-ho' and more aware of the risks lurking alongside the multifarious glories of Africa. Such a one was Major Billy Hull who had been very good to me when I first arrived and who also befriended my parents when they were staying with me in Mbabane. Soon after they left he was struck down by a stroke at the age of eighty-four and lay unconscious in Mbabane hospital for nearly three weeks. People had written him off. The young woman who was his partner in his horse-breeding enterprise sold up all the horses. I went to see him in hospital. He was lying there like a corpse. I held his cold, lifeless hand for a while and thanked him for his kindness to me and my family and then, as I thought, took my last leave. A day or two later, for no apparent reason, he came out of the coma, gradually regained his strength and all his faculties, and before long he was his old self. There was hell to pay over the horses and within six months of his stroke he was driving his car and back in the saddle. A friend of mine had a half-baked theory that every generation born after 1880 was slightly softer than the previous one. People like Billy Hull lent credibility to this proposition.

Jock King, Director of Agriculture
and Billy Hull.

An encounter I was to have in Kenya on my way home on leave several months later pointed the same way. My sailing friend Bill Deverell took me to the Muthaiga Country Club in Nairobi. Whilst we were talking at the bar he drew my attention to an elderly couple sitting by the window. "You see that old chap," he said, "when he was a young man, he fell in love with a girl and asked her father for permission to marry her. "No," replied the father, "you can't." Asked why he was withholding his consent, the father replied, "because you're soft and lack backbone." "Well," said the young man, "if I walk from The Cape to Cairo, will you still consider me soft and lacking backbone?" The father agreed that such an achievement would cause him to revise his opinion, so the young man did his walk and got his girl; there they were, sixty years later, that erstwhile young man and his sweetheart, enjoying a sundowner at the Muthaiga Club, having a few weeks earlier celebrated their diamond wedding anniversary.

In truth, that walk was probably less hazardous when he did it than it would be today, over a hundred years later, for his route would have been mostly through territories under British authority; and law and order was the stock in trade of that rule. Great sections of the continent were not, as today, awash with Kalashnikovs. In 1962 I had the idea of travelling out to Swaziland through Egypt and the Sudan, going up the Nile via Juba and Kosti to Lake Victoria. Perhaps I would be able to divert sufficiently to dally a few days and see the peoples I had read and talked about with Dr Lienhardt: the Nuer, Mandari and, of course, the Dinka. However, the Sudan authorities refused me a visa because of civil unrest and when I tried to plan the trip again for my long leave in early 1965, I was again barred because of civil war, basically the same war which is still raging as I write another forty years on.

As it turned out, I was to enjoy a different distraction on my leave.

One of the orphans at Mlilwane's rescue nursery.

Chapter 13

# Loose Ends

My first tour was coming towards its end and there were a number of initiatives to put to bed before I left for long leave in the UK in January 1965. It was a battle against time. In Africa, fighting such a battle usually means you are on the losing side.

On the national scale, the big event of the period was the opening of the Legislative Council in September 1964. It seemed likely that there would be an NNLC demonstration and I conferred with the police on tactics. Whereas with Frank Loyd's swearing in, four months earlier, it had been possible to suggest to the NNLC leaders that a demonstration was not in their long-term interests, it would have been absurd to use the same arguments about so palpably a political event as the Legco opening. Of course they should be allowed to stage their protest, but they must agree to co-operate with the police so that the conduct of the ceremony was not obstructed and there were no breaches of the peace. When I, a police inspector and small group of constables met the demonstrators at the bridge between Msunduza Township and Mbabane, we were confronted by rather smaller numbers than the crowd which had met Julian Faux at the same spot fifteen months earlier during the strikes and riots. Their leaders agreed to the simple rules we proposed. They marched up the hill to the town centre in a slightly disorganised fashion, singing their jolly political songs, accompanied by the small detachment of police. The day passed off with typical Swazi good humour. Sobhuza did not attend, pleading illness and his speech was read for him. I suspected this was a diplomatic illness and if so it was a wise move on his part. He was keen not to be seen to be too closely connected with the victorious Imbokodvo party, the more easily to be acceptable as future Head of State to the vanquished as well as the victors.

NNLC Protesters at the opening of the new 'Legco'.

Time was running on. A friend in the Secretariat had a poster in his bungalow's loo. It depicted a small boy sitting on his pot and it bore the caption: "The job's not finished till the paperwork is done." I had much more than paperwork to complete before I could go off on leave in January with a clear conscience. There was still no start date for the construction of the new Msunduza road and public toilets. Several of my other projects were also hanging fire. It was one thing to have these works approved; but I wanted to see them underway before I left. Lions do not leave their kill until they are satiated, for fear of hyenas and jackals moving in. There was always the human equivalent of those scavengers on the lookout to snaffle approved funding from projects that they could argue were less urgent than their own pet schemes. So I had to live up to my 'Malindzane' name –'Young man in a hurry'. I was told to learn patience; but some people in Africa became so patient that they were totally ineffective. In a letter home I wrote, "All the forces of Africa seem to be against me – corruption, stupidity, inertia, political exploitation, the PWD (Public Works Department) and the constant enemy, lack of funds to get things done."

Another matter was even more disturbing. The head warden had been attacked in Mlilwane Game Park, stabbed eight times and left for dead. Could this be the start of a new campaign (to a lesser or greater extent politically co-ordinated) aimed at those who worked for European business concerns? The attacker was thought to be a poacher, but we did not know for sure. It raised the question as to how successful we had been in justifying the park to its Swazi neighbours as a resource for the whole nation. I felt a real sense of personal responsibility over this. Perhaps I was being too hard on myself; one of the disadvantages of being a bachelor was the tendency to let disappointments and failures prey upon you. A good wife could tell one to snap out of it and not take oneself so seriously!

Talking about good wives, Diana Simkin, who pretended not to have a clue about anything, took a First and a Third prize in the embroidery classes at the Goedgegun Show. No one knew she could even sew. I had a Second in the photography section with a picture of an impala. Any credit for this should be shared between the impala and Leitz GmbH – impala are the most enchanting creatures and my Leica delivered sharp images.

On my domestic front there were both good and bad developments. Aaron, Abednego's replacement as part-time gardener, was proving both interested and hard working, underlining the extent to which Abednego had been freewheeling; but the excellent Maria, my maid, was off home to have a baby. Swazi attitudes to sex tended to be fairly free and easy, as was to be expected in a society where polygamy was widespread. The Christian teaching of chastity before marriage and fidelity within marriage cut little ice when it was perfectly respectable (and in many circles even socially desirable) for a man to take a second or subsequent wife without regard to the views or feelings of his existing wife or wives. It has to be admitted that many of the Christian churches were casuistic, to say the least, in their attitude towards traditional Swazi morality. Against such a background it is no surprise that teenage Swazi children, as is increasingly the case in the 21st century with their European and American counterparts, regarded sex more or less as a game, although *in theory* they were not meant to go the whole way.

Men, and increasingly women too, when working away from home, felt free to form casual relationships or to use prostitutes even if they had established families back home. No wonder when the AIDS virus hit Southern Africa it had such dire consequences. However, such is the cohesiveness of Swazi society that most illegitimate and orphan children are gathered up into their wider family, usually through the efforts of the grandmothers. This was apparently so in Maria's case for she expected to be back after two months when her mother, not for the first time, would take over the child rearing. Maria's replacement turned out to be a prostitute and lasted less than twenty-four hours. Replacement number two, although adequate, was never in Maria's league. I, and anyone on whom I inflicted my hospitality, counted the weeks until Maria's return.

It was always a pleasure, when out in the District, to visit the local school. There was one I particularly remember, in an inaccessible area I visited about this time during a trip under canvas. It was a three-hundred-pupil primary school in the wild country to the south of Maphalaleni and it seemed the last time an administrative officer had called there had been thirteen years previously. I was therefore something of a curiosity, almost like being a creature from outer space. But we soon established common ground when some of the children noticed my stick, with its tup's horn handle.

I never ceased to be amazed by the rural schools. Despite having negligible facilities and equipment, the teachers were able to generate incredible keenness in the children, who would rise in the dark of the morning to walk, often barefoot, for up to three hours to reach the school where, usually sharing slates and books and sitting on the floor, their eyes bright and in total silence, they would pay rapt attention to their lessons and soak up everything they were taught. I wrote in my notes made at the time, "What a contrast to many of the children one was seeing in UK schools who make a nuisance of themselves, truant when they can and eventually leave, having learnt virtually nothing except a deep pessimism that teaches them to live only for the present."

Our job, as colonial administrators, was to ensure that we left behind systems and attitudes that would allow the bright young generation to flourish and contribute to their new nation. How could we best achieve that end? This was often the subject of our discussion when junior members of the administration came together to chew the fat and put the world to rights. Quite simply, we concluded, our task was to instil self-discipline and idealism in Swaziland's emerging leaders and this could probably only be done by example. Tell people how to do things and they will forget – show them and they will remember (simple *Army Methods of Instruction* practice!). Hopefully, not only would the new leaders follow the good example that had been set by us, but, more importantly the bulk of the population would demand from their leaders the standards which they had come to expect from the British administrators.

So, what sort of an example were we setting? That was a good question. Some people were setting a better example than others. Certainly, tarring the suburban roads in the smart, mainly European parts of Mbabane, while doing nothing about conditions in Msunduza and the other smaller African townships around the capital was an appalling example of a mindset that looked after No 1 and No 1's friends - and to Hell with the less fortunate.

Example was particularly important because, even at the best of times, it was quite hard for Swazis to distinguish between where family duty ended and where corruption began. The duty to kith and kin ranked very high in the Swazi ethos, as in most of Africa. The admirable Dr Sidney Shongwe, on appointment to his post at Hlatikulu Hospital, was inundated by requests from his so-called 'brothers', people with only the most distant ties of kinship, for him to use his influence to secure them employment contracts, preferment etc. He was shocked by the level of this harassment and simply told the supplicants, "I am not your brother. What you ask is impossible, it is corrupt and against the law."

By contrast, for Britishers like myself there was no such dichotomy. Most of us had been imbued from our youth with the belief that corruption of all sorts was abhorrent, irrespective of whether it benefited ourselves or our friends and family. In our 'O' level (as it was then) history studies we had learnt how Warren Hastings, the Governor General of the East India Company, had been impeached before the House of Commons for corruption and we knew the rough outline of his subsequent seven-year trial. In short, for Swazis and other Africans, the issue was clouded by family piety; for a Brit, it was clear as crystal. So when, on the morning I was to hold court in the matter of a liquor licence by a Portuguese café owner and the office messenger brought in a case of cheap *vinho verde* with a card conveying the applicant's compliments, it was a reflex response for me to tell the applicant that because he had tried to bribe me with the case of wine which he might collect as he left, I could not hear his application and was remitting it to the Registrar, who would doubtless deal with it as he thought fit. I think the greasy little man was genuinely shocked at my reaction to 'his kindness'. Later I reflected wryly on how low he had put my price – one case! And *it was not even good wine!* At least Warren Hastings, as he stated in his defence, had been "tempted beyond endurance" and under the circumstances "was astonished at his own moderation".

I think the Portuguese café owner's approach simply reflected that in different places there were different norms, which was actually the essence of Warren Hasting's defence nearly two centuries earlier. Certainly Swaziland was a very different place from Mozambique, or Portuguese East Africa, as it was then called, which was a country of contrasts. Lourenco Marques (and I believe Beira too – though I never knew it) had the feel of a Latin city and it was a joy to go down there for a complete change from Swaziland or South Africa; but there seemed to be no attempt by the Portuguese to improve the lot of the Africans in the colony (although there was no official colour bar) nor, indeed, that of the territory's large Portuguese peasant population. As one drove through rural areas black and white could be seen living side by side, all jumbled up in equal poverty, often intermarried or interbred, many barefoot and in rags.

Whereas we had a fair idea what was happening in South Africa, we had scarcely a clue about Mozambique and had few contacts within the country, official or unofficial. Our police had practically no dealings with their Portuguese opposite numbers even in the border areas. By contrast, there was obviously a dialogue between the Portuguese police force and the South African Special Branch, as I had discovered some weeks previously. The Varcoes and I had agreed to meet for lunch in Lourenco Marques. It was a short journey for them from Stegi. En route I was stopped and put in a police cell at the Portuguese border post and was there for over an hour before I was able to persuade them to phone the duty officer at the Secretariat to confirm my identity. It turned out that the Portuguese police had been tipped off by Pretoria that a radical South African civil rights lawyer was coming their way and the border post officials had decided that I was he.

The Portuguese had no plans for African self-determination in Mozambique. There was the *assimilado* system by which an African, or anyone else who was deemed suitable, could become a sort of 'honorary European'. But this was not what the emerging African middle class wanted. Africans were the majority and their leaders set their hearts on independence. An embryo freedom movement, 'Frelimo', was already established, being largely financed and trained in newly independent Tanzania and activists were starting to trickle through Swaziland en route for guerilla training up north. One day such a group came to my office in Mbabane to announce their presence to me, for they were planning a week's stay in Swaziland before moving up to Tanzania. Amongst them was an artist who had studied in Lisbon on a government scholarship. He had brought some of his paintings with him, hoping to sell them to help meet the group's travelling expenses. His paintings were untypical of African art; their muted colours and economical brushwork evoked, instead, the style of the French Impressionists.

He could probably have had a comfortable and fulfilling life as a painter; but politics is a heady brew and these young people were obviously addicted.

António Salazar would doubtless have claimed that his style of government, which others regarded as dictatorship, best met the needs of Portugal's metropolitan and overseas citizens; but Frelimo and, in the end, even the metropolitan Portuguese decided enough was enough. Although there was a peaceful transition in Portugal, the Frelimo struggle became one of the most bitter and destructive wars in Africa, with fearful atrocities and obliteration of the environment, from which parts of the north of the country, particularly Niassa province, have not yet recovered.

. I wonder if that little group I met in 1964 had any inkling of what suffering their freedom struggle would inflict. I bought one of the artist's paintings. It depicted a gentle African suburban scene and I find it hard to believe that the hand that crafted it could later have been steeped in blood. I suppose in most revolutions the end results turn out very different from the aspirations of the movement's pioneers.

Presumably Athel Long, the Chief Secretary, spoke to Mr Loyd about Msunduza and the latent security risk, not to mention the health and safety issues which it and the other smaller Mbabane townships presented, for, not long after he had arrived, our new Queen's Commissioner asked me to take him round Msunduza. Once he saw the reality of the place for himself, he was quick to realise that this was indeed a serious problem. The facts spoke for themselves. Out of Mbabane's population of 9,000, some 7,000, nearly all Africans but including a few coloureds, lived in the environs of the town on five areas of Crown land, of which Msunduza was by far the largest. A very few people, like Mnt Makhungu Dlamini, whose house was substantial and well built, had freehold title to their plots. A further number had serviced stands on licensed tenure; but the vast majority had moved on to the Crown Land as squatters, putting up makeshift dwellings without services either on their plot or within reasonable reach. Everywhere the situation was deteriorating and we had little means of controlling it. The worst place was Black Msunduza, part of the township, which housed several thousand people. This had no water, roads, electricity or public lavatories. A small stream did double duty as water supply and sewer. Elsewhere the problems were not quite so acute, but throughout the five Crown Land areas public amenities were either non-existent or woefully inadequate.

Squatters' houses.

Mr Loyd's visit brought swift action. The Ministry of Overseas Development was requested to send out a town planner to advise on the Mbabane Crown Lands and I was asked to submit a report on the whole issue to help identify the government's objectives for comprehensive improvement. Before starting on the report itself, I needed to do detailed research. Some of this was illuminating. For instance, I found that all the cubicles in the existing ramshackle public lavatories in Msunduza were so narrow that only the slenderest inhabitants could use them with any ease. All in all, the squatter areas provided a fertile breeding ground for every possible kind of political, social and medical ill health.

My report's recommendations aimed to set up an orderly progression towards acceptable living standards for everyone in the five squatter areas. It would be wise to work through the consent of the local people, I suggested. In Msunduza, at least, the committee could be enlisted to help in obtaining this consent. Much of the work could be done by the people themselves; it would only have lasting value if any new construction was delayed until proper public services were provided, which should be installed by the government as speedily as possible – roads, street lighting, water and sewerage.

Long before in India, Ghandi had identified the changing of people's toilet habits as the key to disease control and thus to civic advancement. It was one thing for people to relieve themselves behind a bush in thinly populated rural areas; in urban situations such conduct was the open sesame to raging epidemics. Therefore what we should plan to provide, first and foremost, was a sufficient number of modern lavatory blocks. Six were proposed, including the one already promised to the Msunduza Committee, which was now about to be started. After the water and sewerage should come the roads and the lighting. Specimen plans for self-build houses were to be provided by the PWD to be used by the people who would be building or commissioning the new houses. All new construction should be under the supervision of sufficient township inspectors who would allocate the new serviced plots and ensure proper control as building progressed. In particular they had to insist that as people moved into their new houses, their old houses and shacks were demolished before they could be reoccupied by people moving in from rural areas. In one or two well-intentioned schemes elsewhere in Africa, squatter-town improvement initiatives had resulted not so much in the upgrading of the townships, as simply in their enlargement. This was the result of there having been no systematic destruction of new house owners' previous shacks, before they became reoccupied.

Ratcheting up people's housing standards demanded discipline on their part and, failing self-discipline, this had to be enforced. The Swazi, as my report rather harshly spelt out, had probably experienced less discipline than practically any other people in Africa. Life had been fairly gentle; *pax Britannica* was administered in a laissez-faire fashion. There was no real pressure on land (to date) and because of the inherent fertility of the soil and plentiful rivers, life for the average rural Swazi was generally not very demanding. It came hard for him when he moved into a town and had to conform to the disciplines necessary when living at close proximity to others.

It was quite an effort to finish the report in good time. But then, shortly before the start of my leave, everything suddenly started to come right. Maria was back, so the household was once more running like clockwork. My *magnum opus* finished, including the costing of its recommendations, which was the most difficult part, I had the time to spend a splendid weekend with the Simkins and Varcoes, complete with their young babies, in Ndumu, the small game reserve at the very north easternmost tip of Natal which the Simkins and I had visited at the start of the year, the domain of the excellent David Pooley. This time we decided to concentrate on watching birds. We saw waders, pelicans and flamingos and all manner of ducks and geese, masses of fish eagles fishing away like fury, yelping with their high pitched cries of "Kow, Kow, Kow-Kow-Kow," lily-trotters (jacanas) messing around in the shallows, large numbers of herons and storks and, in the shoreside vegetation, myriad weaver birds with their woven nests suspended over the water's edge.

When it came to birds, Ndumu more or less threw the book at you. If a bird was in *Roberts' Birds of South Africa*, it was (with obvious exceptions) probably in Ndumu. As for game, like on our previous visit, there were hippos and crocs in profusion and, most notably, nyala – dark striped antelope, stockier and slightly smaller than Kudu, which were rare except in Northern Natal and in the north of the Kruger which we had not encountered on the earlier trip. Once again we were the only visitors, so we had the camp and our friend David to ourselves. And, of course, we had to pay a token visit to David's pride and joy, his white rhinos.

Returning refreshed to Mbabane, I found that the police had caught the poacher who had so nearly killed the head warden in the Mlilwane reserve. It turned out he was not a poacher at all, but a burglar from Mbabane, trying to make good his escape by cutting across the reserve. So it was not a case of the local Swazis having reneged on their undertaking not to use Mlilwane as a handy hunting ground. The warden, happily, had made an amazing recovery from his eight stab wounds and was soon back at work and able to go and talk to the neighbouring Swazis in person. The Swazis have great respect for people whom they regard as having come back from the dead, like Billy Hull a few months earlier; so the whole incident ended up enhancing the head warden's authority and, by association, the reserve's standing as well.

*Easy Rider*, Swazi style.

On the development front work had started on the Maphalaleni road, which would open up the whole valley to vehicular contact with Mbabane. This bode well for marketing irrigated vegetables and other cash crops. As part of the deal the local community was responsible for constructing a causeway over the river, to allow the road to follow an easy gradient right down the valley to the Maphalaleni River's confluence with the Komati. The old chief's brother, Nsambane, was now installed as the area's new chief. He was progressive and his authority was underpinning this endeavour and, apparently, he was offering reasonable security of tenure to members of the newly formed local farmers association.

Besides this road, the tarring of the road up to Msunduza and through the township was under way, as was the construction of the European-style public lavatory block, the forerunner, we hoped, of the five more which should follow if the Mbabane squatter proposals were implemented. In this regard I learned that my report on the Crown Land squatter problem had been approved almost in its entirety and sent, complete with the new Legco's imprimatur, to the Ministry of Overseas Development for them to find the funding.

All of a sudden it felt as if I was being able to make a difference to people's lives. And there was something else to put a smile on my face; I was expecting a visitor.

Chapter 14

# Zelda

It was the summer of 1960; forty-five years on I can still picture her.

On the bank of the Thames at Port Meadow, Oxford, beside a willow, stood this gorgeous girl. Not just beautiful, but stylish too, tall and blonde – more Grace Kelly than Brigitte Bardot in terms of the screen sirens of the time. I later heard her compared to Doris Day, perhaps because of her ready smile, which lit up her face; but Doris Day did not much appeal to me; this girl, instantly and unforgettably, did.

With the girl was Martin Hall, Captain of the Oxford Sailing Team. "John," he called, "come and meet Zelda!" So this was Zelda Garner, Martin's childhood sweetheart, whom he had met when he was fifteen and she thirteen. They had just announced their engagement. "Lucky old Martin," I thought, "talk about being born with a silver spoon in his mouth." Not only had he been blessed with looks (tall, dark and handsome) and wealth (he ran a Mini Cooper, the trendy car of the decade, whereas those of the rest of us who could afford wheels had former delivery vans or ancient Morris Minors). He was also clever (a scholar at Westminster and an exhibitioner at Christ Church, our college). Thus work was no problem for him, neither was the attainment of his half-blue (as sailing was then accorded) for no sooner had he set foot in Oxford than he immediately took a permanent place in the sailing team. His ready charm guaranteed Martin a constant circle of good friends and now he was engaged to marry this lovely girl – "the prettiest girl at the Westminster Ball" as his school matron had described her several years earlier. Matron obviously had a good eye. But it could not have happened to a nicer fellow, as the saying goes, so one could not sustain one's envy for long. It would just have been good if something were left over for the rest of us, especially for me, and especially that girl! However, there did not seem to be any prospects in that regard, and I had to admit they made a handsome couple.

Zelda.

Zelda was at the Guildhall School of Music and Drama, studying acting and stagecraft and when she spoke you realised just how well suited she was for her chosen career. In due course, however, she opted to teach rather than act, as being compatible with family life in a way that acting could never be. But family life did not materialise for her as she expected. After eighteen months the engagement collapsed and Zelda went out to Switzerland to teach drama in an English girls' boarding school, located half way up a mountain in a building that had been a ski hotel before the snow line receded.

With Zelda in Switzerland and me, by this stage, in Swaziland, she became even more of a *princesse lointaine*. I always imagined that she and Martin would come together again, for both of them were devastated at the way their engagement had imploded. Probably they just met too soon.

Martin's sense of devastation obviously healed sooner than Zelda's. While I was at Hlatikulu I learned from *The Times* of his engagement to someone I didn't know. I wrote to Zelda and thereafter over the next eighteen months we conducted a regular correspondence. Our letters generally told each other what we were doing, but they were sometimes enlivened by comments which gave a clue to each other's thoughts and values; occasionally I ventured something vaguely personal: "Was her hair still long and goldenish? And was her face still enlivened by a scattering of freckles around the edges?" I was not rushing my fences, for Zelda was still hurting and grieving. Working up a mountain in Switzerland with just a band of women teachers and the odd middle-aged ski instructor for company probably did not help the situation. Sensibly, after a year's teaching she decided to go off and see the world as an air hostess.

After eighteen months' flying, Zelda had been just about everywhere and was tiring of racketing around. Customarily, on leaving the airline, girls were given a 10% return flight for two people to a destination of their choice. Zelda chose to take her mother to Salisbury in Rhodesia to visit a cousin who had gone out there in the early 1950s. At the end of their holiday, in order to see more of the country, Zelda stayed on to do a term's teaching in Shabani, a mining town west of Bulawayo. I phoned her up and suggested she came down to Swaziland for a visit at the end of her term. To my delight she accepted the invitation.

When the time came, Zelda's long drive to Mbabane was uneventful except for one moment of shock. This came when she was diverted off her route because of road works and lost her way. She stopped to ask an African pedestrian which road to take at a junction and when he lifted his face to answer her question he revealed himself to be an albino with ginger hair, pink skin and pale watering eyes. She had never known such people existed. What worried her was the extent her expression must have betrayed her horror at his appearance.

Despite her detour, Zelda made excellent time and when I came home to the bungalow she had already been effusively welcomed by Jess, the Labrador (fortunately she liked dogs) and given tea and cakes by Maria. Her first sighting of me was of my legs, clad in my khaki colonial shorts, stockings and desert boots, descending the garden steps. Her mother had teased her about this visit, suggesting "This chap John Miller holds a torch for you." But as Zelda told me later (but not that much later) her immediate thoughts on sighting the shorts and the knees was "If Mummy thinks there is anything going to come of this visit, she's way wide of the mark." I had arranged for Zelda to stay with Jack and Meryl Klopper, whom I had known in Hlatikulu, who had now transferred to Mbabane. They were coming to supper. Shorts, knees and colonial stockings notwithstanding, by the time Jack and Meryl arrived Zelda and I were getting on famously, as if we had known each other for years, despite the strange realisation that this was the first time we had ever been alone together in our lives.

I collected Zelda from the Kloppers early each morning. It was the time for registering new voters and people who had failed to register earlier in the year, so I had a full programme going round checking the registration centres most of the week. Zelda came with me. She thus did plenty of Land Rover miles and met masses of Swazis, including one rural chap to whom we memorably gave a lift. As soon as he climbed into the Land Rover it was obvious he had been copiously refreshing himself with Swazi beer in the heat of the day. His sweat reeked to high heaven. It was the worst case of utshwala-induced body odour I ever encountered, but Zelda endured it with good humour. And she continued to look good even in the heat and the dust. Over the next few days she made a considerable impression on the office staff she met, especially Makhungu who, never quite able to rid himself of the 'Bellrigg Castle' fantasy, told me, "You only have to look at her to see she is an aristocrat." Truth be told, Zelda had that rare quality of being able to look totally the part in any surroundings and with all sorts and conditions of people.

We had a night with Peter and Diana, who pronounced Zelda

enchanting; and at the weekend we made a short visit to Lourenco Marques, eating piri piri prawns, bathing in the sea and generally delighting in the Latin atmosphere of the place. On our way home we briefly stalked wildebeest and zebra in the bushveld. High above us were a pair of bataleur eagles working the thermals, their soaring flight matching my soaring spirits. We then drove up the escarpment to have dinner and stay overnight with Jeremy and Wendy Varcoe at Stegi. We found them much obsessed with a large python, which had taken up residence under the stoep and was disinclined to budge. Fortunately they had another guest in the person of the redoubtable Dorothy Mearns, now retired, but for many years the personal secretary to successive resident commissioners. Mike Fairlie had experienced the Mearns' phenomenon at the Secretariat in the 1950s. He described her thus: (*No Time Like the Past*) "an eccentric elf-like spinster of indeterminate age and slight build, with her grey pigtails wound into earphones she had short lived schoolgirl enthusiasms, but remained loyal to all her previous chiefs, whom she adored without exception and had served in one or other of the territories over an unknown number of years." Dorothy counselled Jeremy to let the python be; uncharacteristically he took the proffered advice. 'Do nothing, wait and see,' was not normally his style. I had no fears for Zelda's safety during the night. She was sharing a bedroom with Dorothy and if it came to a confrontation with the python I would have put my money on Dorothy every time! As it turned out, the snake played possum.

On Zelda's last day I had to go down to Lobamba to finalise the seating arrangements for the public part of the last day of the Ncwala. I asked if I could bring Zelda and was surprised to be told I could. We were the only Europeans there. I dealt mainly with A K Hlophe, the Ngwenyama's Private Secretary, by then also a Legco and Exco member. A number of Swazis whom I knew came and talked with us, including a local Isangoma who spoke practically no English. He assumed Zelda was my wife. I told him she was a visitor from the UK. "Well," he replied, "she will be your wife very soon." "What is he saying?" asked Zelda. I thought it would be pushing the pace to answer truthfully, so I told her. "He says he hopes you will enjoy the rest of your visit." "Tell him," she replied, "I'm sure I shall." The Isangoma obviously understood this reply for, without waiting for me to translate, he said to me in siSwati, almost conspiratorially, "You see, she is already on the way to fulfilling what I said will happen." We left him after mutual expressions of goodwill. I very much hoped he had got it right.

It was Maria's day off so we had the house to ourselves that evening and Zelda cooked supper. It was clear that when she left Mbabane next morning it could not be goodbye, only au revoir. So by the time I took her back to the Kloppers that night we had decided to change our individual plans to allow me to spend six days with her in Salisbury in mid-January, en route for Nairobi and the UK.

Apparently after my leave I would be coming back to continue as DO Mbabane. Arrangements had been made for a temporary replacement to keep the office ticking over while I was away. My personal effects were to be stored in one of the bedrooms of my bungalow and the servants should stay in their quarters to look after the place. I made arrangements for them to be paid weekly and this ensured there was someone to whom they could refer if there were any problems. All this was very satisfactory. I loved the job and I found myself reflecting rather wistfully that it would be a very suitable posting for a newly married man; but although I had my hopes, it was still early days on that score.

Three weeks after Zelda's visit to Mbabane my heart leapt when I saw her waiting for me as I came out of the arrivals lounge at Salisbury airport. She was wearing her hair loose around her shoulders the way I liked it and was looking more enchanting than I had ever seen her. We spent the time in the Nyanga mountains south east of Salisbury near the Mozambique border. It was said to be a 'dramatic scenic' area; but the mist was down and it rained practically without intermission. No matter, we enjoyed walking and we liked the rain – a gentle kind rain reminiscent of the West Highlands of Scotland. We were just extraordinarily happy.

It seemed no time at all before my plane was waiting at Salisbury to take me to Nairobi. As I walked out across the tarmac I was kicking myself for not having asked Zelda to marry me. The idiot – why had I left the issue hanging in the air? I have referred much earlier to the way Cupid used an aeroplane to bring Peter and Diana Simkin together and indicated that Cupid would in due course intervene in like fashion on my behalf. Well, it happened in this wise. My plane took off and climbed up into the clear sky above Salisbury. Then, instead of heading northwards, it began to circle the airport. Far below on the runway I saw fire engines and ambulances massing and the Captain came over the tannoy. A light on the control panel was indicating landing gear failure, so we were putting down again at Salisbury. We landed safely and the incident gave me another two days to remedy my earlier omission.

Zelda did not accept my proposal, nor did she refuse me. She was not the sort of girl to come home from Africa and present her parents with a fait accompli. We should go home and meet each other's parents and then she would give me an answer.

So I had to wait; but that, and more besides, is another story!

# The End

# Appendix I

## Swaziland – Some Key Dates and Events
## 1400 – 1982

### 15 / 16th Century

**Dlamini** clan move from Central Africa to an area near Lourenco Marques

### 18th Century

**Ngwane III** leads Swazi to settle near Shiselweni (the south of modern Swaziland)

### 19th Century

**Sobhuza I** (d.1839) avoids confrontation with the Zulus.

**Mswati II** (d.1868) unifies the nation. Starts to grant concessions to Europeans as protection against the nation's enemies.

**Mbandzeni** (d.1889) Concessions run out of hand. Seeks British protection. Refused. British and Transvaal governments jointly guarantee independence of Swaziland.

**Bhunu** (d. 1899) succeeds while a minor. Regency again unsuccessfully seek British protection.

**1894** A Convention, without Swazi assent, transfers administration of Swaziland to the Transvaal, but excluding incorporation.

**1899 Bhunu** dies. **Sobhuza** (d.1982), aged 4 months, chosen to succeed him. Regency. At outbreak of Boer War, Transvaal Government hand over authority to the Swazi Queen Regent.

## 20th Century

**1903** Swaziland becomes British Protectorate.

**1907 Swaziland Concessions Proclamation** return one third of all land concessions to the Swazi Nation. Transvaal Government land becomes Crown Land, but much sold (almost entirely to Europeans) over ensuing thirty years to help balance the territory's budget.

**1909 South Africa Act** provides for eventual transfer of Swaziland, Basutoland and Bechuanaland to South Africa.

**1921 Sobhuza II** installed as King and Ngwenyama.

**1923 Sobhuza** travels to Britain seeking amendment of the Concessions Proclamation – rebuffed.

**1941-5** During **Second World War** nearly 4,000 Swazi serve in British Army in North Africa and Italy.

**1947 George VI** visits Swaziland.

**1953 Sobhuza** attends coronation of Queen Elizabeth II in Westminster Abbey.

**1960** Harold Macmillan's **Wind of Change** speech to South African Parliament.

**1962** Swaziland's Anti-Discrimination Proclamation.

**1961-3** First and Second Swaziland Constitutional Conferences. British Secretary of State imposes a Constitution providing for internal self-government leading to independence. **Protests** by political parties culminating in **strikes** and **intimidation**. 1st Battalion The Gordon Highlanders flown in. Order restored without loss of life. **Sobhuza seeks amendment of Constitution**. When this is refused, conducts his own **Referendum**, where his policies are overwhelmingly endorsed.

**1964 Sobhuza** forms **The Imbokodvo**, a political movement which sweeps the boards in the country's first election.

**1965-8** Many of the main figures in political parties reach an accommodation with Sobhuza. The Imbokodvo dominate the Legislative Council and prepare to take over.

**1968 Swaziland Independence** on September 6th, with Sobhuza as King and a government formed by the Imbokodvo.

**1982 Death of Sobhuza. Mswati III**, a minor, chosen to succeed him.

# Appendix II

## Game Conservation in Swaziland
## 1960 – Present

Animals which had disappeared from Swaziland and have been successfully reintroduced in the Game Parks.

**Elephant**
**Lion**
**Buffalo**
**White Rhino**
**Black Rhino**
**Giraffe**
**Eland**
**Sable Antelope**
**Roan Antelope**
**Tsassebe**
**Nyala**
**Blesbuck**
**Warthog**
**Suni**
**Blue Duiker**
**Red Hartebeest**
**Black Wildebeest**
**Cheetah**
**Hippo**

Animals which were still present in the country in 1960 but have increased naturally since the establishment of the Game Parks.

**Leopard**
**Waterbuck***
**Kudu***
**Impala**
**Vaal Reedbuck***
**Mountain Reedbuck***
**Common Reedbuck**
**Oribi**
**Grey Duiker**
**Bushbuck**
**Blue Wildebeest**
**Red Duiker**
**Zebra**
**Crocodile**
**Steenbuck**
**Klipspringer**

Two species of birds have also been re-established.

**Ostrich**
**Blue Cranes**

*Numbers were augmented by imports from South Africa.

*Details kindly supplied by Ted Reilly of Big Game Parks.*

252

# Appendix III

## Swaziland Since Independence

My narrative finishes at the end of my first tour of duty in Swaziland when I went on long leave to the U.K. I then had a second tour.

On 6th September 1968, after sixty-five years as a British Protectorate, Swaziland became a sovereign state and a member of both the Commonwealth and the United Nations. Its early promise was fulfilled and it became one of the jewels of Africa with its growing prosperity riding on considerable inward investment. Then things started to go wrong and a succession of bad harvests put pressure on the rural population and the AIDS pandemic ran riot.

### HELPING SWAZILAND WHEN IT MATTERS
### - By the Bishop of Swaziland

The country's present situation is succinctly pictured by the Bishop of Swaziland, The Right Reverend Meshack Mabuza, in his analysis printed below.

"The situation in Swaziland may be briefly described in the following terms:

- The HIV/AIDS prevalence rate is 42.6% This is the highest rate in the whole world, and it is said to be the highest level ever reached by any country.

- Out of a population of 1,200,000, 20,000 people die of AIDS related diseases.

- The country has about 70,000 orphans, and these increase at a rate of 10,000 per annum.

- There are about 6,000 orphan headed families. The average size of an orphan family is 4, and the eldest sibling is 11 years.

- 70% of the country's population lives below the poverty line, and the poverty line in the country is drawn at USD 15.00 per month. This is far below the international poverty line of USD 2.00 per day.

- Unemployment runs at about 40%.

The above is just a brief description. The situation is aggravated by our political situation which is undemocratic. For this reason, Swaziland is sidelined by a number of European countries and the USA when it comes to aid in support of HIV/AIDS and poverty.

Our diocese indeed has a programme to respond to the pandemic. Our programme is four pronged:

**1. Prevention** - focusing on abstinence for the unmarried, and faithfulness for married couples.

**2. Care and Support** - for those infected. We lay a great deal of emphasis on hospice care as the hospitals of the country have only 2,000 hospital beds. This means that of the 20,000 who die per year more than 18,000 die without medical care in hospitals.

**3. Counselling** - encouraging peer education and testing to confirm people's HIV status.

**4. Mitigation** - of the effects of the pandemic, some of our parishes have soup kitchens to feed orphans. An orphanage is being envisaged. We also have a small bursary fund to offer sponsorships to orphans who would otherwise not see the inside of a classroom because of their misfortune."

He concludes "I am outlining briefly the situation in our diocese to show how desperate our situation is. Any assistance, no matter how big or small, has an important place and a genuine need to answer"

## HOW TO HELP

I think there are many people who are shocked by the suffering of ordinary men, women and children in Africa, but want their help to go where there is a proper trail of accountability which takes the donated funds direct to the point of need. I believe that the Diocese of Swaziland's HIV/AIDS and Orphans programme is just such an operation. I commend the Diocese's programme to anyone who feels moved to help the Swazi people in their time of need.

**The address is:**   The Swaziland Diocese HIV/AIDS
and Orphans Programme
P.O. Box 118
Mbabane
Swaziland
Africa
**E-mail:**   bishopmabuza@africaonline.co.sz

The most convenient way of remitting donations to the Swaziland Diocese HIV/AIDS and Orphans Programme is through the good offices of:

The Anglican Consultative Council
St Andrew's House
16 Tavistock Crescent
London W11 1AP

**Tel:**   0207313 3900
**Fax:**   0207313 3999
**Email:**   aco@anglicancommunion.org

It is best to use their Gift Aid form (copy attached). That way the money is securely transmitted to the Diocese's HIV/AIDS and Orphans account and the donation is enhanced through the Gift Aid process (currently 28p per £1 given). Donations should be transmitted, together with a completed Gift Aid Declaration to:

ACC Account – Sort Code 160038 – Account No. 00100576
Account Name: Bishop Mabuza's Swaziland Aids Fund

**ANGLICAN CONSULTATIVE COUNCIL**
Charity Commission Registration No. 276591

**GIFT AID DECLARATION FOR GIFT TO ACC FOR
BISHOP MABUZA'S AIDS FUND**

[To be completed by individual donors who are United Kingdom Tax Payers]

Donor's full name ...................................................................................

Address ...................................................................................................

.................................................................................................................

.................................................................................................................

.................................................................................................................

I hereby declare *(delete the part not applicable)*:

1. That all donations I shall make/have made to the Anglican Consultative Council from 6 April 2000 onwards should be treated as Gift Aid donations until I notify you otherwise.

2. That my donation of £ ................... dated ................... should be treated as a Gift Aid donation.

Signed .....................................................................................................

Date ........................................................................................................

Notes: 1. You must be a United Kingdom taxpayer and pay tax sufficient to cover the amount of tax recoverable on the donation(s) made in the tax year. (currently 28p per £1 given)

2. If you pay tax at the higher rate you can claim further relief in your Self Assessment Tax Return.

3. If your circumstances change and you cease to be a United Kingdom taxpayer or pay insufficient income or capital gains tax to cover the amount reclaimable by the council, you can cancel your declaration.

# Appendix IV

## Other Useful Addresses

**Swaziland High Commission**
20 Buckingham Gate
London
SW1E 6LB
Tel: 0207 630 6611

**Swaziland Tourism Authority**
P O Box A1030
MBABANE
Swaziland
Tel: + 268 404 9693 / 404 9675
E-mail: secretary@tourismauthority.org.za
Web: www.welcometoswaziland.com

**Big Game Parks**
P O Box 311
MALKERNS
Swaziland
Tel: + 268 528 3944
E-mail: conservationhq@biggameparks.org

**Trade Promotion Unit**
**Ministry of Foreign Affairs and Trade**
P O Box 518
MBABANE
Swaziland
Tel: + 268 404 5180 / 2
Fax: + 268 404 3833
E-mail: tpuswd@realnet.co.sz

# Appendix V

## Chapter Header Silhouettes

Chapter 1 **Black browed Albatross**, one of the sights on the voyage to Cape Town.

Chapter 2 **Pied Kingfisher**, which I watched in the early morning fishing off the jetty at Knysna.

Chapter 3 **Cape Lourie**, its primaries are the red feathers which the Dlamini clan wear in their hair.

Chapter 4 **Secretary Bird**, a sub-species could be found in the Secretariat at Mbabane in the 1960s which habitually kept its in-tray empty and its nose clean and never strayed far from its desk.

Chapter 5 **Cape Swallows**, gave the DC's Residence at Mankaiana a happy feel and enjoyed being fed bread on the lawn.

Chapter 6 **Long-Tailed Widow Birds,** the males lose their tails in winter.

Chapter 7 **Cape Glossy Starlings**, dominated the bird table at Doug and Elsa's home at Mhlume.

Chapter 8 **Guinea-fowl**, "only the guinea-fowl shows true caution" (*Sobhuza II*).

Chapter 9 **Hoopoe**, drills for worms with its long curved beak and calls "hu-pu-pu".

Chapter 10 **Fish Eagle**, whose call is "one of the characteristic sounds of Africa" (Roberts).

Chapter 11 **Blue Crane**, one of the most ornamental of birds, it has no need of a "make-over" before a big occasion – often kept as a garden pet but said to blot its copy-book by pecking at children's feet or eyes.

Chapter 12 **Ostrich**, rather than bury its head in the sand, in my experience more likely to bury its great rasping single claw in your gut.

Chapter 13 **Goliath Heron**, Fish Eagles like to chase them just for the fun of it despite their size.

Chapter 14 **Bataleur Eagle**, In the bushveld its soaring flight matched my soaring spirits.

# Glossary

*(Sw) Swazi*     *(Afr) Afrikaans*

**Amadube** *(Sw)*

Zebras: the name of the multi-racial tennis club in Mbabane

**apartheid** *(Afr)*

the South African Nationalist party's policy of separate development for different races

**baas** *(Afr)*

boss

**Bantustan** *(Afr)*

semi-autonomous African reserve created by the South African Nationalist Party while in power 1948-94

**Boer** *(Afr)*

White South African of Dutch descent

**dagga** *(Sw)*

cannabis

**dassie** *(Afr)*

rock rabbit, hyrax

**Devonshire Course**

training course for colonial administrators run at Oxford and Cambridge

**District Commissioner (DC)**

administrative officer in charge of a District

**District Officer (DO)**

DC's assistant

**donga** *(Afr)*

ravine created by soil erosion

261

| | |
|---|---|
| **European Advisory Council** | a consultative body operative in the pre-Legco years |
| **Government Secretary** | No.2 in the administrative hierarchy and the Resident Commissioner's deputy. Restyled "Chief Secretary" in 1963 |
| **Imbokodvo** *(Sw)* | grinding stone; taken as the name for the Swazi National Council's political party (or "national movement" as Sobhuza preferred to call it) |
| **impi** *(Sw)* | regiment, detachment of warriors |
| **isangoma** *(Sw)* | soothsayer |
| **isona** *(Sw)* | witchweed |
| **jojo** *(Sw)* | male widow-bird |
| **khaya** *(Sw)* | home, homestead |
| **koppie** *(Afr)* | hillock |
| **Mau Mau** | uprising (1951-60) in Kenya among the Kikuyu and, to a much lesser extent, the neighbouring Meru and Embu |
| **Mlamuli** *(Sw)* | the symbol of protection and reconciliation |
| **Mnt** *(Sw)* | abbreviation of Mntwanenkosi – son of the King, i.e. "Prince" |
| **morgen** *(Afr)* | measurement of land (approximately 2 |

acres – slightly less than 1 hectare)

**Nkulunkulu** *(Sw)*        God (the Great, Great One)

**nkundla pl. tinkundla** *(Sw)*        regional meetings

**pronking** *(Afr)*        vertical leaping practised by springbok

**Residency**        official home of the Resident Commissioner, later (1963) re-designated Government House; the term was also used for the home of a District Commissioner

**Resident Commissioner**        The head of the administration in a Protectorate. In Swaziland, re-designated (1963) as "Queen's Commissioner", with equivalent powers to a Governor in a colony.

**rinderpest** *(Afr)*        cattle plague similar to the "murrain" of the Middle Ages

**rooinek** *(Afr)*        "red neck" i.e. new-comer, especially a Briton

**Roma**        University of Basutoland, Bechumaland and Swaziland

**Secretariat**        the protectorate's administrative headquarters

**shikane** *(Sw)*        female widow-bird

**sibhaca** *(Sw)*        energetic dance-style developed by the

|  | Bhaca people |
| --- | --- |
| **Sibaya** *(Sw)* | royal cattle Kraal, by tradition the meeting place for discussion of matter of national importance. |
| **siza** *(Sw)* | a lend lease system applied to livestock |
| **stoep** *(Afr)* | verandah |
| **Swazi National Council (SNC)** | a body that traditionally advised the Ngwenyama |
| **triple-gait** | midway between a trot and a canter |
| **tsotsi** *(Sw)* | spiv, gangster |
| **Umhlanga** *(Sw)* | Reed Dance |
| **umlimi** *(Sw)* | Agricultural Field Officer |
| **utshwala** *(Sw)* | millet beer |
| **wattle** | a type of mimosa whose bark is used in tanning. It grows well in the high veld and was a valuable cash crop; but it is now largely replaced by synthetic materials. |
| **xoxa** *(Sw)* | discuss serious matters |
| **yebo** *(Sw)* | yes |

# A Brief Bibliography

Barker, Dudley / *Swaziland* / HMSO / 1965

Fairlie, M J / *No Time like the Past* / Pentland Press / 1992

Ferguson, Niall / *Empire* / Penguin-Allen Lane / 2003

Garnett, Mary / *Take your Glory Lord* / One Way Publications (Australia)
(Life Story of William Duma – ISBN 086883 078X) / 1992

Grimble, Sir Arthur / *A Pattern of Islands* / John Murray / 1952

Haggard, Sir Henry Rider / *King Solomon's Mines* / Blackie & Son Ltd. / 1961

Hailey, Lord / *Native Administration in the British African Territories* / HMSO / 1953

Huxley, Elspeth / *The Merry Hippo* / Chatto & Windus / 1963

Kirk-Greene, Anthony / *On Crown Service* / IB Tauris / 1999

Kuper, Hilda / *Sobhuza II Ngwenyama and King of Swaziland* / Duckworth / 1978

Mackworth-Praed and Grant / *African Handbook of Birds* / Longmans / 1962

Marwick, Brian / *The Swazi* / Cambridge University Press / 1940

Meinertzhagen, Richard / *Kenya Diary 1902-1906* / Eland Books / 1984

McCall Smith, Alexander / *No. 1 Ladies Detective Agency* / Polygon / 1999

Roberts / *Birds of South Africa* / South African Bird Book Fund / 1961

Richmond, Anthony H / *The Colour Problem* / Pelican / 1961

Scutt, Joan / *Story of Swaziland* / Swaziland Printing and Publishing Co. / 1966

# Index

# Index

# Index

# Index

Shiselweni – 180, 200

Shongwe, Dr Sidney and June – 49, 106, 135, 232

Sibhaca dancing – 123

Simkin,      Peter – 33-5, 37-40, 46, 54, 58, 65-6, 79, 130, 132-6, 161, 191-3, 197, 238, 244, 246

            Diana – 209, 230

            Michael – 79, 209

Siphofaneni Hot Springs – 141-2, 164

Siswati language (see Swazi language)

*Siza-ing* cattle – 82

Smuts, General Jan – 37

Sobhuza I, (Somhlolo) – 138

Sobhuza II, Ngwenyama of Swaziland – 38, 39, 40, 41, 68-9, 87, 90-1, 100, 118, 122, 139, 143-4, 152, 155, 157, 158, 164-6, 167-8, 178, 180, 198-9, 202, 214, 229

Soil erosion – 29, 31, 81

South Africa – 19, 43, 144, 155, 157, 166, 168, 178, 201, 209, 234

South African Nationalist Party, Government – 30, 37, 87, 144, 148, 154, 185

South African Broadcasting Corporation – 147

South Lancashire Regiment – 170

*Solinye* – 110

Somers, The Lord – 216-20

Somhlolo (see Sobhuza I)

Special Constables – 154, 158

Springbok – 221

Sputnik – 76

Stalk-borer beetle – 118

Starling, Doug and Elsa – 148-51

Starlings, Cape Glossy – 150

Stebbing, John – 165

Stegi – 85, 200, 245

Stephenson, Sir Hugh – 216

Stephens, RP (Bob) – 35, 40

Stern, Michael – 49

Sturgis, John and Jeanette – 104, 125, 130-2, 139, 174

Sudan – 226

Swaziland – *passim* – key dates – 249

Swazi Inn – 136

Swazi language – 16, 61, 111, 146

Swazi names for Europeans – 62-3

Swazi National Council (SNC) – 35, 38, 40, 42, 43, 61, 73, 99-100, 141-3, 152, 164, 165, 178, 199, 201, 202

Swaziland Democratic Party (SDP) – 39, 140, 145, 153, 214

Swaziland Progressive Party (SPP) – 38, 214

Swaziland Railway – 42

# T

Tanganyika (Tanzania) – 146, 147, 170, 234

Tavern Hotel, Mbabane – 67, 170

Tax – poll tax – 44, 59, 127

# Index

# Index

# The Author

John Miller was born in 1937 and grew up in Dumfries and Galloway in southern Scotland. He went to school at Charterhouse, and did National Service (subaltern in the Royal Scots Fusiliers – now The Royal Highland Fusiliers) before going up to Oxford to read French and German. Then, after a year's training at the "Devonshire Course", he was one of the last Colonial Service cadets to be posted to Africa. This book is the story of his first tour of duty in Swaziland from 1962 to 1965.

Following a second tour, he trained and practised as a Solicitor (Writer to the Signet) in Edinburgh, and later farmed in South Norfolk. He ended his working life with seventeen years as Chief Executive of St Matthew Housing, a charitable housing association, based in Norwich. Married with two grown-up children, his interests include racing small sailing boats, walking, gardening and bird watching. This is his first book.

# Credits